HP-UX Tuning and Performance:

Concepts, Tools, and Methods

ISBN 0-13-102716-6

90000

9 780131 027169

Hewlett-Packard® Professional Books

HP-UX Tuning and Performance:
Concepts, Tools, and Methods

Robert F. Sauers
Peter S. Weygant
Hewlett-Packard Company

http://www.hp.com/go/retailbooks

Prentice Hall PTR
Upper Saddle River, NJ 07458
http://www.phptr.com

Library of Congress Catalog-in-Publication Data

Sauers, Robert (Robert F.)
    HP-UX tuning and performance : concepts, tools, and methods /
Robert Sauers, Peter Weygant.
      p. cm. -- (Hewlett-Packard professional books)
    ISBN 0-13-102716-6
    1. Hewlett-Packard computers--Programming. 2. UNIX (Computer
file) I. Weygant, Peter. II. Title. III. Series.
    QA76.8.H48 S28 1999
    005.2'82--dc21
                                                        99-29396
                                                            CIP

Editorial/production supervision: *Vanessa Moore*
Cover production: *Talar Agasyan*
Cover design: *Design Source*
Cover design director: *Jerry Votta*
Manufacturing manager: *Alexis R. Heydt*
Marketing manager: *Lisa Konzelmann*
Acquisitions editor: *Jill Pisoni*
Editorial assistant: *Linda Ramagnano*
Project coordinator: *Anne Trowbridge*
Manager, Hewlett-Packard Retail Book Publishing: *Patricia Pekary*
Editor, Hewlett-Packard Professional Books: *Susan Wright*

Prentice-Hall International (UK) Limited, *London*
Prentice-Hall of Australia Pty. Limited, *Sydney*
Prentice-Hall Canada Inc., *Toronto*
Prentice-Hall Hispanoamericana, S.A., *Mexico*
Prentice-Hall of India Private Limited, *New Delhi*
Prentice-Hall of Japan, Inc., *Tokyo*
Prentice-Hall (Singapore) Pte. Ltd., *Singapore*
Editora Prentice-Hall do Brasil, Ltda., *Rio de Janeiro*

To my wife Kay
and my son Matthew—
I couldn't have done this
without your support and encouragement.
—Robert F. Sauers

For Richard McClure—
Thanks for your patience and understanding.
—Peter S. Weygant

Contents

List of Figures

List of Tables

Preface

Maximizing the performance of Unix systems is a challenge that requires a specialized understanding of operating system behavior and an intimate acquaintance with system tools that assist in tuning. This book brings you some of this complex knowledge in chapters that provide general background, hardware and software performance concepts, reference material on performance tools, and detailed practical suggestions for application development and tuning.

Part 1 offers a performance management methodology as a way of introducing the world of performance management. Part 2 presents an array of performance monitoring tools, some of them specific to HP-UX, and some of them available on other Unix operating systems as well. Part 3 describes bottleneck analysis, and relates operating system concepts to tuning strategies that use the tools presented in Part 2. Finally, Part 4 sketches the complex topic of application tuning. Tuning the operating system is often not enough; designing for performance is equally important.

Hewlett-Packard's HP 9000 computer systems (both Series 700 workstation and Series 800 servers) use the HP-UX operating system. This is a version of Unix that is based on both System V Unix and BSD (Berkeley) Unix. The authors are most familiar with HP-UX, and therefore, the specific operating system architecture and tuning suggestions presented in this book apply directly to HP-UX. However, HP-UX conforms to the *IEEE Portable Operating System Standard (Posix)* P1003.1 and P1003.2. It also conforms to the *System V Interface Definition (SVID) Release 3* (based on System V Release 4) and the *X/Open Portability Guide*. Because of this conformance to both *de jure* and *de facto* standards by the HP-UX operating system, the concepts presented in this book may be applied to other versions of the Unix operating system, although the specifics may differ.

Acknowledgments

In preparing this book, Bob Sauers had responsibility for the technical content, and Peter Weygant provided assistance with writing, editing, formatting, and graphics. But a number of individuals also deserve credit for their help. We owe a particular debt of gratitude to Hewlett-Packard engineers Dan Dickerman, Doug Grumann, and Michael Kunz, who read and commented on the manuscript, offering invaluable suggestions for technical changes and additions. They helped us detect and repair many defects. We hasten to add that the authors are solely responsible for any errors or deficiencies that remain.

Many others have our thanks as well. D. Paul Klein and Chris Cooper of Hewlett-Packard gave a very helpful course on HP-UX 11.0 internals. Brent Henderson from HP's Performance Analysis Tools Group graciously provided us with invaluable information about the application profiling tool *CXperf*. Mark Cousins and Steve Stichler helped with management support from Hewlett-Packard. Pat Pekary and Susan Wright, editors at HP Press, and Jill Pisoni, editor at Prentice Hall PTR, offered encouragement throughout the project, and helped push it through to completion. Vanessa Moore of Prentice Hall and Bethany Kanui of Kanui Communications provided much-needed assistance in editing and formatting.

Finally, thanks to the hundreds of students who participated in performance tuning classes given by Bob Sauers over the years. Their questions, insights, and real-world point of view helped to shape this book from the start.

Performance Management Methodology

Part 1 describes a performance management methodology that is based on the data that can be obtained from Unix computer systems. Here are the chapters:

- Introduction to Performance Management
- Performance Management Tasks
- A Performance Management Methodology
- Kernel Instrumentation and Performance Metrics

## CHAPTER 1

Introduction to Performance Management

Application developers and system administrators face similar challenges in managing the performance of a computer system. Performance management starts with application design and development and migrates to administration and tuning of the deployed production system or systems. It is necessary to keep performance in mind at all stages in the development and deployment of a system and application. There is a definite overlap in the responsibilities of the developer and administrator. Sometimes determining where one ends and the other begins is more difficult when a single person or small group develops, administers and uses the application. This chapter will look at:

- Application developer's perspective
- System administrator's perspective
- Total system resource perspective
- Rules of performance tuning

1.1 Application Developer's Perspective

The tasks of the application developer include:

- Defining the application
- Determining the specifications
- Designing application components
- Developing the application codes
- Testing, tuning, and debugging
- Deploying the system and application
- Maintaining the system and application

1.1.1   Defining the Application

The first step is to determine what the application is going to be. Initially, management may need to define the priorities of the development group. Surveys of user organizations may also be carried out.

1.1.2   Determining Application Specifications

Defining what the application will accomplish is necessary before any code is written. The users and developers should agree, in advance, on the particular features and/or functionality that the application will provide. Often, performance specifications are agreed upon at this time, and these are typically expressed in terms of user response time or system throughput measures. These measures will be discussed in detail later.

1.1.3   Designing Application Components

High-level design should be performed before any code is actually written. Performance should begin to play a part at this point in the development process. Choices must be made as to what operating systems services are to be used. Trade-offs such as ease of coding versus algorithm efficiency appear to be easily made at this stage, but they can often negatively affect performance once the application is deployed.

Not considering performance at this phase of the life cycle condemns the application to a lifetime of rework, patches, and redesign. The designer should also be considering ways to design instrumentation for transaction rate and other application-specific measurements that cannot be made by general-purpose tools.

1.1.4   Developing the Application Codes

After high-level design is complete, the developer creates the actual codes in one or more computer languages. Codes are based on the application specifications, including performance specifications, developed in conjunction with users.

1.1.5   Testing, Tuning, and Debugging

All too often, performance does not become an issue until the application has been written and is in the testing phase. Then it quickly becomes apparent that the application performs poorly or will not meet the response or throughput requirements of the user.

1.1.6   Deploying the System and/or Application

If not discovered sooner, performance deficiencies normally become quite apparent once the system and/or application is deployed out to the user community. Complaints that the performance is poor may be frequent and loud once the system is fully operational.

1.1.7 System and Application Maintenance

Once the system is operational, the developers work on making changes in the application, which may include adding new features, fixing bugs, and tuning for performance. It is often too late to have a big impact on performance by making slight modifications to the application. Developers may have to consider large-scale application redesign in order to meet performance specifications. This area begins the overlap between the duties of the developer and the system administrator.

1.2 System Administrator's Perspective

The tasks of the system administrator include:

- Making the system available to others
- Monitoring the usage of the system
- Maintaining a certain level of performance
- Planning for future processing needs

1.2.1 Making the System Available to the Users

This may include such responsibilities as loading the system and application software, configuring devices, setting up the file system, and adding user and group names.

1.2.2 Monitoring the Usage of the System

Measuring the utilization of various system resources is done for several reasons. Monitoring CPU and disk utilization can provide the basis for chargeback accounting. Identifying and documenting the various applications being used allows management to understand the trends in resource usage within the system. And of course, monitoring is the quickest way to detect problems.

1.2.3 Maintaining a Certain Level of System Performance

System administrators often see performance tuning as a response to user complaints. After monitoring and analyzing system performance, administrators must take appropriate action to ensure that performance returns to acceptable levels. System or application tuning may be necessary to improve responsiveness.

1.2.4 Planning for Future Processing Needs

This involves predicting the size of systems needed either for new applications or for growth of existing applications.

Almost any change to a system or application will have some impact on performance. Proposed changes must be weighed against the potential resulting change in performance. Performance management is the process of measuring, evaluating, and modifying the level of performance that a system and application provide to their users, and assessing the effect of proposed changes. It is important to understand that performance management is a proactive and not a reactive function. It is not very pleasant to be told by either the users or management that the computer system is not living up to expectations, and that you, the system administrator or developer, need to do something about it.

1.3 Total System Resource Perspective

To understand performance management, it is necessary to understand the various system resources that interact to affect the overall performance of the system. Traditionally, system administrators viewed performance as the interaction of three system resources: *CPU*, *memory*, and *disk*. Figure 1-1 shows this view. The Central Processing Unit, or CPU, is the hardware that

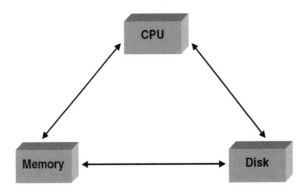

Figure 1-1   Interaction of System Resources

executes the program codes, which exist as one or more *processes*. Each process may run as one or more *threads*, depending on the operating system (OS) version or variant. The part of the OS that controls the CPU resource is the process management subsystem, which handles the scheduling of the processes that want to use the CPU.

Memory is the part of the computer that stores the instructions and data. Physical memory is typically semiconductor Random Access Memory (RAM). Virtual memory includes physical memory and also the backing store (which is the term for the overflow area used when memory is fully utilized) that is typically on disk. The Memory Management Subsystem controls this resource. Processes may be swapped and/or paged in and out as demands for memory change.

The disk resource includes all of the hard disk drives attached to the computer system. These disk drives may be of various capacities and interface types. From a performance standpoint, the disk resource involves the movement of data between the computer and the disks rather than the utilization of the space on the disk. The File System and I/O Management sub-systems control the disk resource. Although the disk resource is a specific case of the general resource known as I/O, the most important I/O resource is the disk, and most of the I/O tuning that can be done is related to the disk resource.

When one of these resources is completely consumed and is the source of a performance problem, then we often conclude that there is a bottleneck. For example, if memory is completely utilized and response is slow, then there is a memory bottleneck. However, reality is always more complicated. We will see later that it is not sufficient to use 100% utilization as the sole criterion for defining a resource bottleneck.

Figure 1-1 shows the primary resources: CPU, memory, and disk. The double-sided arrows between them are meant to emphasize that the resources are interrelated and that relieving a given bottleneck will often change the system to a different bottleneck. Several years ago, one of the authors was involved in a performance problem on a database server system. Analysis showed that the CPU was saturated and was limiting the throughput of the database. After the system was upgraded with a faster CPU, the performance was limited by the disk subsystem. It was then necessary to better distribute the tables of the database across multiple disk drives. It is often the case that one system resource that is bottlenecked can mask another resource problem.

1.4 Rules of Performance Tuning

Here is the first of several "Rules of Performance Tuning."

RULE 1: When answering a question about computer system performance, the initial answer is always: "It depends."

(These rules will often be referred to by just the number, or the short form. So, here we would say: "**Rule #1**" or "It depends.") The following shows the application of the rule in a typical consulting situation.

From Bob's Consulting Log—On arriving at a customer site for a performance consultation, one of the first questions we were asked was, "What will happen if I add 20 users to my system?" The answer was, of course, "It depends!" Implicit in this question, though unspoken, was the fact that performance was actually *satisfactory* at the time. But the customer did not know whether any resources were at or near the saturation point.

Of course, when you say, "It depends," you have to qualify the dependencies—what does good performance for added users depend on? Does each extra user require additional memory, or does the application support additional users without requiring more memory? Will more data storage be needed for the new users? This book aims to show you how to understand what the dependencies are, to ask the right questions, to investigate, to weigh the dependencies, and then to take appropriate action.

The weighing of dependencies brings us to the second "Rule of Performance Tuning."

RULE 2: Performance tuning always involves a trade-off.

When an administrator tries to improve the performance of a computer system, it may be necessary to modify operating system parameters, or change the application itself. These modifications are commonly referred to as performance tuning, that is, tuning the system kernel, or tuning the application. Tuning the kernel involves changing the values of certain *tunable parameters* in what is called the *system file* followed by relinking the kernel and rebooting the system. Application tuning involves adjusting the design of the application, employing the various compiler optimization techniques, and choosing the appropriate trade-offs among the various kernel services that will be discussed more fully in Part 4. Application tuning also may involve adjusting any tunable parameters of the application itself, if any are available.

System tuning requires an understanding of how the operating system works, and a knowledge of the dependencies that affect performance. Choosing a particular modification always involves trading off one benefit for another. For example, tuning to improve memory utilization may degrade file system performance. Understanding the needs of the application and this interaction between memory and file system permits the selection of the appropriate trade-off. Cost or risk may also be involved in the trade-off. Choosing RAID disk configurations for data integrity may be less expensive than alternative mirroring solutions that often improve performance. It may be more cost-effective to purchase a CPU upgrade rather than spend days or weeks analyzing how the application could be changed to improve performance.

In the case of a bottleneck, it is necessary to strike a balance between the demand for a resource and the availability of that resource. In order to relieve a given bottleneck, we must either increase the availability of a resource or decrease demand for it. Figure 1-2 shows this balance. A more complex view analyzes the demand for and availability of resources over time. Shifting some of the demand for a resource from a high demand time period to one of lower demand is a way of balancing resource and demand without reducing the total demand. One way to view this graphically is shown in Figure 1-3.

The traditional view of system resources is, however, incomplete. HP-UX systems are often used in a distributed environment where many computer systems are joined in a cooperative network. Other important resources, such as the network and graphics, are not included in the traditional view.

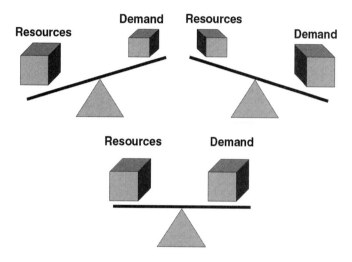

Figure 1-2   Balancing Resources and Demands

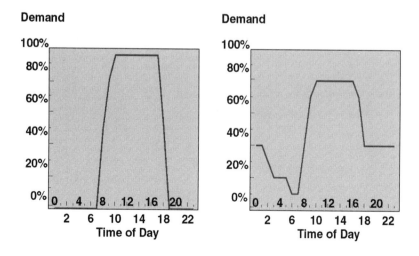

Figure 1-3   Balancing Demand Over Time

A fuller view of system resources is shown in Figure 1-4. Again, the double-sided arrows denote that all the resources are intertwined, and that relieving one bottleneck will likely result in a new one.

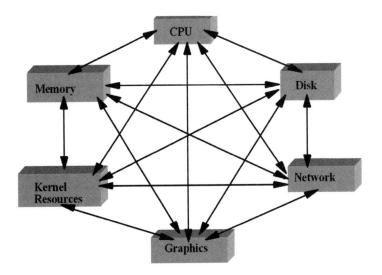

Figure 1-4 Complete View of System Resources

The general I/O resource, which includes direct-connected terminal I/O and magnetic tape, is *not* included in Figure 1-4. Network-connected terminals, such as those connected via a terminal server, are included in the network resource. However, network-connected terminals use the same *termio* subsystem as direct-connected terminals. The *termio* subsystem can consume a large amount of the CPU resource to process the characters as they are transmitted from the terminals.

The network resource includes system-to-system connections, network-connected terminals, and other smarter clients such as PCs. Network transports such as Ethernet, SNA, and X.25 are included here. Applications that consume this resource include virtual terminal, file transfer, remote file access, electronic mail, X/Windows or Motif applications, and networked inter-process communication (IPC) methods such as sockets and remote procedure calls (RPCs).

Client/Server applications are very complex. One must consider the traditional resource consumption on the server and client systems, plus the network resource consumption and latency involved in communication between the client and server programs.

Kernel resources are system tables that provide the mechanism for file access, intrasystem interprocess communication (IPC), and process creation.

The graphics resource typically involves specialized hardware and software that provides graphics capabilities. This resource will not be discussed in detail in this book. The tuning possibilities for the graphics resource are limited to upgrading to a faster CPU, upgrading to faster graphics hardware, or tuning the specialized graphics software, for which the typical user does not have the source code (X-11, PHIGS, etc.).

It is useful to look at each of these resources separately for the purpose of analysis. The various performance monitoring tools, which will be discussed in Part 3, provide data from a particular set of metrics, and may not provide data for all the system resources shown above. It will be demonstrated that no one tool provides all the data needed to monitor overall system performance.

An important aspect of resource analysis is that it is invasive, as shown in another rule.

RULE 3: Performance cannot be measured without impacting the system that is being measured.

Rule #3 is a loose interpretation of the Heisenberg principle. Physicist Werner Heisenberg discovered that he could not measure both the speed and the position of an atomic particle, since the act of making the measurement perturbed the system that was being measured. This is also true of computer systems. The following is an example from Bob's consulting experience.

From Bob's Consulting Log—I was called in to evaluate a database server system used for OLTP. There were several hundred users on the system, and memory was configured at 128 MB. There had been complaints of poor performance. I did preliminary measurements with *vmstat* and *glance*. Then I started using *gpm*, the graphical version of *glance*, for more detailed measurements. The system started thrashing and exhibiting a very different behavior: application processes were being starved of CPU. The system was already at the verge of a severe virtual memory problem, and I pushed it over the edge by running *gpm*, which consumes much more virtual memory than the other tools (over 5 MB).

Making measurements consumes resources. The level of resource consumption caused by performance data collection and presentation depends upon:

- The type, frequency, and number of measurements
- Data presentation method (text and/or graphics)
- Whether the data is being stored to disk
- The source of the data (to be discussed later)
- General activity on the system (the busier the system is, the more data is generated)

Different tools consume varying amounts of memory, CPU, and disk bandwidth (if the data is being recorded in a file). It is important to realize that it is not possible to collect performance data without consuming resources and even changing the *system* that is being measured. There may not be sufficient system resources available to run the tool. The added overhead due to using the tools may push the system over the edge. In that case, what is being measured is no longer the same system. For instance, if memory consumption is already very high, and the tool requires a large amount of memory just to run, memory thrashing may occur if it is not already occurring, and change the characteristics of what is being measured. The "Catch-22" with this situation is that the poorer the system's performance, the more measurements must be made to provide information about what the system is doing. One must decide what level of impact is acceptable in order to acquire the necessary information.

Finally, there is no single tool for all your needs.

RULE 4: No single performance tool will provide all the data needed to solve performance problems.

The perfect performance tool that solves all performance problems in all situations simply does not exist. It is necessary to develop familiarity with multiple tools so that all needs can be met. In fact, it is sometimes useful to cross-check measurements between the various tools to ensure that the tool itself is reporting information correctly. In other words, if the data doesn't make sense, question the tool!

## CHAPTER 2

Performance Management Tasks

Performance Management is a job function that may be performed by the System Administrator, or by a person whose job is to monitor system performance. In either case, it is a process that starts when the computer purchaser considers what system to buy, and it continues throughout the life of that system. Unfortunately, the role of performance management is sometimes left until a performance crisis occurs, as in the following.

From Bob's Consulting Log—We were called in to a situation where performance was so bad that users and management were complaining loudly. However, the problem had existed for several months, and no one had bothered to collect any performance data, so it was impossible to tell if the situation had suddenly become worse, or if it had degraded gradually. Worse still, there was no log of changes to the system to help in figuring out whether some system adjustment had degraded performance.

Performance management tasks include:

• Workload estimation

• Benchmarking

• Performance characterization

• Performance forecasting or prediction

• Application optimization

• Capacity planning

• Performance problem diagnosis

Each of these tasks fits into the performance management system life cycle that is shown in Figure 2-1.

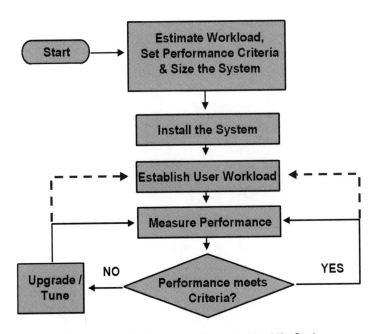

Figure 2-1   Performance Management Life Cycle

2.1 Workload Estimation

Workload estimation begins when a new application is being designed, or when an existing application is to be ported to a new system platform. Examples of data required for workload estimation are:

- Number of users
- Types of transactions
- Mix of transactions
- Transaction rate
- Amount of data
- Throughput (amount of work to be accomplished in a given time interval)
- Response time (acceptable average amount of time per transaction)

When a similar workload does not exist, workload estimation involves guessing the values for the data listed above. Otherwise, the data should be estimated based on real values from a working application and system.

2.2 Benchmarking

Performance criteria are typically set along with the workload estimation. Both are needed to appropriately size the system. *Benchmarking* is sometimes conducted to prove that the system sizing accurately meets the workload and performance criteria. Benchmarking is a very complex and time-consuming activity that tests the system and application in a controlled environment. Deciding whether to use an industry-standard benchmark or to define and create a custom user-benchmark is very difficult. There are trade-offs associated with each. For instance, industry standard benchmarks can be very useful in comparing systems from different vendors, and in determining relative performance differences among several systems from the same vendor. However, the industry-standard benchmark is not usually an accurate reflection of the actual application environment. Only a well-defined and characteristic subset of the actual application environment used as a benchmark will provide an accurate prediction of performance. This process is usually quite expensive to define, create or port, and execute. The trade-off, then, is one of time and money versus accuracy.

There are commercially available tools that can simulate users, transactions, and batch jobs to help execute the benchmark. Nevertheless, benchmarking requires a significant investment in hardware, software tools, and time for design and implementation.

2.3 Performance Characterization

After the system and application are installed, and users begin putting a real workload on the system, *performance characterization* is done, first with baseline measurements and later with historical measurements. The performance professional keeps monitoring system performance and checks it against the performance criteria that were set before the system was installed. Some organizations use Service Level Agreements to guarantee a certain level of performance to the user organizations. In order to monitor compliance with Service Level Agreements, it is necessary to continually monitor performance against the performance criteria. It may become necessary to upgrade the hardware, to tune the operating system, or to optimize the application to comply with the terms of the Service Level Agreement. This is a two-way agreement in which the user organization defines and fixes the workload, and the performance organization guarantees the level of performance. Performance monitoring becomes an on-going task that continues throughout the life of the system.

2.4 Performance Prediction or Forecasting

Performance managers may want to predict when resources may be saturated on the system. This prediction is based on historical performance evidence of the current application and the current growth rate of the business. This task is often called *performance prediction* or *forecasting*. By accurately predicting resource consumption, necessary hardware or software upgrades may be ordered in advance and installed before users complain that performance is degrading unacceptably as the workload naturally increases.

2.5 Application Optimization

Application optimization is an important activity before and during application development and when performance problems arise. Knowledge of the operating system is necessary so that decisions can be made about selecting various system services. Compiler optimization features can be used to improve application performance in certain circumstances. Profiling tools can be used to determine where an application is spending its time. Databases, for instance, may include tools that provide information that can be used to tune the application to improve performance. Part 4 will be dedicated to a discussion of application optimization.

2.6 Capacity Planning

Capacity planning techniques may also be a part of the performance professional's job. Capacity planning involves answering "What if?" questions such as:

- What size system will be needed if 50 more users are added?
- How will response time degrade if a new application is added to the system?
- Will performance improve if the CPU is upgraded to a faster model?
- Do I add an application server or upgrade an existing one?

Capacity planning is a complex activity that requires an intimate knowledge of the application and accurate measurements of system resource utilization related back to the business transactions.

Capacity planning software packages that are commercially available use either modelling or simulation techniques to project answers to the "What if?" question. Use of capacity planning software requires measurement and analysis of data from tools such as *PerfView/Analyzer* or *sar*, both of which are discussed in Chapter 5, "Performance Tools." Measurements are made at certain key times, such as peak periods during the day, as well as during peak business cycle periods such as end-of-month, end-of-quarter, and end-of-year.

Further discussion of capacity planning is beyond the scope of this book.

2.7 Performance Problem Resolution

Each of the preceding activities is proactive in that an attempt is made to predict and prevent performance problems. Even if the system is currently performing satisfactorily, performance management is required so that changes in performance can be readily and speedily detected. Unfortunately, no matter how much planning is accomplished, *performance problem resolution* is still needed when problems arise. Performance problems manifest themselves when users complain of poor response time or when the user department complains that the workload cannot be processed in the appropriate time. Problems often arise at very inopportune times, and therefore create emotional, reactive, and time-constrained environments. For these reasons, performance problem resolution requires crisis management skills and techniques. It is too late to employ performance management techniques when a performance crisis occurs. The type, quantity, and frequency of data collected in the course of performance problem resolution is also quite different from the data collected during performance management activities. Therefore, performance problem resolution is often a large part of the performance professional's role.

All of the activities that are part of performance management require performance tools to provide objective data that shows what the system and application are doing, and how well (or not so well) it is performing. A variety of performance tools will be discussed in great detail in Chapter 5.

## CHAPTER 3

A Performance Management Methodology

Although performance management and crisis management require different techniques and data collection, the same basic methodology can be used for both. Performance management uses the following steps:

- Assessment
- Measurement
- Interpretation and analysis
- Identification of bottlenecks
- Tuning or upgrading the system

The flow chart in Figure 3-1 summarizes the performance methodology that will be discussed in detail, step-by-step.

3.1 Assessment

Assessment often involves asking lots of questions, as the following shows.

From Bob's Consulting Log—I spent the entire morning asking people a lot of questions about the application, the system configuration, and how users perceived the performance problem. At lunch, the person who hired me said he was surprised that I had not yet logged onto the system. I told him my approach is to ask questions first and collect system data second. Later that day, I did obtain some data from the system, but the most important clue to the nature of the problem came from interviewing the users.

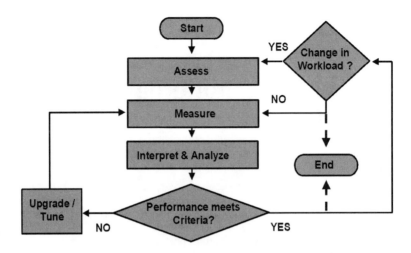

Figure 3-1   Performance Management Methodology

These questions are necessary to help you understand your limits as a performance professional, as well as those things that you can change. The following items must be learned during the assessment phase:

- System configuration
- Application design
- Performance expectations
- Known peak periods
- Changes in the system configuration or the application
- Duration of the problem, if applicable
- The options
- The politics

3.1.1   System Configuration

System configuration includes both hardware and software configuration. The number of disk drives, how data is distributed on the disks, whether they are used with mounted file systems or used in raw mode, the file system parameters, and how the application makes use of them—all these are examined during a system configuration assessment. Memory size, the amount of lockable memory, and the amount of swap space are scrutinized in assessing the virtual memory system configuration. You will need to know the processor type and the number of CPUs in the system. Finally, the kernel (operating system) configuration must be understood, and the values of tunable kernel parameters should be identified. Knowing all these items in advance will make carrying out the various performance management functions much easier.

3.1.2 Application Configuration

Understanding the design of the *application* is equally important. It may not be possible for you as a performance specialist to thoroughly understand the design and workings of the application. Optimally, however, there should be someone with whom the application design can be discussed. Such things as inter-process communication (IPC) methods, basic algorithms, how the application accesses the various disks, and whether it is compute- or I/O-intensive are examples of the knowledge you will need. For instance, with relational databases, it is important to understand whether the RDBMS supports placing a table and the index that points to it on different disk drives. Some RDBMS products support this and some do not; when this capability is present, it is an important tuning technique for improving database performance.

You should expect consumer complaints and comments to be in terms of the application. However, measurements will be based upon the available metrics, which are mostly kernel-oriented. If you can't translate system measurements into application-specific terms, it will be difficult to explain in a meaningful way what the measurements indicate in terms of necessary changes in the system.

3.1.3 Performance Expectations

You will need to learn the *performance expectations* of the system's users. It is very important to know, in advance, the measurable criteria for satisfactory performance. This is the only way to know when performance tuning is successful and when it is time to monitor performance rather than actively attempt to improve it. Objective rather than subjective measures must be elicited. Being told that response time must be less than two seconds and is currently five seconds or more is much more useful than being told that performance is "lousy."

Understanding performance expectations is a complicated task. The perception of actual system performance and the definition of satisfactory performance will change depending upon one's perspective and role.

3.1.3.1 Response Time

Users of the system typically talk about poor response time. They are mostly concerned with how long it takes to get a response from the system or application once the enter key is pressed. For instance, a user who is entering invoices into an accounts payable system expects to have data verification and data insertion completed within several seconds, at most. Engineers who use a computer-aided design application expect to see the image of the part being analyzed rotated in real-time. Otherwise, they get frustrated with what they consider to be poor performance. Response time is the most commonly used measure of system performance and is typically quoted as one of the following:

- An average of a fractional second (sometimes called sub-second) or seconds
- A certain confidence level
- A maximum response time

Typical confidence levels are 90%–98%. For example, one would say that the desirable average response time is 2 seconds, 95% of the time, with a maximum transaction response time of 5 seconds.

What is a good value for response time? While the automatic answer "It depends" is certainly true, it is useful to have a range of values for response time to use as a guideline. Users of a text editor or word processing package don't want to have to wait to see the characters echoed on the screen as they are typed. In this case, sub-second response time of approximately 250 milliseconds would be considered optimal. In a transaction processing environment one must understand the environment before developing good response time values. Some of the factors are as follows:

- Transaction complexity

- Number of users

- Think time between transactions

- Transaction types and ratios

Transaction Complexity   This deals with the amount of work which the system must perform in order to complete the transaction. If the transaction is defined as requiring three record lookups followed by an update, that transaction is much more complex than one that is a simple read. The complexity associated with typical CAD applications is very high. Many CPU cycles and perhaps disk I/Os are necessary for simple interactive tasks, such as rotating a model of an object on the display.

Number of Users   The number of users influences the sizing of any system that is required to support a given workload and response time.

Think Time   As the think time between transactions increases, more work can be supported by the system in the idle periods between transactions. *Heads down* environments provide almost no think time between transactions. This is a typical data input environment. Conversely, customer service environments often provide very long think times, since most of time the customer service representative is speaking with the caller by telephone and casually accessing various databases as the telephone conversation proceeds.

Transaction Types and Ratios   It is necessary to look at the types of transactions and the ratios of the number of each transaction type to the total. Read-intensive applications can provide rapid response times to queries. Insert- and particularly update-intensive applications require more CPU cycles and often disk I/Os to complete the transaction. Table 3-1 gives guidelines for acceptable response times.

Table 3-1 Typical Application Response Times

Transaction Type	Acceptable Response Time in Seconds
Interactive CAD applications	< 1
Text editing or word processing	1/4
Read-intensive low complexity	< 1
Read-intensive medium to high complexity	1–2
Update-intensive low to medium complexity	5
Update-intensive high complexity	5–15
Long think-time environments	2–3
Batch run	N/A

Users perceive performance as poor when update response time exceeds 5 seconds and when there is no preparation to be done by the user to get ready for the next transaction. Read performance must be no more than 1–2 seconds to keep users satisfied.

After installing the computer system and the application, some system administrators or performance managers have been known to create dummy workloads on the systems before letting any users access the applications or the system. The initial users perceive a certain response time following their inputs. As more users are added, the dummy workload is reduced, thus providing a constant response time to the users. This trick attempts to address another issue with the perception of actual performance. Users prefer consistent responsiveness rather than variable responsiveness. If someone decides to run some resource-intensive batch jobs while interactive users are on the system, interactive performance will typically degrade. End-of-month processing will usually consume a very large amount of system resources, making it necessary to either keep the interactive users off the system while it is being run, or to run it in off-hours.

Users can tolerate and accept consistently poor response time rather than response that is good one minute and poor the next. The acceptable variance in response time changes as the average response time itself changes. Users will tolerate an average response time of 1.5 seconds with a variance of ± 1 second much less than they will tolerate an average response time of 3 seconds with a variance of ± .25 second. One problem associated with attempting to prevent variability in performance is that when throughput is favored in tuning the system, the chance of experiencing variability in response time is greatly increased.

Predictability is another way of looking at consistency of performance. Predictability makes the job of the performance professional easier when forecasting future resource consumption. It also allows the appropriate setting of expectations for performance, as the following analogy shows.

The public transportation department announces that buses on a particular bus route are scheduled to arrive at each stop an average of every ten minutes. In a given thirty minute period, three buses arrive all at once and the next one arrives forty minutes later. This schedule meets the stated criteria. However, it will make the people waiting for the fourth bus very unhappy. It would be much better for the waiting passengers if the buses were to arrive consistently 10 minutes apart. It would also be perceived well if the buses were to arrive predictably at certain clock times.

3.1.3.2   Throughput

Information system *management personnel* are typically interested in throughput, rather than response time. If the demands of the organization require that a certain amount of work must be processed in an average day, then management is concerned whether the system can process that workload, rather than caring whether response time is one second or two seconds. Throughput is often quoted as work per unit time. Examples of throughput measures are:

- 3000 invoices processed per hour
- 5 CAD modeling runs per day
- All end-of-month processing must complete within 3 days
- Overnight processing must complete in the 9 off-peak hours

It is not possible to develop guidelines for good throughput values. Throughput is driven by business needs, and the system must be sized to support those requirements. Capacity planning is done to ensure that as business requirements grow, the system will be able to handle the workload. It should be easy to predict in advance whether a system will be able to provide a specified throughput. The workload is considered a batch workload and the average time to complete a unit of work can be measured with a simple benchmark.

In reality, the situation is never that simple. Users are typically very vocal, and poor response time often reaches the ears of management. The point of this discussion is that the definition of performance may change from person to person; attitudes about response time and throughput must be examined to determine what users consider to be acceptable performance. Although the overall methodology is the same, tuning for response time and for throughput are different. Another way of putting this is that there is one strategy for approaching performance, but there are many different tactics.

3.1.4   Known Peak Periods

It is useful to identify *known peak periods* in advance, so that unusual spikes in the data can be readily explained. For instance, it is often mentioned that resource utilization in an office environment peaks at 11:00 a.m. and between 2:00–3:00 p.m. during the normal work day. Processing requirements typically grow at the end of the month or the end of a quarter. Expecting peaks at these times can save time when analyzing the data. Additionally, if the peaks are absent, it may be a clue that something unusual is preventing full system utilization.

3.1.5   Sudden Changes

Anyone who has worked in technical support has experienced callers complaining that the system "suddenly" is no longer working correctly or that performance has suddenly degraded. The following is a familiar dialog:

From Bob's Consulting Log—

Consultant: Has anything changed in the application or the system?
Client: No, nothing has changed.
Consultant: Are you sure that nothing has changed?
Client: I'm quite sure nothing has changed.

(Three days later, after a lot of investigation...)

Consultant: Did you notice that your DBA dropped some indexes?
Client: Oh! I didn't think **those** changes would make a difference.

The task of investigating changes that may have been made to the system is quite an art. However, the importance of this part of the assessment should not be minimized.

3.1.6   Duration of the Problem

When doing performance problem diagnosis, identifying the *duration of the problem* involves several issues:

- How long does the performance problem last?
- When does the performance problem occur?
- How long has the performance problem existed?
- When did it begin?

It is important to understand *the length of time that the problem lasts* to detect whether it is a spike in resource utilization, or whether the problem occurs constantly. Tuning in each of these situations requires a different approach.

Knowing *when the performance problem occurs* means that data collection can be planned and minimized, as an alternative to collecting performance data for days or weeks to capture data when the problem manifests itself.

Finally, *the length of time that the performance problem has existed* influences the probability of determining whether anything in the system or application has been changed. If the problem has existed for a long time (weeks or months) it is very unlikely that any changes will be discovered. One can also question the seriousness of the situation if the users have been living with the problem for months.

3.1.7   Understanding the Options

Understanding the options lets you determine what recommendations should be offered. If there is no capital budget for purchasing computer hardware, you can look for other ways to resolve the performance problem. Perhaps tuning the operating system or application is a viable alternative to upgrading the CPU to a faster model. In contrast, if time constraints dictate that the problem must be resolved quickly and deterministically, then upgrading the CPU to a faster model would probably be more expeditious than spending an unpredictable amount of time attempting to improve or redesign the application.

3.1.8   Understanding the Politics

It may be necessary to *understand the politics of the organization* before revealing the cause of the problem or before recommending the changes to be implemented. Knowledge of the politics may help narrow the scope of the question you are trying to answer. It may be that the user organization wants to gain more control of the system, and it is trying to gather evidence to support this cause. The MIS department may be trying to allocate computing resources fairly, and it may not be possible to make changes that improve the situation for only one group. Finally, you may have been called in simply to provide objective data to justify the purchase of a larger, faster system.

3.2 Measurement

The next phase of the performance management methodology involves measuring actual system or application performance. For this phase, performance tools are used to perform the data collection and presentation.

Measurement is based upon the answers to several interrelated questions that must be answered before any data is collected.

- Which performance tools are available?
- What is the purpose of the measurement?
- Is the measurement baseline- or crisis-oriented?
- How long should the data be collected, and at what intervals?
- What data metrics are to be collected?
- How well are the metrics documented?
- How accurate are the data presented by the tool?
- Are certain system resources already saturated?
- How do these measurements relate to the organization's business needs?

3.2.1 Tool Availability

Some performance tools come standard with the HP-UX Operating System. Others are available as separately purchasable products. The availability of the various tools on the system being measured will constrain the answers to the other questions. Tool familiarity also affects the answer to this question. Comfort and experience with using a tool often limits the use of other tools even if other tools are more useful in a given situation. However, the best tool for a given purpose should be used to make the measurements, even if that tool must be purchased.

3.2.2 Purpose of the Measurement: Baseline versus Crisis

The purpose of the data collection must be determined in advance in order to select the correct set of tools for gathering the data. It is important to measure performance on the system when performance is acceptable. This type of measurement is called a *baseline measurement.* Think of a baseline as a signature or profile which can be used for purposes of comparison at those times when performance is not acceptable or is degrading. Baseline measurements require fewer metrics and a longer sampling interval, because a particular problem is not being investigated. Instead, the goals are to characterize system performance only, and to watch for trends.

An analogy to baseline measurements is a routine physical exam. The physician takes certain vital signs like blood pressure, pulse rate, temperature, and blood tests, including cholesterol counts. A visual inspection by the physician is correlated with the internal measurements and an historical record is kept to monitor trends over time. Any unusual symptoms are investigated immediately, so that the physician can treat the problem before it becomes chronic.

Baseline measurements should be reviewed to develop conclusions about system performance without the immediate goal of altering performance by tuning the system or application. Baseline measurements should be archived for historical purposes. They can then be used to:

- Review performance trends over time
- Compare against current performance when investigating or diagnosing current performance problems
- Provide data for performance forecasting
- Develop and monitor service level agreements
- Provide data for capacity planning

Data collected and archived over time does not typically need to be as voluminous and detailed as for performance problem resolution.

Performance crises usually result from failing to manage performance. *Crisis measurements* (those typically made during performance problem diagnosis) require much more detail, so that performance problems can be adequately investigated. The additional detail involves additional metrics as well as more frequent measurement, resulting in a much larger volume of data. The purpose of crisis measurements is to characterize *current* system performance in detail so that appropriate tuning can be done. Managing a performance crisis is much more difficult when there are no baselines against which a comparison can be made.

Baseline measurements should be made, archived, and reviewed periodically so that future performance crises can be prevented, and dangerous performance trends acted upon, before they become serious. As the data ages, less and less detail is required. As changes in the system occur, for example, adding users or making changes in the application, new baseline measurements should be taken. Another tactic is to compare baselines from similarly configured systems, to help understand the variances before problems occur.

Baseline measurements can help provide the necessary translation between the language of performance tools and the needs of users. If the data can be presented and reviewed prior to a crisis, then communication during the crisis should be easier.

Baseline measurements should include information that is not related to existing sources. For instance, reviewing the "Other Application" category in MeasureWare can indicate if new work is being added, or whether the trend is to move work away from existing applications.

3.2.3   Duration and Interval of the Measurement

Some tools are good for displaying performance metrics in real-time. Other tools are better for collecting performance metrics in the background over a long period for casual analysis later. If performance problem diagnosis is the goal of the data collection, and the problem manifests itself consistently or after a short time, then real-time performance tools would be the best choice. The amount of data produced by real-time performance tools is quite large. Therefore, this type of data should not be gathered for long periods of time since there is a large storage requirement, and it is difficult to review large volumes of data. Performance problems that cannot be readily reproduced, or those that occur unpredictably or only occasionally, will warrant longer-term data collection. Tools that provide summarization and detail capabilities are the best choice

If performance characterization or forecasting is the goal, longer-term trending tools would be the tools of choice. The tools chapter will discuss in detail the individual tools and when they are best used. The duration of the measurement should greatly influence selection of the tool or tools that will be used to collect the data.

The measurement interval must also be determined. Sampling intervals for baseline measurements should be measured in minutes or hours rather than seconds to reduce the volume of data that will be collected. Sampling intervals for crisis measurements or for performance problem resolution need to be shorter and are measured in seconds. If performance problems are of short duration, i.e., tend to spike, sampling intervals must also be short: typically one to five seconds. The shorter the sampling interval, the higher the overhead of making the measurement. This is of particular concern if one or more of the system resources are already saturated.

3.2.4   Particular Metric Needs

Performance tools come from various sources, and people get used to using certain ones, depending on their background. These then become their favorite tools, whether or not they are best for the job. Some tools were written for specific purposes; for example, *vmstat* was written specifically to display virtual memory and CPU metrics, but not disk statistics. The tool chosen should be useful in diagnosing the performance issue at hand.

3.2.5   Metric Documentation

There are several hundred performance metrics available from the kernel. These metrics were developed over time, and some are better documented than others. Some of the metrics may have a one-line description that is incomprehensible. Only by reviewing kernel source code can one hope to determine the meaning of some of the more esoteric metrics. Of course, the availability of kernel source code is limited, as is the desire to review it.

For example, the manual page for the tool *vmstat* defines the field *at* as the number of address translation faults. Those of us who are familiar with hardware components of modern computers might readily conclude that this field counts the number of Translation Lookaside Buffer (TLB) faults. This would be a very desirable metric, since it would give one indication of how well the CPU address translation cache is performing. Unfortunately, only by reviewing the kernel source code can one determine that the *at* field in the *vmstat* report is really referring to the number of page faults, a virtual memory system metric.

Good documentation is needed to determine what metrics are important to the purpose of the measurement, and to learn how to interpret them.

3.2.6   Metric Accuracy

In order to understand completely why some performance metrics are inaccurate, one must understand how the kernel is designed. For instance, although most CPU hardware clocks measure time in microseconds, the granularity of the HP-UX system clock is 10 milliseconds. The kernel records CPU consumption on a per-process basis by noting which process was running when the clock ticked. That process is charged for consuming CPU time during the *entire* clock tick, whether or not it used all of the tick. So, the saying "Garbage in, garbage out" applies to performance tools in a loose sense. If the source of the data is inaccurate, the data will be inaccurate.

The standard Unix performance tools use the kernel's standard sources of data. Newer methods have been developed by Hewlett-Packard to more accurately characterize system performance. Tools developed by HP get their data from the new sources in the kernel, which provides for greater metric accuracy. The IEEE POSIX (P1004) committee, the Open Group, and the Performance Working Group (PWG) are all reviewing HP's implementation for adoption into a standard that could be implemented in other versions of Unix.

3.2.7   Saturation of Certain System Resources

When one or more system resources are saturated, it may be necessary to concentrate on particular metrics in order to determine the source of the saturation. However, merely invoking a performance tool causes additional overhead. The tool chosen should be one that does not exacerbate the saturation of the resource of concern. Tool overhead will be discussed more fully in Part 2.

3.2.8   Relationship between the Metric and the Application

Metrics by their nature usually count how many times some piece of code or hardware is used. The relationship of a given metric to a particular application and to the needs of its users must be established by analysis and interpretation of the data, plus a complete understanding of the application.

3.2.9   Qualitative versus Quantitative Measurements

One last point about measurements. The preceding discussion involved quantitative measures of how the system is performing. Other, equally important measures of system performance are qualitative in nature. There is a management style called "Management by Wandering Around," or MBWA, in which the manager visits a wide variety of managed personnel and asks questions that help to monitor the pulse of the organization. In the performance arena, MBWA becomes "Measuring by Wandering Around."   Talk to the users. Ask them how they perceive system and application performance. Find out *why* they might feel that performance is bad. Watch how they interact with the system. It's possible that the users may be interacting with the system in a way that the application designers never imagined, and that is causing the application to behave poorly.

Another type of qualitative measurement can be made by interacting with the system directly and noting its responsiveness or the lack of it. Logging on the system, initiating a simple command like *ls* for a directory listing and noting the response might result in a qualitative measure of interactive performance.

3.2.10   Summary

In summary, the reasons for making measurements are:

• Measurements are key to understanding what is happening in the system.

• Measurements are the *only* way to know what to tune.

In addition, it is necessary to measure periodically in order to proactively monitor system and application performance so that problems can be prevented or resolved quickly.

3.3 Interpretation and Analysis

After making the measurements, it is necessary to review the voluminous amount of data that was collected. Some of the performance tools present the data as tables of numbers. Other tools offer summarization of the data in graphical form. Regardless of the presentation method, interpretation of the data is complex. One must first understand what the metrics mean. Then, it is necessary to know how to interpret the numbers, in other words, what number indicates a performance problem. This is no easy task! **Rule #1** comes into play here. A good value or a bad value for a given performance metric *depends* upon many factors.

From Bob's Consulting Log—I was involved in a sizing exercise where we had to determine what system was needed to support the application running 125 users with a response time of < 5 seconds. We started out with a basic system and looked at the load average metric, which was 250. We also saw that the response time was well above 5 seconds (some took 5 minutes!), and we were only simulating 75 users.

After upgrading the CPU to a faster one, we re-ran the test, and the load average dropped to 125. We were now able to simulate all 125 users, but response time was still unsatisfactory. Finally, we upgraded to the most powerful processor currently available. Now, the load average was 75. Most people would cringe at that number, saying response time should be terrible. However, all transactions completed in under 5 seconds for all 125 users. The moral is: Don't be scared by large numbers. What really matters is that you meet the performance requirements of the application.

The value for a given metric that can be considered good or bad will be discussed in depth in the tuning section for each major system resource.

Some of the general factors that affect setting rules of thumb for performance metrics are:

- Type of system: multi-user or workstation
- Type of application: interactive or batch, compute- or I/O-intensive
- Application architecture: single system or client/server, multi-tiered, parallel system
- Speed of the CPU
- Type of disk drives

3.3.1   Multi-User versus Workstation

A multi-user system experiences many more context switches than a workstation normally does. Context switches consume some of the CPU resource. Additionally, the high number of users typically cause a lot of I/O, which puts demands on the CPU and disk resources. Workstations that are used for graphics-intensive applications typically have high user CPU utilization numbers (which are normal) but lower context switch rates, since there is only one user.   Applications on a multi-user system usually cause random patterns of disk I/O. Workstation applications often cause sequential patterns of disk I/O. So, these factors affect the optimal values for the CPU and disk metrics.

3.3.2   Interactive versus Batch, Compute-Intensive versus I/O-Intensive

Workstations can support highly interactive applications, for example, X/Windows or Motif applications that require a lot of interaction. These can be business applications, such as customer service applications that provide several windows into different databases. Alternatively, technical applications such as Computer-Aided Design (CAD) programs support interactive input to draw the part on the screen. Compute-bound applications on a workstation sometimes act like batch applications on a multi-user systems. Batch applications consume a large amount of CPU, as do compute-intensive applications. Interactive applications cause many more context switches and more system CPU utilization than do batch or compute-intensive applications. Batch applications use less memory than highly interactive applications. Compute-intensive applications can touch more pages of memory than individual I/O-intensive applications. The optimal values for the CPU and memory metrics are affected by these factors.

3.3.3   Application Architecture

An application may be architected in several ways. It can be monolithic, that is, one large program that runs entirely on a single system. Parallel applications are designed to make better use of the components of the single computer system (especially an SMP system) to improve throughput or response. In contrast, an application can be distributed as in a multi-tiered client/server environment. In this case, parallel processing does not necessarily provide the same benefits. For these reasons, understanding the architecture necessary before deciding what measurements to make and how to interpret the data.

3.3.4   Speed of the CPU

The faster the CPU, the greater the CPU resource that is available. Applications can get more work done during the time-slice they are allocated, and may be able to satisfy their current need for the CPU resource completely, rather than having to wait for another turn. This factor affects the run-queue metric.

3.3.5   Type of Disks

Newer technology disk drives are faster and can support more I/Os per second than can older disks. The number of disk channels also affects the number of disk I/Os that are optimal.

3.4 Identifying Bottlenecks

With all these factors in mind, the goal of data interpretation and analysis is to determine whether there is a particular bottleneck. Once a particular bottleneck is identified, tuning to improve performance can be initiated. Characteristics of bottleneck are:

• A particular resource is saturated.
• The queue for the resource grows over time.

- Other resources may be starved as a result.
- Response time is not satisfactory.

3.4.1   Resource Saturation

Resource saturation is often thought of as 100% utilization. The entire resource is consumed. Additional requests for the resource are required to wait. However, this is not sufficient as proof of a bottleneck. Two examples reinforce this point.

Disk utilization is determined by periodically monitoring whether there are any requests in the queue for each disk drive. The total number of requests in the queue is not factored into the disk utilization metric. Although 100% disk utilization is an indicator of a busy disk, it does not mean that the disk cannot support more I/Os.

The idle loop in the kernel is used to compute CPU utilization. On a workstation executing a compute-intensive application, CPU utilization is probably 100% for a long period of time. However, if no other processes are waiting for the CPU, and response time is satisfactory, there is no bottleneck.

There are utilization metrics for the CPU, memory, and disk resources.

3.4.2   Growing Resource Queue

Resource queue growth over time is a strong indicator of a bottleneck, in conjunction with the utilization metric. The queue for a resource tends to grow when demand increases and when there is not enough resource available to keep up with the requests. It is easier to develop rules of thumb for queue metrics than for utilization metrics.

3.4.3   Resource Starvation

Resource starvation can occur when one resource is saturated and another resource depends upon it. For instance, in a memory-bound environment, CPU cycles are needed to handle page faults. This leaves less of the CPU resource for application use.

3.4.4   Unsatisfactory Response Time

Unsatisfactory response time is sometimes the final arbiter of whether or not a bottleneck exists. The CPU example given above demonstrates this point. If no other processes are waiting for the CPU, and the application produces the results in a satisfactory time period, then there is no bottleneck. However, if the CPU is saturated and response or throughput expectations are not being met, then a CPU bottleneck exists.

3.4.5   Bottleneck Summary

Multiple metrics should always be reviewed to validate that a bottleneck exists. For example, the CPU utilization metric is a measure of saturation. The run queue metric is a measure of queue growth. Both metrics are needed to establish that a CPU bottleneck is present. Multiple tools should be used to validate that there is not a problem with a particular tool yielding mis-leading data. Consider the following analogy.

A three-lane highway is built to accommodate a certain maximum traffic flow, for example, 20 vehicles per minute distributed across the three lanes. This would be considered 100% utilization. Additional traffic entering the highway would be forced to wait at the entrance ramp, producing a queue. Suppose that a tractor/trailer over-turns and blocks two lanes of the highway. Now, the same amount of traffic must fun-nel through the one remaining open lane. With the same number of cars on the road, the highway is now more than saturated. The queue builds at the entrance ramps. Resource starvation occurs, since two lanes are closed. The time it takes to travel a given distance on the highway now becomes unacceptably long.

Once a bottleneck is identified, it can possibly be alleviated. However, alleviating one bottleneck may result in the emergence of a new one to investigate.

3.5 Tuning or Upgrading

Once the bottleneck is identified, there are two choices. Either the amount of the resource can be increased, or the demand for the resource can be reduced. Tuning techniques will be discussed along with the particular bottlenecks. However, there are some general tips that can be applied to tuning bottlenecks:

- Determine whether the data indicate a particular bottleneck.
- Devise a simple test for measuring results.
- Do not tune randomly.
- Use heuristics and logic in choosing what to tune.
- Look for simple causes.
- Develop an action plan.
- Change only one thing at a time.
- Prioritize the goals.
- Know when to stop tuning.

3.5.1   Determine Whether There Is a Particular Bottleneck

This is the first tip to apply. Using the multiple characteristics of a bottleneck, determine if the data indicate a particular bottleneck. There is no use in tuning disk I/O on a system that is CPU bound.

3.5.2   Devise a Simple Test for Measuring Results

When something in the operating system or application is tuned, it is advisable to quantita-tively measure whether performance has improved or degraded. The test should be simple, short, and repeatable, so that it can be performed as each tuning step is taken.

3.5.3   Do Not Tune Randomly

There was once a system administrator who always tuned the size of the buffer cache, no matter what the bottleneck. Tuning the wrong thing can make the situation worse rather than better. Use knowledge of how the kernel works to help decide the cause of the bottleneck. Always try to visualize what the data *should* look like and compare it to the actual data before assuming that a cause has been found.

3.5.4   Use Heuristics and Logic

Use heuristics to select the most likely cause of the bottleneck. Experience can point to a particular bottleneck rather quickly. Watching the access lights on the disk drives can quickly indicate which disk drives may be saturated even before you look at the metrics. Use the qualitative measures as well as the quantitative metrics. Logically work through the possible causes and potential tuning solutions. Experience in tuning systems will tell which tuning alternatives offer the largest probability of success.

3.5.5   Look for Simple Causes

By looking for simple causes, easier and less expensive solutions can be tried. This is the K. I. S. S. principle: Keep it Simple, Stupid! Simple causes tend to occur more frequently, and simple solutions should be tried first. For example, tuning a system parameter is easier and less costly than modifying the design of an application. Either tactic might result in performance improvements, but one is clearly a better solution than the other.

3.5.6   Develop an Action Plan

Write up an ordered, prioritized list of measurements and tuning actions. The list can sometimes be turned over to other people for execution. Include contingencies in case some of the steps do not result in improvement. Analyze the results after performing each step of the plan.

3.5.7   Change Only One Thing at a Time!

Otherwise, the cause of the bottleneck cannot be found. If you attempt to tune multiple things at once, the benefits from one type of tuning can be counteracted by the degradation caused by a different type of tuning.

3.5.8   Prioritize Goals

Often, you may have multiple goals when developing a tuning solution. Prioritizing the goals can solve the problem caused by different goals requiring different solutions. It is usually possible to tune for response time or for throughput, but not both. In a transaction-processing environment, one should tune for the most frequent type of transaction, or the most important.

3.5.9   Understand the Limits of the Application's Architecture

Some applications cannot fully utilize a system. An example is a single-threaded process flow, designed with no parallelism. Adding a CPU to such an application may not increase performance.

Instrumenting an application to provide performance metrics can also create this problem, if the instrumentation is not created with parallelism in mind. For example, incrementing a single global counter may be a choke point, as in the following code design:

```
while not done {
    do transaction work
    lock
    increment global counter
    unlock
}
```

3.5.10   Know When to Stop

Finally, knowing when to stop tuning is very important. Setting the performance expectations in advance is the easiest way to establish completion. Baselines can be used to help establish that performance has returned to a normal level. The "eternal hope syndrome" will not occur if the performance expectations are met through tuning.

From Bob's Consulting Log—I spent several days at a customer site improving performance by a factor of 50%. Once the customer saw the extent of the improvement, she insisted I do additional work to improve things even more. Soon it became clear that we had already maxed out the performance improvement and then wasted several more days trying to eke out just a little bit extra.

It is not useful to spend a lot of time on gaining 1% improvement in performance. Optimizing a part of the application that is only executed once and consumes less than 5% of the total execution time is just not worth it.

## CHAPTER 4

Kernel Instrumentation
and Performance Metrics

Themability to make measurements is crucial to any performance management activity. Without measurements, there is no objective data that shows where a system bottleneck is. Also, there is no way to objectively evaluate the effects of tuning the system or the application. The only alternative is to tune randomly, but even with random tuning, the outcome cannot be evaluated without measurements.

This chapter discusses several topics related to how performance data is gathered, and which items of data are interesting:

- Approaches to measuring
- Kernel instrumentation
- Performance metrics categories

4.1 Approaches to Measuring

Making measurements involves gathering data and processing it so that it is usable. There are several common approaches to acquiring data to measure activity in a computer system. They fall into two groups:

- External hardware monitors
- Internal software monitors

4.1.1   External Hardware Monitors

External hardware monitors usually involve probes, such as printed circuit boards which plug into the computer backplane or attach directly to the integrated circuits on the CPU board itself. These hardware monitors are triggered by events such as instruction execution or hardware interrupts. The accumulation of data typically occurs so rapidly that some external storage mechanism is required to save the data in real-time so that it can be analyzed later.

Advantages (+) and disadvantages (-) of hardware monitors are as follows:

+ Extremely accurate
+ Non-invasive to operating system
+ No overhead

- Expensive to build
- Difficult to set up and use
- Requires specialized hardware
- Hardware must be redesigned with each change of CPU
- Large volume of data
- Difficult to tie individual data items to individual processes
- Difficult to measure resources other than the CPU
- Difficult to relate to the user's application

Although hardware monitoring provides very accurate results, these disadvantages preclude its use outside of laboratory environments.

4.1.2   Internal Software Monitors

Internal software monitors are created by placing instrumentation points within the source code of the operating system kernel to acquire the performance data. Advantages (+) and disadvantages (-) of software instrumentation are as follows:

+ Relatively easy to implement
+ Easy to monitor many different resources, including networks
+ Easy to link individual processes with the data
+ Can easily be turned on or off
+ Can run safely in production environments
+ Run on various models of CPU without change
+ Conducive to general purpose software analysis tools

- Is invasive to the operating system
- Contends for the same resources that it is measuring, which affects accuracy

Data from internal software monitors is so general-purpose and easy to analyze that this kind of instrumentation is quite common on Unix systems. HP-UX incorporates three types of software instrumentation: sampling, counters and event traces.

4.1.2.1   Periodic Sampling

Sampling is normally performed by the kernel. The kernel schedules itself periodically to take a sample, which is like taking a picture of what is happening. Each sample will contain particular information that is measurable and desired by some performance tool.

The software clock on HP-UX systems ticks at a rate of 10 milliseconds. Since counting is synchronous with respect to the system clock, accuracy of the counting is limited to the clock rate. Today's computer hardware operates at much higher frequencies than in the past: 400 MHZ or more. Since Reduced Instruction Set Computers (RISC) typically complete one hardware instruction every hardware clock cycle, a computer operating at 100 MHZ would complete as many as 10 million instructions in one 10 millisecond software clock cycle. In this case, multiple short-lived processes could be created, perform their work, and terminate. The counting mechanism would not accurately account for these short-lived processes.

There are several ways of addressing this situation. An obvious solution would be to have the software clock tick more often. Although easy to implement, it is not a common solution. This is because the kernel does a lot of work when the software clock ticks, and a faster clock rate would cause higher overhead but would not provide the process-accounting accuracy desired. A more difficult solution would involve inventing a new method of capturing performance information in Unix.

Sampling is performed by Unix systems whenever the system clock ticks. When the clock ticks, the kernel takes note of which process, if any, is running, and allocates CPU time for the entire tick to that process. It also keeps track of what state the kernel is in so as to allocate global CPU utilization to the appropriate state. The kernel takes care of other housekeeping at the same time; for example, it checks to see if a higher priority process is ready to run. Sampling is commonly used for global and per-process CPU utilization and disk utilization metrics.

Process profiling, used for application optimization, also employs a sampling technique which is incorporated into the kernel. At the clock tick, the kernel determines which procedure or system call the process is currently executing, so that the profiler can determine how much time is being spent on which part of the process. Profiling will be discussed in more detail in Part 4.

4.1.2.2   Event-Driven Sampling

Rather than acquiring data based on a time interval, event sampling occurs whenever the event happens. For instance, if a page-out or a context switch occurs, it is counted immediately. Since event-driven sampling is related to the event rate, it has an inconsistent overhead. It is highly accurate, however, and especially useful for process profiling: whenever a procedure is called, a counter is incremented.

4.1.2.3   Counters

Counters are commonly found in various Unix systems to measure kernel activity. They were inserted into the kernel code at certain *interesting* points by the originators of the System V and Berkeley Unix variants, and were designed for use with specific performance-analysis tools.

This same instrumentation can be found today on almost every version of Unix. Because of this, one advantage of these counters is that they are considered "standard" on multiple versions of Unix.

Counters can be thought of as answering the questions: "How Many" and "How Much?" They record the number of times a particular event occurs, or how much of a particular resource is used. Answering the question "What?" is up to the tool when it is accessing a particular counter. Examples are the number of page-outs (a virtual memory function) that occur and the amount of CPU that a process has used. The kernel merely increments a counter during the execution of a particular section of code. Counters are almost always turned on, counting the occurrence of various events and providing very little detail. The overhead of collecting this information is unknown and cannot be measured with software tools, but it is estimated to be a very low, and an acceptable cost of monitoring system performance. Additional resources are consumed to access and report the data.

Because HP-UX is a combination of Berkeley and System V Unix, it contains counters to support both the Berkeley and System V performance tools which will be discussed in the next chapter. For example, in HP-UX 10.0, the majority of the standard counters can be found in the file */usr/include/sys/vmmeter.h*. (Note that accessing these counters on an SMP system may yield incorrect results.) A number of structures and individual counters defined in this include file produce measurements of the CPU and of memory resources. These counters are used by all the standard Unix performance tools. However, most of these tools have been changed to access these counters by calling *pstat(2)* instead of referencing them directly.

4.1.2.4   Accessing Counters through /dev/kmem

Counters are typically accessed through the pseudo-driver */dev/kmem*. This pseudo-driver provides access to kernel run-time memory by a user process with appropriate permissions. As an example of how counters can be accessed directly, it is possible to create a program that reads the data in the structure *vmtotal* which is defined in *vmmeter.h*. Acquiring data from the instrumentation defined in *vmmeter.h* alone is a time-consuming, multi-step process:

1. Determine the metric names by perusing the numerous system include files.

2. Call *nlist( )* for each metric name to find the address in the kernel.

3. Open the */dev/kmem* special device file.

4. For each of the metrics:

   - Position the driver to the address.

   - Read the variable or structure.

5. Report the results.

The code shown below gives an example of the old way of accessing performance metrics. It may be the only way to access counters on some non-HP operating systems. The technique is not recommended for use with HP-UX 10.0 and later, and it is no longer supported.

```
#include <nlist.h>
#include <fcntl.h>
#include <unistd.h>
main()

struct nlist nl[2];
struct vmtotal vmt;
int ierr;
int fd;
int value;
int address;

nl[0].n_name = "vmtotal";
nl[1].n_name = "";

if ((ierr = nlist("/vmunix",nl)) == -1) {
    printf("error from nlist call\n");
    exit(1);
    }
if (fd = open ("/dev/kmem",O_RDONLY)) == -1) {
    perror(open:   ");
    exit(2);
    }
if ((ierr = lseek(fd,nl[0].n_value,SEEK_SET)) == -1) {
    perror("lseek:   ");
    exit(3);
    }
if (ierr = read(fd,vmt,sizeof(vmt)) == -1) {
    perror("read:   ");
    exit(4);
    }
close(fd);
printf("Structure vmtotal:   ... ... ..
```

4.1.2.5   Accessing Counters through pstat(2)

Due to the overhead required to read the data periodically for all of the desired metrics, some vendors have developed a system call like the *pstat(2)* call in HP-UX. *Pstat(2)* transfers a block of data to the user process all at once, at much lower overhead. However, *pstat(2)* is not intended for use by the casual application programmer, because kernel source code is required to fully understand all of the counters. It is the job of the various performance reporting tools to document the counters they report. Making calls to *pstat(2)* is the only supported way to access performance metrics with a user-written or non-HP application.

The following code illustrates one way of using *pstat* to obtain performance data:

```
#include <sys/pstat.h>
#include <sys/param.h>
{
#define BURST ((size_t) 10 )
    struct pst_pstatus pst[BURST];
    int i, count;
    int idx = 0; /* index within the process context */
    while ( count = pstat_getproc(pst,sizeof(pst[0],BURST,idx)) > 0) {
        for (i=0;i<count;i++) {
            (void) printf ("pid=%d, command=%s\n",
                pst[i].pst_ucomm);
            }
            idx = pst[i].pst_ucomm;
        }
    if (count == -1) perror ("pstat-getproc: ");
    }
```

See the *pstat(2)* man page for a description of the many ways to invoke *pstat(2)*. This man page is very complete, even showing example code for calling wrapper routines that make the calls easier and more self-documenting. Here are a few of the wrapper routines, and the data they return:

- *pstat_getdisk()*—per-disk information
- *pstat_getproc()*—process table entries
- *pstat_getprocessor()*—per-CPU statistics
- *pstat_getshm()*—shared memory information
- *pstat_getvminfo()*—virtual memory statistics

4.1.2.6   Advantages and Disadvantages of Counters

Here are the advantages and disadvantages of counters:

+ Easy to implement
+ Reasonably standard across Unix implementations
+ Low fixed CPU consumption to do the counting
+ Minimal memory consumption to maintain the counters
+ Interval of data collection is up to the tool
+ Volume of data depends upon sampling interval and counters requested

- Minimal information
- Medium CPU consumption to access all counters
- Time-stamping must be performed by the tool that reads the data
- Sampled counters are incremented synchronously with respect to the system clock

4.1.2.7 Event Traces

HP is currently unique in that it employs a second method for instrumenting the HP-UX kernel This method is being reviewed by a number of organizations and vendors for inclusion in other Unix variants. The approach is to generate event traces that answer the following questions:

- Who? What process caused or initiated the event?
- What? What is the event? (for example, a disk read operation)
- When? When did the event occur? (a very accurate time-stamp)
- How much? How much or how many were requested? (for example, number of bytes read)

One can easily assume that such additional detail does not come free. Event traces generate a lot of data that must be read from the kernel and then analyzed and reduced into usable performance data. Event traces are similar to data generated by hardware monitors in terms of greater volume and the need to reduce the data.

Event traces also have advantages (+) and disadvantages (-):

+ Increased detail over counters shows the user of the resource.
+ Chronological time-stamp is maintained by the kernel.
+ Interval of data collection is up to the tool.
+ Tracing can be turned on or off.
+ Tracing is asynchronous with respect to the system clock.

- Event trace buffers consume kernel memory.
- Variable CPU consumption is required by the kernel to collect the information.
- Event traces are more difficult to implement than counters.
- There is a high volume of data which must be analyzed and reduced.
- Events must be read quickly or data will be lost.

Since event traces are asynchronous with respect to the system clock, they can be generated more frequently than every 10 milliseconds. This means that the measurements can be much more accurate than those from counters, because specific events initiate the traces. For example, a trace might be generated when a process is created and when it is terminated, so that we have a more accurate measurement of elapsed time.

4.2 Kernel Instrumentation and Measurement Interface

In HP-UX, event traces are generated by the kernel using a mechanism called Kernel Instrumentation (KI). They are written into a circular buffer in the kernel for each occurrence of events such as:

- System call (operating system intrinsic)
- Context switch (from one user process to another)
- Pageouts
- I/O events

There are more than three hundred different system calls in HP-UX that normally occur at a rate of thousands of calls per second. Context switches occur quite often, sometimes hundreds or thousands of times per second. Therefore, HP-UX event traces can result in a large amount of data generated. The overhead associated with kernel-generated event traces, although larger than that of counters, provides so much additional detail that it is worth it. This overhead is a function of the workload on the system and cannot be measured directly, even though event traces are not always turned on.

The KI is turned on selectively by a user process called *midaemon*. Each instrumentation point in the kernel can be turned on or left off as necessary for collecting various types of data. Certain event traces are enabled and read by *midaemon*. This process runs at a real-time priority of 50, which gives it higher priority than normal timeshare processes. (Process priorities will be discussed in the chapter on CPU.) *Midaemon* needs this higher priority so that it can read the circular event trace buffer written by the KI before it overflows. After the event trace buffer is read, it must then be analyzed to reduce the large volume of data. This task is also performed by *midaemon*, which summarizes the data and makes it available through a library called the *Measurement Interface* (MI). In fact, that is where the name *midaemon* originated. All of the HP performance tools use the MI to gather their data.

Since *midaemon* is a user process, the overhead associated with reading, analyzing, and reducing the event traces to manageable form can be directly measured. It is usually less than 3%, although the exact amount of overhead is workload dependent. Computer professionals who come from the mainframe environment see performance data collection as a "cost of doing business" and would generally consider anything less than 10% overhead acceptable.

4.2.1 Acceptable Overhead

What should you consider *acceptable overhead*? Here, you can apply **Rule #1**: "It depends." Specifically, what is acceptable changes based on the kind of system and the kind of application. The answer will vary for

- Workstations
- Servers
- Single-user systems
- Multi-user systems
- Systems running scientific or engineering applications
- Systems running business applications

Also recall **Rule #3**: "Performance cannot be measured without impacting the system being measured." Remember that it is impossible to collect performance data without consuming resources and thus changing the *system* that is being measured.

4.3 Performance Metrics Categories

Metrics can be categorized by their scope within the system being measured. They can also be viewed from the perspective of the type of data they provide.

4.3.1 Categories of Metrics by Scope

Instrumentation in the kernel provides metrics that fall into several categories:

- Global performance metrics
- Per-process performance metrics
- Application performance metrics
- Subsystem metrics
- Process profile metrics

Within each of these categories, data from the major kernel subsystems may be available. This data may include CPU utilization metrics, virtual memory utilization metrics, disk utilization metrics, network utilization metrics, and kernel resource utilization metrics.

4.3.1.1 Global Performance Metrics

These are the most basic types of metrics. They reveal what is happening on the system from a global perspective, that is, the *what* can be detected, but not the *who*. The particular process consuming the resource cannot be found using global data. Global metrics are reported by all of the *standard* Unix tools, as well as HP-written tools.

4.3.1.2 Per-Process Performance Metrics

These provide various levels of detail about individual processes. Thus, the *who* can be determined as well as the *what*. Per-process information takes more of the CPU resource to acquire, so **Rule #2** gets invoked: there is a trade-off between acquiring more information and using more of the CPU resource to get it. The *ps* command and System V Accounting are the only standard Unix commands that report per-process information. There are several HP-written tools that report per-process information.

4.3.1.3 Application Performance Metrics

These are an HP invention, and are not generated by the kernel. Simply stated, application metrics are obtained by summing per-process metrics for an arbitrary grouping of processes, where the arbitrary grouping is defined by the performance manager. Only HP-written tools provide application metrics.

4.3.1.4   Subsystem Metrics

The choice of subsystem metrics will depend on the reason for making the measurement. Whereas global and application CPU, memory, and disk utilization measurements may be sufficient for performance characterization and forecasting, per-process CPU, memory, and disk utilization are most useful in performance problem diagnosis. Remember that if the purpose of the measurement is performance problem diagnosis, more metrics and more detailed metrics are necessary.

4.3.1.5   Process Profile Metrics

Both counting and sampling methods are used for application profiling at the procedure level. Procedure calls are counted by caller and procedure called, and the time spent in each procedure is sampled as described above. Profiling will be discussed in greater detail in Part 4.

4.3.2   Categories of Metrics by Type of Data

Three types of data can be gathered for all the subsystems and categories mentioned above. They are saturation metrics, queue metrics, and rates.

4.3.2.1   Saturation Metrics

Saturation metrics indicate how much of a resource is being utilized. An example would be the percentage of global or per-process CPU utilization.

4.3.2.2   Queue Metrics

Queue metrics show the amount of waiting for a resource by requests or processes. Examples include the CPU run queue and the disk I/O queue.

4.3.2.3   Resource Rates

Rates are the requests for a resource per unit of time. They indicate how often an event is occurring. Examples include I/Os per second, context switches per second, and interrupts per second.

4.4   Summary

It is impossible to carry out performance management unless system performance can be measured. Measuring system performance requires some method of instrumentation. Software instrumentation is the most practical method for measuring system performance, even though it is invasive to the operating system, that is, it will often affect the performance of the system being measured. The amount of effect is called the overhead of the measurement. The smaller the overhead of the measurement, the more accurate it will be.

An important goal of performance tools is to minimize the overhead of the tool so that the performance data presented accurately reflects the state of the system. Different tools have different amounts of overhead. The state of the system will determine the real impact that the tool imposes on the system. As the system becomes busier, the greater the chance that the tool will impact the system that is being measured.

The instrumentation in the various kernel subsystems provides different categories of data. Tool selection must be made based on the purpose of the measurement and the data presented by the tool. Information about which performance tool shows which type of data, and which metrics, will be presented in the next chapter.

## PART 2

Tools and Metrics

P art 2 presents information about a variety of performance monitoring tools—some of them specific to HP-UX, and some available on other Unix operating systems. The chapters are:

- Survey of Unix Performance Tools
- Performance Tools Alphabetical Reference

Survey of Unix
Performance Tools

There are many different performance tools available for Unix systems in general, and for HP-UX in particular. This chapter presents a broad overview of tools by type. The goal of this chapter is to familiarize the reader with how the tools are used, and the metrics that they display; however, we will not go into the meaning of each of the metrics. Metrics will be discussed in the chapter on the bottleneck to which they apply. The following topics are presented:

- Choosing the right tools
- Multipurpose diagnostic tools
- CPU diagnostic tools
- Disk diagnostic tools
- Memory diagnostic tools
- Performance characterization tools
- Performance prediction tools
- Application optimization tools
- Network diagnostic tools
- Capacity planning tools

These tools have come from a variety of sources; Chapter 6 contains tables listing all the available tools discussed in this book, with information about their origins.

5.1 Choosing the Right Tools

Deciding which tools to use under which conditions probably seems difficult at this point. We will demonstrate that some tools are better than others under certain circumstances, and depending upon particular needs. Recall **Rule #4**: "No single performance tool will provide all the data needed to solve performance problems." The major performance tools and their relationship to the data sources are shown in Figure 5-1. These tools provide most of the information that is available about the system and processes running on it

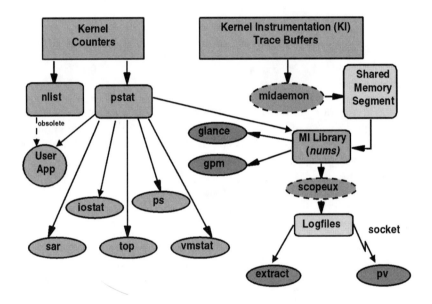

Figure 5-1   Performance Tools and Data Sources

Most of the tools in Figure 5-1 use data that is provided by two basic Unix elements: the kernel counters in */dev/kmem*; and the kernel instrumentation trace buffers monitored by *midaemon*. In general, tools can be grouped into categories based on the kinds of questions they help to answer:

- Diagnostic: "What is going on now?"
- Performance Characterization: "What happened last month compared with this month?"
- Performance Prediction: "When will I run out of CPU?"
- Application Optimization: "Why is this process so slow?"
- Network Diagnostic: "Which system is heavily loaded?"
- Capacity Planning: "What will happen if I add 20 users?"

Each category is described below, together with the most useful tools for addressing the problem. Note that because some tools fit into more than one category, they may be described more than once.

5.2 Multipurpose Diagnostic Tools

Diagnostic tools provide a snapshot of system or subsytem behavior at particular moments. Although data from diagnostic tools can also be used to compare system activity over longer periods, the tools are designed primarily to provide current data.

Diagnostic tools are of many different types, some offering a general, multipurpose set of metrics covering many subsystems, others with more specialized uses. The most important multipurpose tools are *GlancePlus/UX*, *GlancePlus/Motif*, *PerfView* and *sar*. Also included in this group are time-related tools, such as *uptime*, *time*, and *timex*.

5.2.1 GlancePlus/UX

GlancePlus/UX is an interactive performance tool that displays numerous metrics organized on a number of different screens. *Glance* is available for HP-UX, Solaris, and AIX, and comes in two versions: character-mode and Motif. The Motif version is called *gpm* and will be discussed separately, since it has a number of additional features.

Due to the number of metrics and features provided, *glance* occupies more memory than the standard Unix tools. Following the adage that nothing worth anything comes without cost, *glance* is not included with the OS, and must be purchased separately.

Glance displays both process and global information, a great advantage over the standard Unix tools. When process information is displayed, multiple criteria are available to limit the output to processes of interest, such as those that correspond to particular CPU, memory and disk thresholds. In addition, filters are available to restrict the output to a particular user, tty, or process name. *Glance* is generally invoked without parameters. However, it does have some command-line options and is invoked in the following way:

glance [-j interval] [-p dest] [-f dest] [-maxpages n] [-command]
[-nice n] [-nosort] [-lock] [\<midaemon control parameters>]

The command line parameters are:

- *-j \<interval>*—specifies the data refresh interval
- *-p \<dest>*—enables printing to the print spooler printer destination
- *-f \<dest>*—enables printing to a file
- *-maxpages \<n>*—limits the number of pages to be printed
- *-command*—selects the initial metric screen
- *-nice \<n>*—nice value at which glance runs
- *-nosort*—don't sort processes on the process screen
- *-lock*—locks glance into memory

For quicker *glance* startup, *midaemon* or *scopeux* should be run from the */sbin/rc*d/mwa* script. Alternatively, create the */sbin/rc*d/mwa/midaemon* file so that *midaemon* starts up at boot time. *Glance* resides in *opt/perf/bin* on HP-UX versions 10.0 or later, versions 11.x or later, and Solaris 2.X.

5.2.1.1   Glance Screens of Metrics

Glance has the following screens of metrics, which may be selected by pressing the labelled softkey or by typing the single letter shown below:

- *a*—All CPU detail (for SMP systems)
- *c*—CPU detail
- *d*—Disk detail
- *f*—Single process open file detail
- *g*—Global process list
- *i*—Disk I/O by file system
- *j*—Adjust data refresh interval
- *l*—LAN detail
- *m*—Memory detail
- *M*—Single process memory regions detail
- *N*—Global NFS activity
- *n*—NFS detail by system
- *o*—Change process list filtering (thresholds)
- *s*—Single process detail
- *t*—System table utilization
- *u*—Disk queue lengths
- *v*—Disk LVM detail
- *w*—Swap detail
- *W*—Single process wait states detail
- *y*—Renice a process

Since it is desirable to present performance data in a timely manner, *glance* is "nastied" by default with a nice value of -10, so that it has a higher priority than most timeshare processes. Bear in mind, however, that there are times on a very busy system when *glance* may be delayed in its report of the data. You should resist the temptation to run *glance* with a realtime priority, because doing so would have a severely negative impact on system performance. Interactive processes should usually not be given a realtime priority.

Glance is meant to run interactively to diagnose performance problems. Although it is possible to print a particular screen of metrics, either once or continuously, it is recommended that screen printing be done continuously only when the refresh interval is 60 seconds or longer, since the printing may have an impact on system performance (Remember **Rule #3:** "Performance cannot be measured without impacting the system being mesasured.") Additionally, the Adviser can be used to print a customized set of metrics to a file.

The overhead that *glance* imposes on the system is as follows:

- CPU—depends on the data refresh interval and the number of running processes
- Memory—depends on the number of running processes

5.2.1.2 Per-Process Information in glance

One important advantages of *glance* is its wealth of per-process information. Not only can one determine what is happening on the system; one can also determine who is using it. Detailed process information includes the following:

- CPU utilization
- System call rate
- Context switch rate (voluntary and involuntary)
- Paging and swapping rates
- Some particular system call rates
- I/O rates, amounts, and types
- Detailed global information on CPU, memory, disk, LAN, NFS

CPU utilization is further broken down into:

- User (normal)
- User (niced or nastied)
- User (real-time priority)
- System (system calls)
- System (context switch)
- System (interrupt processing)
- System call rates
- Context switch rates
- Load averages
- The bar graphs for CPU, memory, disk, and swap

At a glance (pun intended), the CPU, memory, disk, and swap utilization may be seen. CPU utilization is broken down into System (S) and User (U), Nice (N) and RealTime (R). It should be noted that *glance*'s concept of Nice CPU utilization differs from that of other performance tools in that it reports both the "nasty" and "nice" forms of *nice* as Nice (N) CPU utilization and (A) Negative Nice ("nasty"). The performance tools *sar*, *iostat* and *top* use the kernel's concept of Nice CPU utilization, which considers only those processes that have used the "nice" form of *nice* to degrade their process priority.

Memory utilization is broken down into the amount of memory consumed by the System (S), Users (U), and the Buffer Cache (B). The Buffer Cache portion of the bar is most useful on those systems that support a Dynamic Buffer Cache, since the amount of memory consumed by it will fluctuate.

The disk bar shows peak disk utilization of the busiest disk during the interval, broken down into File System I/O (F) and disk I/O due to Virtual Memory System operations (V).

Rather than display paging or swapping activity, the swap bar shows the amount of space that is Reserved (R) or Used (U) on each of the swap devices. Many Unix operating systems allocate swap space immediately when the process is *exec*'d, or when it grows in size. This paradigm wastes CPU time by allocating space on the swap device even if it is never used. HP-UX allocates space on the swap device only when it needs to page or swap the process out. Therefore, in order to follow the standard Unix paradigm of making sure that swap will be available if it is ever needed, HP-UX reserves the swap space at *exec* time, or at the time of process growth (*malloc(3)* or *sbrk(2)*) merely by decrementing a global counter that represents the total amount of swap space available.

5.2.1.3   Advantages and Disadvantages of *glance*

Advantages (+) of *glance* include:

+ Filters for the process list. The process list may be sorted alphabetically by name, by CPU utilization, or by disk utilization. Additionally, the process list may be limited by user name, tty name, and thresholds for CPU, disk, and memory utilization by the individual process.

+ Extensive online help. Although a manual is available for *glance*, there is little need for it because all the necessary information is available online. Understanding the meaning of a particular metric or screen is as simple as invoking the online help facility.

+ Availability for HP-UX, AIX, and Solaris. The Motif version of *glance*, called *gpm,* is available on all of these Operating Systems. The character-mode version is available only for HP-UX.

The disadvantages (-) of *glance* include:

- More overhead than traditional simple tools. This point is an example of **Rule #2**— "Performance tuning always involves a trade-off." You can't collect detailed performance data without cost. *Glance* collects and displays much more detailed information than is available from the standard performance tools. In doing this, however, it consumes more CPU and memory than the simpler tools.

- Limited logging of data. *Glance* will optionally log the current screen data for each interval to a spooled printer or to a disk file. Because of the overhead, logging should only be invoked when the screen-refresh interval is 60 seconds or longer

- Relatively slow startup. If *midaemon* is not running, *glance* must first start it up. *Glance* then checks its on-disk databases to see if the information is still compatible with the currently running kernel; if not, it must recreate the databases. All this activity results in a clearly perceptible startup time.

The CPU overhead associated with running *glance* depends on the refresh interval and the number of running processes. Longer intervals use less overhead. Memory overhead depends on the number of running processes, because *glance* keeps information about all running processes in its user memory to reduce CPU overhead. The counters and other metrics accessed by *glance* are collected by *midaemon*; some of them are turned on only when *midaemon* is running.

Figure 5-2 shows the *GlancePlus* report screen for Resources by Process ID 1, *init*.

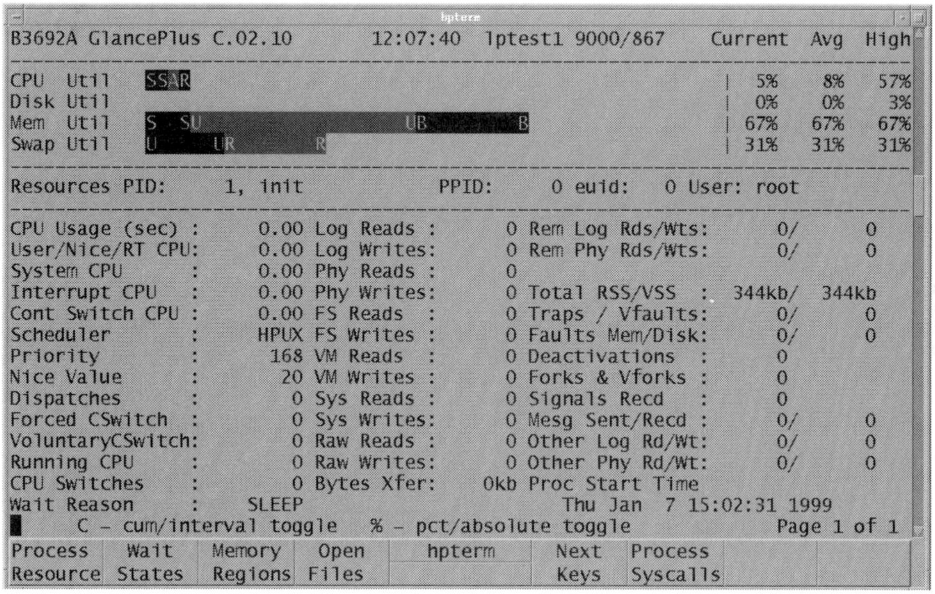

```
                                              hpterm
B3692A GlancePlus C.02.10          12:07:40  1ptest1 9000/867     Current   Avg   High

CPU  Util  SSAR                                               |   5%    8%    57%
Disk Util                                                     |   0%    0%     3%
Mem  Util  S  SU                       UB          B          |  67%   67%    67%
Swap Util  U       UR           R                             |  31%   31%    31%

Resources PID:         1, init            PPID:     0 euid:    0 User: root

CPU Usage (sec) :      0.00 Log Reads :       0 Rem Log Rds/Wts:      0/       0
User/Nice/RT CPU:      0.00 Log Writes:       0 Rem Phy Rds/Wts:      0/       0
System CPU      :      0.00 Phy Reads :       0
Interrupt CPU   :      0.00 Phy Writes:       0 Total RSS/VSS  : 344kb/  344kb
Cont Switch CPU :      0.00 FS Reads  :       0 Traps / Vfaults:      0/       0
Scheduler       :      HPUX FS Writes :       0 Faults Mem/Disk:      0/       0
Priority        :       168 VM Reads  :       0 Deactivations  :      0
Nice Value      :        20 VM Writes :       0 Forks & Vforks :      0
Dispatches      :         0 Sys Reads :       0 Signals Recd   :      0
Forced CSwitch  :         0 Sys Writes:       0 Mesg Sent/Recd :      0/       0
VoluntaryCSwitch:         0 Raw Reads :       0 Other Log Rd/Wt:      0/       0
Running CPU     :         0 Raw Writes:       0 Other Phy Rd/Wt:      0/       0
CPU Switches    :         0 Bytes Xfer:     0kb Proc Start Time
Wait Reason     :     SLEEP                       Thu Jan  7 15:02:31 1999
█       C - cum/interval toggle    % - pct/absolute toggle                Page 1 of 1
Process    Wait    Memory    Open        hpterm      Next    Process
Resource  States   Regions  Files                    Keys   Syscalls
```

Figure 5-2 *GlancePlus* Resources by PID—Report Screen

5.2.2   GlancePlus Motif

Gpm is the Motif version of *glance*. It is bundled with *glance* and provides more features than the character-mode version. *Gpm* uses color to indicate severity and signal alarms, and provides a short-term history in graphical format. Also, some new metrics and screens are shown by *gpm*. Since *gpm* is a Motif application, the DISPLAY environment variable must be set before invoking *gpm*. It is invoked with the following syntax:

**gpm [-nosave] [-rpt <name>] [-sharedclr] [-nice <nicevalue>]
[-lock] [<midaemon control parameters>]**

The command line parameters are:

- *-nosave*—Do not save configuration changes at exit.

- *-rpt <name>*—Display one or more report windows at startup.

- *-sharedclr*—Have *gpm* use a shared color scheme in case of color shortage at the cost of disabling user color configurability.

- *-nice <nicevalue>*—Change the *nice* value at which *gpm* runs (default -10).

- *-lock*—Lock *gpm* into memory.

Figure 5-3 shows the *GlancePlus Motif* main screen.

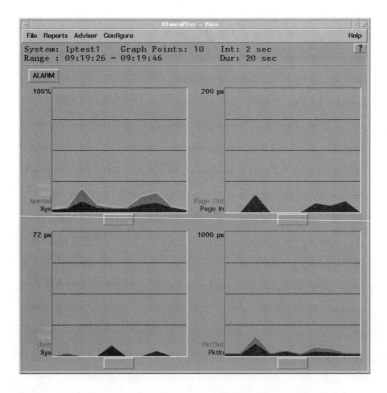

Figure 5-3   *GlancePlus Motif*—Main Screen

For quicker *gpm* startup, *midaemon* or *scopeux* should be run from the */sbin/init.d/mwa* script. Alternatively, create the */sbin/init.d/midaemon* file so that it starts up at boot time. *Gpm* resides in *opt/perf/bin* on HP-UX versions 10.0 or later, versions 11.x or later, and Solaris 2.X.

Since *gpm* is a Motif application, its functions are selected from a menu bar at the top of the main control window. This control window displays four graphs that show the utilization of the major system resources of CPU, memory, disk, and network. Notice that the fourth graph shows different data than the fourth bar shown at the top of each *glance* screen; *glance* shows swap utilization, whereas *gpm* shows network data. Figure 5-3 shows the main screen of Glance-Plus Motif.

Gpm displays metrics on the following screens, which are called report windows. They may be selected from the menu bar on the control window, and are shown as the menu items to be selected with the mouse.

5.2.2.1   Reports / Resource History

This window contains four line graphs, by default, showing CPU, memory, disk, and network utilization over the last 'n' samples. The look of this window can be changed with Configure. Each graph has several lines representing types of each resource; that is, the CPU graph shows Normal, System, Realtime, and Nice CPU utilization.

5.2.2.2   Reports / CPU / CPU Graph

This graph shows a history of the one-minute Load Average metric which is one measure of a CPU bottleneck.

5.2.2.3   Reports / CPU / CPU Report

The CPU report is a table of the various global CPU metrics, such as the seven types of CPU utilization, the one-minute Load Average, and the system call rate. This report, shown in Figure 5-4, is identical to the *glance* CPU (c) screen. The CPU report is most useful in a Uni-processor environment.

5.2.2.4   Reports / CPU / CPU by Processor

This report is most useful in a Symmetric Multi-Processor (SMP) environment, because it contains metrics that do not appear on the CPU Report. It shows CPU utilization, the one-, five-, and fifteen-minute load averages, the context switch rate, fork rate, and last PID all by processor number. It is the same as the *glance* All CPU screen (a).

5.2.2.5   Reports / Memory Info / Memory Graph

This window graphs the three most important indicators of a memory bottleneck: Page Outs, Swap Outs, and the number of processes blocked on Virtual Memory (Wait Queue).

5.2.2.6   Reports / Memory Info / Memory Report

Similar to the *glance* Memory (m) screen, this report displays the important global memory metrics. The Buffer Cache Read Hit Ratio, a disk metric, is also shown in this report. The metrics are shown as current, cumulative since *gpm* started up, and percent.

```
┌─┐                      GlancePlus - CPU Report                              ┌─┐
├─┘                                                                          └─┤
│  File  Reports                                                       Help   │
│  System: lptest1    Last Update: 09:20:45    Int: 2 sec          ┌─┐ ? │    │
│                                                                            │
│  Top CPU User: gpm                             PID: 17685                  │
│                                                                            │
│  State            Current    Avg.     High     Time    Cum Time           │
│                                                                            │
│  Normal             0.5%      1.5%    10.4%     0.0        1.47            │
│  Nice Nice          0.0%      0.0%     0.0%     0.0        0.00            │
│  Negative Nice      1.5%      3.0%    29.1%     0.0        2.84            │
│  RealTime           1.5%      1.6%     4.5%     0.0        1.56            │
│  System             1.5%      3.3%    32.4%     0.0        3.18            │
│  Interrupt          1.0%      1.2%     2.7%     0.0        1.17            │
│  Context Switch     0.0%      0.4%     1.2%     0.0        0.36            │
│  V Fault            0.0%      0.3%     2.4%     0.0        0.31            │
│  Trap               0.0%      0.0%     0.5%     0.0        0.01            │
│  Idle              94.0%     88.6%    95.0%     1.9       84.39            │
│                                                                            │
│  Activity          Rate    C Rate      High                               │
│                                                                            │
│  Syscalls         246.0     448.3     3648.7                               │
│  Interrupts       356.5     353.2      516.5                               │
│  Cont Switches     44.0      52.5      144.2                               │
│                                                                            │
│  Queues          Length     Avg.       High                               │
│                                                                            │
│  Load Average      10.1      10.1       10.1                               │
└────────────────────────────────────────────────────────────────────────────┘
```

Figure 5-4   *GlancePlus Motif*—CPU Report

5.2.2.7   Reports / Disk Info / Disk Graph

This window contains a graph of the percent utilization of the busiest disks. The chapter on "Disk Bottlenecks" will demonstrate that the Disk Queue metric is more useful than the data presented here.

5.2.2.8   Reports / Disk Info / Disk Report

This report is like the *glance* Disk (d) screen. It shows global disk metrics including Logical I/O rates, Physical I/O rates, and User and System I/O rates.

5.2.2.9   Reports / Disk Info / I/O by Disk

This window lists metrics such as Disk Queue Length and utilization, along with Physical, Logical, Virtual Memory, File System, System, and Raw I/O rates. Although similar to the *glance* Disk Queue (u) screen, this screen shows several new metrics as well.

5.2.2.10   Reports / Disk Info / I/O by File System

Like the *glance* I/O by File System (i) screen, this report indicates the I/Os that are associated with each mounted file system.

5.2.2.11   Reports / Disk Info / I/O by Logical Volume

Since the Logical Volume Manager (LVM) feature of HP-UX can result in a File System or Raw Volume being split or striped across multiple physical disks, disk metrics related to each Logical Volume are useful to monitor in conjunction with the Physical Disk rates. This report is like the *glance* Disk by Logical Volume (v) screen.

5.2.2.12   Reports / Network Info / LAN Graph

The LAN graph window shows the LAN packet I/O rates, percent LAN Errors and percent LAN Collisions. Collisions are a measure of Network saturation, and Errors are a measure of Network quality. Both cause degradation in network throughput.

5.2.2.13   Reports / Network Info / Network by LAN

In the presence of multiple LAN cards on the system, it is useful to determine the distribution of I/Os, collisions, and errors across each LAN when looking at network loading. The *glance* LAN (l) screen shows similar information.

5.2.2.14   Reports / Network / NFS Global Activity

This report shows Network File System (NFS) global activity from *this system's* perspective, as well as metrics such as Read and Write Queues, Idle Biods, and response time. It is similar to the *glance* global NFS (N) screen.

5.2.2.15   Reports / Network / NFS by System

Since it is useful to display the amount of NFS acitivity generated by particular systems, this report shows the NFS I/O rates for each system with an NFS-mounted file system. It is important to distinguish whether these rates are generated as an NFS client or an NFS server. This information can be seen on the *glance* NFS by system (n) screen.

5.2.2.16   Reports / Network / NFS by Operation

NFS uses various access methods, including remote file access and remote procedure calls. NFS activity is shown by particular NFS operation in this report.

5.2.2.17   Reports / System Table Info / System Tables Graph

One of the system-tuning functions involves monitoring the utilization of the various system tables whose size is tunable. This report graphs the percent utilization, over time, of the process, system file, shared memory-identifier, message-identifier, semaphore-identifier, file lock, and pseudo-terminal tables. It also graphs the utilization of the global swap space.

5.2.2.18   Reports / System Table Info / System Tables Report

Along with the metrics shown in the System Tables Graph, this report displays utilization of the inode table, maximum shared memory, message buffer memory, and the file system buffer cache. It is similar to the *glance* System Tables (t) screen.

5.2.2.19   Reports / Swap Space

The amount of swap space available and used by swap device or swap file system is shown in this report. It is similar to the *glance* Swap (w) screen.

5.2.2.20   Reports / Application List

MeasureWare has a feature that aggregates certain metrics for user-defined collections of processes, which are called Applications. The application definition list is shown in this report.

5.2.2.21   Reports / Process List

If you know a resource bottleneck exists, you want to determine which process or processes are causing it. The process list is the first step in making this determination. This screen is similar to the Global (g) screen in *glance*, but drilling down to the Single Process (s) screen works differently.

Since *gpm* is a Motif application, double-clicking with the mouse on the line showing a particular process will display the Single Process window. Single-clicking the mouse on one or more lines of individual processes will highlight these processes and lock them onto the Process List. This makes important processes much easier to follow.

The arrangement of the columns can be changed to suit the preference of the user or the needs of the performance problem. Sorting and filtering processes in this list is discussed under "Reports / Process List / Configure" in later sections.

5.2.2.22   Reports / Process List / Admin / Renice

The superuser or owner of the process can easily change the nice value of individual processes after selecting the process from the Process List. Changing the nice value of a running process will directly impact the priority of the running process, and indirectly impact the amount of CPU that the process receives. Only the superuser can assign a "nasty" nice value that will improve the priority of the process, thus increasing its opportunity to use the CPU.

5.2.2.23   Reports / Process List / Admin / Kill

A runaway process can be killed by highlighting it in the Process List and selecting Admin / Kill.

5.2.2.24   Reports / Process List / Reports / Process Resources

This report window is like the Single Process (s) screen in *glance*. It lists the per-process CPU, memory and disk performance metrics for the selected process.

5.2.2.25   Reports / Process List / Reports / Process Open Files

It is sometimes desirable to see which files are being accessed by a process. This report window, like the *glance* open file (F) screen, shows all the files that a process currently has open. It also shows the current file offset position, which can be watched to see random or sequential file activity.

5.2.2.26   Reports / Process List / Reports / Process Wait States

The various wait states for a process can help identify the reason why a process is running slower than expected. For instance, if a process is blocked waiting for Semaphores, the reason might be a locking or serialization problem with the application. This information can be seen in *glance* by selecting the Process Wait States (W) screen. The wait states are shown as the percent of time during the interval in which the process was waiting in that particular state.

5.2.2.27   Reports / Process List / Reports / Process Memory Regions

Finally, the sizes and locking status of the various memory regions for a process can be seen in this report window. This information can be used to determine which kinds of memory pages in use by the process are included in the Resident Set Size (RSS) and Virtual Set Size (VSS) of the process. *Glance* shows this same information in the Process Memory Regions (M) screen. An important metric in this screen is the amount of memory locked. This can be used to see what processing may be causing memory bottlenecks.

5.2.2.28   Reports / Process List / Configure / Column Arrangement

All the columns shown in the Process List report window can be rearranged to suit the user. You can also choose columns to be locked at the left of the screen when the display is scrolled horizontally.

5.2.2.29   Reports / Process List / Configure / Sort Fields

This screen lets you define how to sort the processes in the Process List based on the values in one or more columns.

5.2.2.30   Reports / Process List / Configure / Filters

Filters can be used to determine which processes are to be listed in the Process List. Filters are based on comparison of the individual column metrics to threshold values. Comparisons include "equal to," "less than," "less than or equal to," and the like. Processes that exceed a particular threshold can be highlighted with the color of your choice. This screen provides a powerful way of limiting the potentially hundreds of processes that would normally show up in the process list.

5.2.2.31   Configure / Colors

The colors used on the various graphs, as well as the colors for the alert levels, may be chosen by the user if there are enough colors available in the X/Server. This might depend upon how many other windows are open, and the number of colors used in those windows.

5.2.2.32   Configure / Measurement

The interval associated with data refresh can be set in minutes and seconds.

5.2.2.33   Configure / Icon

When *gpm* is iconified, the icon is an active representation of the four major resource measurements. The contents of the icon can be changed from line graph to bar graph or kiveat (radar) plot.

5.2.2.34   Configure / Main Graph / Horizontal, Vertical, Pie, History

The graphs displayed in the initial control window can be changed from the Resource History line graph to a horizontal or vertical bar chart, or a pie chart.

5.2.3   GlancePlus Motif Adviser

Gpm has a feature called the Adviser that is unique among performance tools. The Adviser is a customizable set of rules that determine when and if a performance problem exists. The Adviser bases its decisions on user-specified *symptoms* that are defined in terms of the *interval* time period, and *alarms* that are defined for longer periods of time. Symptoms and alarms can ease the performance management of complex systems by warning operators of impending performance problems by sending *alerts*. The Adviser can be accessed and configured through the following menu items:

5.2.3.1   Adviser / Symptom Status

This window shows the status of all symptoms during the current interval.

5.2.3.2   Adviser / Alarm History

This window shows a textual list of alarms that have been generated since startup or rest time.

5.2.3.3   Adviser / Adviser Syntax

The actual syntax of the alarms is shown and may be edited in this window. If you prefer, the syntax can be saved to a file, edited with the editor of choice, and then reloaded into *gpm*. Alarm syntax consists of a symptom name, a probability value, a time period, an alert for a major resource, and a reset value. The following is an example of how to code an alarm based on the size of the run queue:

```
if runqueue > 74 for 5 minutes {
    start YELLOW ALERT CPU
    reset
    }
```

The variable *runqueue* is defined as a symptom in the Symptom Window.

5.2.3.4   Adviser / Adviser Syntax / Window / Symptom Window

The rule-based symptoms are displayed and can be edited in this window, or edited with an editor by saving the rules to a file. Symptoms are named, and consist of a collection of rules that are based on specific metrics. The exact metric names can be found by using the online help facility, or you can create your own variable names. For example, to create a rule based on the size of the CPU Run Queue, one would define a new symptom variable called *runqueue* and set it to a probability of 75 if the length of the CPU run queue exceeds 10:

```
SYMPTOM runqueue
RULE gbl_pri_queue > 10 probability 75
```

5.2.4   Advantages and Disadvantages of GlancePlus Motif

The advantages (+) and disadvantages (-) of *gpm* include those of *glance* as well as the following:

+ Colors and color graphical presentation. Color is used by *gpm* to indicate the severity of an alert (*red* for alert, *yellow* for warning, *green* for OK) and for showing types of resource utilization. Color improves the readability of the data and the detectibility of problems. Color graphics are much easier to assimilate than tabular data. One can quickly get an idea of health of the system, and in some cases view critical historical information (last 'n' intervals).

+ Extensive process list filtering and sorting. The process list can be filtered by <u>any</u> of the metrics displayed in the window, based on mathematical comparisons. The process can be highlighted by configurable color. Also, the process list can be sorted by any of the window metrics.

+ Customizable alarms and advice. Alarms can be generated based on default and user-defined rules that can be customized for the particular system environment.

- Significant memory consumption. Since *gpm* is a Motif application, it must allocate memory for each of the windows that are being displayed, resulting in a minimum Resident Set Size of 2.5 MB and a Virtual Set Size of 6.5 MB. So **Rule #3** applies here: "Performance cannot be measured without impacting the system being measured." You probably should not use *gpm* to diagnose a severe memory bottleneck.

- Very limited logging capability. Data presented by *gpm* cannot be logged, by default, to the disk or to a printer. By creating new Adviser syntax, individual metrics can be printed to standard out (which can be redirected to a file) or to the alert window.

As with *glance*, the CPU overhead associated with running *gpm* depends on the refresh interval and the number of running processes. Longer intervals use less overhead. Additional CPU overhead is generated by the Motif calls in displaying the windows and graphics, as with any Motif-based application.

Memory overhead depends on the number of running processes, because *gpm* keeps information about all running processes in its user memory to reduce CPU overhead. Additional memory is consumed for each currently displayed window. The counters and other metrics accessed by *gpm* are collected by *midaemon,* and certain ones are turned on only when *midaemon* is running.

5.2.5   sar (System Activity Reporter)

Sar originated in System V Unix. It is now available as part of many Unix systems, including some Berkeley-based Unix systems. *Sar* retrieves all of its metrics via the */dev/kmem* or *pstat(2)* interface, although in HP-UX, some of the counters are specific only to *sar.* As with most of the counter-based performance tools, overhead is minimal as long as the sampling interval is 30 seconds or more.

Sar was designed to log data in the background to a binary-format disk file using the program */usr/lib/sa/sadc.* Therefore, *sar* and *sadc* are useful when collecting data over long periods of time, for purposes such as baselines or general performance characterization.

5.2.5.1   Running sar Interactively

In interactive mode, to report current metrics, *sar* must be invoked with command-line parameters:

sar [-AabcdMmquvwy] <interval in seconds> [number of iterations]

Forgetting to supply these parameters results in a cryptic error message:

can't open /usr/adm/sa/saxx

where xx is a two-digit number that is the same as the number of the month. This message means that *sar* expects a daily system activity file to exist in the directory */usr/adm/sa.* Optionally, a different file to be analyzed can be specified with the -*f* option. By default, data for CPU utilization (the -*u* parameter) will be displayed interactively, storing the data to a binary output file:

sar -o <filename> <interval in seconds> [number of iterations]

Note that the results are also listed to the standard output while the data is being logged to the binary-format file interactively, displaying previously recorded data:

sar [-AabcdMmquvwy] [-s starttime] [-e endtime]
[-i interval in seconds to report] <-f binary data file>

5.2.5.2   Running *sar* in the background

Sar may be invoked in the background only through the program */usr/lib/sa/sadc*. By default, binary output is written to the daily system activity file */usr/adm/sa/saxx* where *xx* is the date of the month, with no output to the *standard output*. This mode is most often invoked in the superuser's *crontab* file to run at midnight every day. The data in this file is then displayed by invoking *sar* in the interactive mode.

WARNING: There are two problems with *sadc* log files: First, the data files will grow without bound, and therefore may be quite large. Sufficient disk space on the */usr* file system must be available to accomodate these files. Second, each month, the *sadc* files are overwritten since the names include only the day of the month. Procedures must be in place to archive these files to tape before they are overwritten.

The command-line parameters for *sadc* are different from those for *sar*. *Sadc* is invoked as follows:

sadc <interval in seconds> [number of iterations] [output file name]

Note that there are no metric parameters for *sadc* because it collects *all* of the various metrics. Additionally, two shell scripts, *sa1* and *sa2* can be found in the directory */usr/lbin/sa*. These shell scripts may be modified, and are supplied to invoke *sadc* in the most common way.

The following is the code in */usr/lbin/sa/sa1*:

```
#! /usr/bin/sh
# @(#) $Revision: 72.3 $
#          sa1.sh

DATE=`date +%d`
ENDIR=/usr/lbin/sa
DFILE=/var/adm/sa/sa$DATE
cd $ENDIR
if [ $# = 0 ]
then
     exec $ENDIR/sadc 1 1 $DFILE
else
     exec $ENDIR/sadc $* $DFILE
fi
```

Here is the code in */usr/lbin/sa/sa2*:

```
#! /usr/bin/sh
# @(#) $Revision: 72.1 $
#     sa2.sh

DATE=`date +%d`
RPT=/var/adm/sa/sar$DATE
DFILE=/var/adm/sa/sa$DATE
ENDIR=/usr/sbin
cd $ENDIR
$ENDIR/sar $* -f $DFILE > $RPT
find /var/adm/sa \
    -name `sar*' -o -name `sa*' \
    -mtime +7 -exec rm {} \;
```

5.2.5.3   Command Line Options

The various metrics are displayed based on command-line parameters. Any combination of command-line metric parameters is permitted. These command line parameters are:

- *-A*—All metrics

- *-a*—File system lookups

- *-b*—Disk logical, physical & raw reads/writes; buffer cache hit ratios

- *-c*—System call rates

- *-d*—Disk I/Os and queue lengths by disk drive

- *-M*—CPU utilization by CPU in an HP-UX SMP environment (used with *-u* or *-q*)

- *-m*—Message and semaphore operations

- *-q*—Run queue

- *-u*—CPU utilization

- *-v*—Kernel table utilization

- *-w*—Swapping and context switching

- *-y*—Terminal I/O

Although *sar* can collect data in intervals as small as one second, for reasons of volume of output and system overhead it is recommended that the interval be reduced according to purpose. If the purpose is performance characterization, intervals of 5 minutes (300 seconds) or even 1 hour (3600 seconds) may be satisfactory. Intervals of 5 to 30 seconds are recommended for problem diagnosis.

The following is a listing of basic sample output from *sar*:

```
HP-UX lptest1 B.10.20 A 9000/867      01/13/99

16:12:13    %usr     %sys     %wio     %idle
            device    %busy    avque    r+w/s  blks/s  avwait  avserv
            runq-sz %runocc swpq-sz %swpocc
            bread/s lread/s %rcache bwrit/s lwrit/s %wcache pread/s pwrit/s
            swpin/s bswin/s swpot/s bswot/s pswch/s
            scall/s  sread/s  swrit/s   fork/s   exec/s  rchar/s  wchar/s
             iget/s namei/s dirbk/s
            rawch/s canch/s outch/s rcvin/s xmtin/s mdmin/s
            text-sz  ov  proc-sz  ov  inod-sz  ov  file-sz  ov
             msg/s  sema/s
16:12:14       1        1       0       98

              1.0       99     0.0       0
                0       87     100       0      0       0        0      0
             0.00      0.0    0.00     0.0     71
              627       14      23     0.00    0.00   540388          0
                0        8       0
                0        0       0       0      0       0
              N/A      N/A 112/276       0  476/476      0  237/800      0
             0.00     0.00
```

5.2.5.4   Advantages (+) of *sar*

The biggest advantage of *sar* is familiarity. Many people have used it to diagnose system performance, because it was the only tool available. Many scripts (*awk, sed,* and *shell*) have been written to analyze and summarize data from *sar*. Another important advantage is that among all the performance tools, *sar* provides several unique metrics, described in the next few sections (the command line options are shown in parentheses).

Table Overflow Information (-v)   In addition to showing the number of entries currently being used for the process (proc), text, system file (file), and inode tables, *sar* also indicates the number of times that an entry was requested, but was unavailable because the table was full. This information is given in the "ov" column in the output. An application receives an error and an error message is written to the console when one of the tables overflows. These messages may include:

• *Cannot fork* (the process table is full)

• *File table overflow* (the system file table is full)

• *Inode table overflow* (the inode table is full)

Sar counts the number of occurrences of table overflow during the measurement interval.

Warning on Inode Table Overflow: The inode table is a cache. Recently used entries for files that have already been closed may remain in the table, until an entry is needed to open another file. Therefore, this metric may *always* show the table as full. There are three ways to determine whether you need to increase the inode table size:

1. Look at the "ov" column in the output.
2. Look for system console messages saying "inode table overflow."
3. Look for application errors related to an inability to open files.

Read and Write Buffer Cache Hit Ratios (-b) Several of the tools report read buffer cache hit ratio. Only *sar* reports the read and write buffer cache hit ratios separately.

Semaphore and Message Queue (IPC) Operation Rates (-m) The IPC operation rates are often important to know, especially for relational databases, which make frequent use of these CPU-consuming system services. The rates show the frequency of system call invocation, and do not refer to the number of semaphores or message queues that are currently allocated.

5.2.5.5   Disadvantages (-) of *sar*

The major disadvantages of *sar* include:

- No per-process information. *Sar* collects only global metrics. Therefore, it is possible to determine *what* is occurring, but not *who* is causing it.
- There is little virtual memory information. Only global paging-in and -out rates and swapping-in and -out rates are shown by *sar.* Currently, the HP-UX version of *sar* reports only swapping rates. *Sar* is limited in its ability to diagnose memory bottlenecks.
- The output produced by *sar* is difficult to analyze and parse. Its output is command-line parameter-specific, so that analysis depends on the options chosen. In addition, *sar* writes a blank in a field rather than a zero, which makes it difficult to look for data in fields. The output can be improved by using the *sar -o* option, which places all the data in columns. However, very long lines can be generated.
- Graphics and tabulation require other tools. *Sar* does not offer any graphics features. It merely produces output with so many lines per interval chosen. Other tools must be used to change the data into more suitable forms. There is also no per-process information.
- The binary output file format can have different versions. *Sar* must match *sadc* in revisions.
- The *sar* data must be analyzed on the system where it was acquired, because it needs information from */stand/vmunix*.

The CPU overhead consumed by *sar* is only dependent upon the interval. This is because all the data is collected all the time, even if it isn't being displayed. Longer intervals consume less CPU, and memory consumption is fixed. The counters used by *sar* are always turned on, so that overhead is not measureable and is constant.

5.2.6   time

Time reports on the time required for the execution of a command. Output includes real time, user time, and system time. *Time* is either an external command or a built-in function within some of the shells. The external command */usr/bin/time* may be invoked by full path name, and is the version used by the obsolete Bourne shell. The Posix, Korn, and C shells use a built-in function that is a variation of */usr/bin/time*. Unfortunately, none of the output formats are the same. But the built-in functions consume less resources, because they do not fork another process. Typical output is shown below for an execution of the MC/ServiceGuard *cmviewcl* command. The output of the ServiceGuard command is shown first, following by the timing data.

```
lptest1 B.10.20 # time cmviewcl

CLUSTER        STATUS
cluster3       up                                      ServiceGuard
                                                        Command
   NODE            STATUS        STATE                  Output
   lptest1         up            running

     PACKAGE        STATUS        STATE        PKG_SWITCH    NODE
     xclock         up            running      enabled       lptest1
     xmeditor       up            running      enabled       lptest1

   NODE            STATUS        STATE
   lptest2         up            running

real         0.49
user         0.10                                       time data
sys          0.04
lptest1 B.10.20 #
```

5.2.7   timex

Like *time, timex* reports on the time required for the execution of a command, but has additional options that provide more information. Option *-s* prints *sar* data for the interval in which the program ran, and *-p* prints process accounting information for the interval in which the program ran. The following example shows *time* data and the *sar* data as provided through use of the *-s* option.

```
lptest1 B.10.20 # timex -s cmviewcl

CLUSTER       STATUS                              ServiceGuard
cluster3      up                                  Command
                                                  Output
  NODE          STATUS        STATE
  lptest1       up            running

    PACKAGE       STATUS        STATE       PKG_SWITCH    NODE
    xclock        up            running     enabled       lptest1
    xmeditor      up            running     enabled       lptest1

  NODE          STATUS        STATE
  lptest2       up            running
```

```
real      0.49
user      0.10                                    timex data
sys       0.04
HP-UX lptest1 B.10.20 A 9000/867    01/13/99

16:01:32    %usr    %sys    %wio    %idle
        bread/s lread/s %rcache bwrit/s lwrit/s %wcache pread/s pwrit/s
        device  %busy   avque   r+w/s   blks/s  avwait  avserv
        rawch/s canch/s outch/s rcvin/s xmtin/s mdmin/s
        scall/s sread/s swrit/s  fork/s   exec/s rchar/s  wchar/s
        swpin/s bswin/s swpot/s bswot/s pswch/s
         iget/s namei/s dirbk/s
        runq-sz %runocc swpq-sz %swpocc
        text-sz  ov  proc-sz  ov  inod-sz  ov  file-sz  ov
         msg/s   sema/s
            62      35       0       4
             0       0       0       0       0       0       0       0

             0       0       0       0       0       0
             0     149      49    7.27    7.27       0       0
          0.00     0.0    0.00     0.0       0
            35     149      58
           0.0       0     0.0       0
           N/A     N/A 113/276      0 476/476    0 236/800    0
          0.00    0.00
```

Another example shows the use of the *-p* option. (Note that for the *-p* option to work with the *timex* command, the command */usr/sbin/acct/turnacct on* must first be used to enable process accounting.)

```
timex -p cmviewcl

CLUSTER       STATUS
cluster3      down

  NODE          STATUS       STATE
  lptest1       down         unknown
  lptest2       down         unknown

UNOWNED_PACKAGES

    PACKAGE       STATUS       STATE        PKG_SWITCH   NODE
    xclock        down                                   unowned
    xmeditor      down                                   unowned


real        2.75
user        0.16
sys         0.04


START AFT: Fri May 14 14:07:57 1999
END BEFOR: Fri May 14 14:07:59 1999
COMMAND                         START    END         REAL     CPU     CHARS    BLOCKS
NAME          USER     TTYNAME  TIME     TIME        (SECS)   (SECS)  TRNSFD   R/W
#cmviewcl     root     ttyp1    14:07:57 14:07:59    2.74     0.19    61656    0
lptest1 B.10.20 #
```

5.2.8   uptime

Uptime is most useful for quickly displaying load average metrics. It shows the current time, the length of time the system has been up, the number of users logged on to the system, and the average number of jobs in the run queue over the last one, five, and 15 minutes.

Uptime has very low overhead. Partial sample output is shown below; load average data is shown in larger *italic* type.

```
$ uptime -lw
 3:52pm  up 265 days,  4:55,  81 users,  load average: 1.03, 1.27, 2.07
User      tty            login@  idle   JCPU   PCPU  what
dts       ttyrc         10:16am  2:58                -ksh
sganesh   ttyp1          6:51pm 21:00                -ksh
john ttyp2            12:41pm 24:59                -ksh
barb ttyp3             5:28pm190:24   1:18   1:18  /usr/local/lib/synchronize/HP
800/bin/synchronize -server hps
annasu    ttyp4          7:39am  8:13                -ksh
whine     ttyp6         11:12am  4:34                -ksh
```

5.3 CPU Diagnostic Tools

Many tools provide data about currently executing processes and CPU load. Some important examples are *ps, xload*, and *top*. *Glance* and *sar* also supply CPU-related metrics.

5.3.1 ps

Used for process status display, *ps* is perhaps the best known and most commonly used of all the performance tools. Its many options (see the man page on *ps*) allow for very specific display of process information. The following is an example showing output of **ps -ef** on a workstation. This display is limited to processes owned by UID *peterw*:

```
  UID    PID  PPID  C    STIME TTY       TIME COMMAND
peterw 14336 14335  0  Jan  8 ttyp2      0:00 rlogin lptest1 -l root
peterw 14323 14322  0  Jan  8 ttyp2      0:00 -ksh
peterw 13146 13145  0  Jan  8 ?          0:06 /usr/bin/X11/hpterm -ls -sl 255
peterw  4743  3825  2 12:16:51 ttyp4     0:00 ps -ef
peterw 13147 13146  0  Jan  8 ttyp1      0:00 -ksh
peterw  2239     1  0 09:03:41 ?         2:21 /opt/adobe/fmsgml155/bin/makersgml
peterw  3824  3823  0 11:04:59 ?         0:01 /usr/bin/X11/hpterm -ls -sl 255
peterw 14271 13147  0  Jan  8 ttyp1      0:00 rlogin lptest1 -l root
peterw 13140 13106  0  Jan  8 ?          0:15 dtwm
peterw 13106 13092  0  Jan  8 ?          0:00 /usr/dt/bin/dtsession
```

Ps also shows information about Process Resource Manager (PRM) groups.

5.3.2 top

Top displays the top processes on the system and periodically updates the information. It also provides global information, including:

• The number of processes in particular states

• Global CPU utilization by type (one line for each CPU in an SMP system).

It then lists the running processes ordered by CPU utilization. On an SMP system, *top* shows the CPU number to which the process is currently assigned. *Top* uses the *vi* commands **j** and **k** to navigate between screens.

Top is the only tool to report BLOCK and SWAIT CPU utilization, which have meaning only on a symmetric multi-processing (SMP) system. These metrics refer to the amount of time the kernel spends waiting for spinlocks or kernel semaphores, respectively. They are a measure of SMP contention. (SMP architecture is described in "Multi-Processing" on page 129.)

Top's display includes system data, memory data, and process data. Raw CPU percentage is used to rank the processes. The following example shows the top ten processes on a workstation:

```
$ top -n 10

System: hpmfac89 Mon Jan 11 11:08:28 1999
Load averages: 0.14, 0.14, 0.12
124 processes: 122 sleeping, 1 running, 1 stopped
Cpu states:
 LOAD    USER    NICE    SYS    IDLE   BLOCK  SWAIT    INTR   SSYS
 0.14    0.2%    0.0%   0.0%   99.8%   0.0%   0.0%    0.0%   0.0%


 Memory: 32672K (8116K) real, 55592K (28060K) virtual, 7708K free  Page# 1/9

TTY    PID USERNAME PRI NI    SIZE    RES STATE    TIME %WCPU   %CPU COMMAND
  ?   1226 root     154 20    692K   180K sleep  105:16  0.17   0.17 dtgreet
  ? 13140 peterw    154 20   1528K  1532K sleep    0:15  0.14   0.14 dtwm
  ?   3859 peterw   154 20    616K   784K sleep    0:00  0.14   0.13 hpterm
 p5   3911 peterw   178 20    388K   268K run      0:00  0.45   0.12 top
  ?    930 root     154 20   6100K   932K sleep   66:28  0.10   0.10 rpcd
  ?   1178 root     154 20    868K   468K sleep   56:27  0.08   0.08 opcle
  ?   1210 daemon   154 20   2436K   232K sleep   24:36  0.07   0.07 X
  ?      3 root     128 20      0K     0K sleep   25:24  0.07   0.07 statdaemon
  ?   1176 root     154 20   2576K   284K sleep   25:41  0.05   0.05 opcmsga
  ?    993 root     120 20    236K   116K sleep    7:52  0.05   0.04 xntpd
```

NOTE: On SMP systems with many CPUs, the global per-CPU list takes up more of the display with fewer lines of process information.

5.3.3   xload

An X-Windows graphical display of CPU load over time appears in *xload*. An example is shown in Figure 5-5.

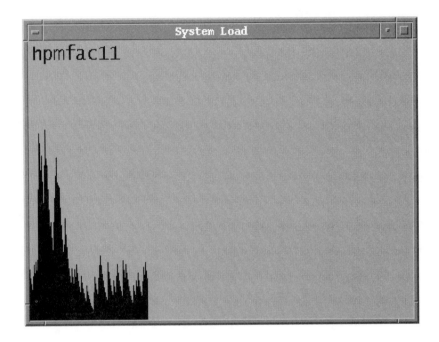

Figure 5-5   Graphic Display of CPU by *xload*

5.4   Disk Diagnostic Tools

Disk diagnostics include *bdf*, *df*, and *iostat*, which also provides data on terminal I/O. *Glance* and *sar* also provide disk-related data.

5.4.1   bdf and df

Bdf is the name given to the Berkeley version of the *df* (disk free) command in HP-UX. It is listed as a performance metric for its resource consumption metrics of on-disk inodes and file system disk space.

Because it reports disk space consumption in KB rather than blocks (512 bytes), *bdf* is often preferred over *df* . It can be used to manage file system capacity for two reasons: to avoid running out of space, and to prevent file system block allocation performance degradation, which occurs when the file system is more than 90% full.

The *-i* option to *bdf* displays HFS on-disk inode utilization as well as file system data space utilization. An inode is the data structure on disk and in memory which describes the location and number of blocks required for each file in an HFS file system. By default, one HFS inode is created for every 6 KB of disk space in the file system (HP-UX 10.x and later; earlier systems used an inode for every 2 KB). This default worked well when disks were small and there were typically many small files. With today's larger disks and larger files, the default causes a lot of disk space to be wasted.

Each on-disk inode consumes 128 bytes of space, which seems small; however, on a 2 GB volume, over 333,000 inodes are created by default. On a 2 GB volume, this translates to 42 MB that is allocated specifically for inodes and cannot be used as data space. Very seldom are there 333,000 files in a file system. Even if there were 33,000 files (10% of the inodes allocated, but still a large amount) in a file system, over 38 MB of disk space would still be unused, and unavailable for data.

This space consumption is particularly wasteful when large files consume most of the disk, because very few inodes are actually needed to describe the few large files. The way to tune these situations will be described in Chapter 10, "Disk Bottlenecks."

Here is an example of output from the *bdf -i* command:

```
Filesystem          kbytes    used   avail %used  iused   ifree %iuse Mounted on
/dev/vg00/lvol3      83733   71263    4096   95%    4232    9208   31% /
/dev/vg00/lvol1      95701   17997   68133   21%      21   15339    0% /stand
/dev/vg00/lvol8     307421  113513  163165   41%    2693  142011    2% /var
/dev/vg00/lvol7     331093  240790   57193   81%   13617   39375   26% /usr
/dev/vg00/lvol6      30597    7969   19568   29%     114   15118    1% /tmp
/dev/vg00/lvol5     247157  220125    2316   99%    4048   35504   10% /opt
/dev/vg00/lvol4      19861      53   17821    0%       6    3450    0% /home
```

NOTE: In-core and on-disk inodes for a JFS (VxFS) file system are dynamically allocated. JFS inode utilization is not shown by *bdf*.

5.4.2   iostat

Iostat is a Berkeley Unix-based tool that displays disk and terminal I/O statistics. Like its counterpart, *vmstat*, *iostat* displays no per-process information. Instead, it displays global information on per-spindle disk I/O rates by default, and terminal I/O rates optionally. *Iostat* is invoked as follows:

• Interactively:

iostat [-t] [interval in seconds] [number of iterations]

• By saving data to a file:

iostat [-t] [interval in seconds] [number of iterations] > output-file-name

The *-t* parameter means list terminal I/O (hardwired terminal devices and pseudo-terminals) and CPU utilization.

By default, *iostat* reports the results every second. Except in few cases, one second is too frequent. Even for the purpose of diagnosing problems, five seconds or thirty seconds are much more reasonable intervals, and use less CPU overhead.

For terminal I/O, *iostat* reports the number of characters input and the number of characters output during the last interval, as well as user, system, and *nice* CPU utilization. Note that *nice* CPU utilization counts CPU time for those processes which have used the "nice" version of *nice*; this differs from the way MI-based tools like *glance* report nice CPU utilization.

For disk I/O, *iostat* reports the following data by disk spindle:

• *bps*—Kbytes transferred per second
• *sps*—Seeks per second which should be the same as I/Os per second
• *msps*—Millseconds per seek. On modern disks that have such features such as command queueing, *msps* no longer makes sense as a performance metric. This metric is hard-coded to a value of 1.

The disk I/O metrics are reported horizontally for all disks, making the report line quite long; it may be so long that it exceeds the maximum 256-byte line length, and therefore might be truncated on large systems with many disks. Other tools that provide a greater volume of similar information are now available. This has dramatically decreased the usefulness of *iostat*.

Because *iostat* is not controlled by any Unix standard, its output may change from one operating system release to the next.

5.5 Memory Diagnostic Tools

Memory data are provided by memory diagnostic tools including *size*, *vmstat* and *ipcs*, as well as by *glance* and *sar*.

5.5.1   size

Size produces section size information for each section in the object files. The size of the text, data and BSS (uninitialized data) sections are printed along with the total size of the object file. Two examples of output from the *size* command are shown below; the first provides a summary, and the second, using the **-v** option, provides the information in more detail.

```
hpgsyha9/B.11.00:size scopeux
443507 + 92120 + 11305 = 546932

hpgsyha9/B.11.00:size -v scopeux

        Subspace              Size      Physical Address     Virtual Address

        $SHLIB_INFO$          86167             4096                4096
        $MILLICODE$            9016            90264               90264
        $CODE$               132772            99284               99284
        $CODE$               132884           232056              232056
        $CODE$                30784           364944              364944
        $LIT$                   448           395728              395728
        $UNWIND_START$        41440           396176              396176
        $UNWIND_END$           9992           437616              437616
        $RECOVER_END$             4           447608              447608
        $PFA_COUNTER$             8           450560          1073745920
        $DATA$                75508           450568          1073745928
        $SHORTDATA$            1404           526080          1073821440
        $PLT$                  9816           527488          1073822848
        $DLT$                  5368           537304          1073832664
        $GLOBAL$                 16           542672          1073838032
        $SHORTBSS$             1025               0          1073838048
        $BSS$                 10280               0          1073839080

        Total                546932
```

5.5.2   swapinfo

Swapinfo prints information about device and file system paging space. The word "swap" is a misnomer, since HP-UX actually implements virtual memory through paging, not swapping. Sample output from the *swapinfo* command is shown below:.

```
hpgsyha9/B.11.00:swapinfo
             Kb        Kb        Kb     PCT   START/      Kb
TYPE      AVAIL      USED      FREE    USED   LIMIT RESERVE  PRI  NAME
dev      307200         0    307200     0%       0       -    1  /dev/vg00/lvol2
reserve       -     81696    -81696
memory   196360     29172    167188    15%
```

5.5.3   vmstat

Vmstat is a tool that is familiar to people using BSD-based Unix systems. It produces output of one line of information per interval, and includes CPU and virtual memory metrics. *Vmstat* is invoked as follows:

• Interactively:

vmstat [-dS] [interval in seconds] [number of iterations]

• By saving data to a file:

vmstat [-dS] [interval in seconds] [number of iterations] > output-file-name

• With special non-interval options:

vmstat [-fsz]

The command line parameters for *vmstat* are as follows:

• *-d*—Per-disk information

• *-f*—Forks and pages of virtual memory since boot-up

• *-S*—Display swap information as well as paging

• *-s*—Display the total count of paging-related events

• *-z*—Zero out the counters

By default, *vmstat* reports the results every second. Except in few cases, one second is too frequent. Even for the purpose of diagnosing problems, five seconds or thirty seconds are much more reasonable intervals, and use less CPU overhead.

The major advantage of *vmstat* is that it produces a great deal of data in a single line of columnar output. This data is organized into the following groupings of metrics:

• Queues (run, blocked, and runnable but swapped out)

• Virtual memory metrics (page faults, paging and swapping rates)

• Scheduler metrics (context switches and interrupts)

• CPU utilization metrics (user, system, and idle)

Although it is quite useful in monitoring virtual memory, *vmstat* is limited in that it does not display process information. Therefore, one can determine that memory is a potential problem, but not which processes might be causing the problem.

A typical output from *vmstat* is shown below:

```
$ vmstat -dS
         procs                memory                    page
   faults          cpu
     r      b      w      avm     free    re    at    pi    po    fr    de    sr      in
     sy     cs    us sy id
     0     41      0     5832      985     4     4     0     0     0     0     0     140
    315     32     0  0 99

Disk Transfers
   device      xfer/sec
   c0t6d0          0
```

The first line of output from *vmstat* (except when invoked with the **-f**, **-s**, or **-z** options) shows the various metrics as an average since bootup or reset time. This information is generally ignored when diagnosing problems.

You should be careful in interpreting the data from *vmstat*, because the headings are cryptic one-, two-, three-, or four-letter mnemonics, and are very poorly documented. For instance, someone who is familiar with CPU hardware might conclude that the column *at*, which is documented as the number of address translation faults, might give a rate of Translation Lookaside Buffer (TLB) faults, because address translation is the function of the TLB. The number of TLB faults would provide a very useful measure of the efficiency of a critical system component. Unfortunately, that is not what *vmstat* is reporting; instead, it is reporting the number of page faults.

Another example is the *avm* column. Because it is a memory metric, and is placed next to *free,* one might conclude that *avm* stands for available memory, but in fact, *avm* stands for active virtual memory. It takes looking at the *vmstat* source code to determine that *avm* is the sum of text, data and stack pages in use for all processes, not including shared library or shared memory pages! Also note that two columns are labeled identically: *sy,* is the number of system calls; and *sy*, the percent of system CPU utilization.

The most important data obtained from *vmstat* are:

- *r*—The number of processes in the run queue
- *b*—The number of processes blocked for any reason
- *w*—The number of processes swapped out but are runnable
- *free*—The number of free memory pages
- *re*—The number of virtual memory page reclaims
- *at*—The number of virtual memory page faults
- *pi/po*—The number of pages paged in and out

- *si/so*—The number of pages swapped in and out (in HP-UX 10.0 and later, these refer to deactivations and reactivations)

- *in*—The number of interrupts

- *cs*—The number of context switches

- *us*—Percentage of user CPU utilization

- *sy*—Percentage of system CPU utilization

In general, the output produced by *vmstat* is easily parsed by *awk* for use with spreadsheets or other programs for summarizing and averaging the data over long periods of time. Sometimes the numbers exceed the number of columns allotted, however, and will use up the space between columns; this can make it difficult to parse the output.

The CPU overhead associated with running *vmstat* is relatively small, but depends on the interval. The counters used by *vmstat* are always turned on, so that overhead is not measureable and is fixed. Longer intervals use less overhead; memory overhead is constant.

5.5.4   ipcs

Both *ipcs* and *ipcrm* are tools that let you manage interprocess communication, although *ipcrm* is not a measurement tool; *ipcrm* lets you delete an IPC object. *Ipcs* provides a report on semaphores, message queues, and shared memory. Sample *ipcs* output is shown below:

```
$ ipcs
IPC status from /dev/kmem as of Wed Jan 13 15:44:06 1999
T     ID     KEY        MODE        OWNER     GROUP
Message Queues:
q      0 0x3c1c0234 -Rrw--w--w-     root      root
q      1 0x3e1c0234 --rw-r--r--     root      root
Shared Memory:
m      0 0x2f180002 --rw-------     root      sys
m      1 0x411c0209 --rw-rw-rw-     root      root
m      2 0x4e0c0002 --rw-rw-rw-     root      root
m      3 0x41201041 --rw-rw-rw-     root      root
m      4 0x00000000 --rw-------     root      sys
m    205 0x431c1b43 --rw-rw-rw-    daemon    daemon
Semaphores:
s      0 0x2f180002 --ra-ra-ra-     root      sys
s      1 0x411c0209 --ra-ra-ra-     root      root
s      2 0x4e0c0002 --ra-ra-ra-     root      root
s      3 0x41201041 --ra-ra-ra-     root      root
s      4 0x00446f6e --ra-r--r--     root      root
s      5 0x00446f6d --ra-r--r--     root      root
s      6 0x01090522 --ra-r--r--     root      root
s    519 0x4c1c1b43 --ra-r--r--    daemon    daemon
```

5.6 Performance Characterization and Prediction Tools

The goal of performance characterization is to obtain a baseline of activity for a system or subsystem, and then compare it with activity at various times. The emphasis is placed on making comparisons rather than on taking snapshots. Prediction takes the process one step further by extrapolating future performance out of the data from past runs.

5.6.1 MeasureWare

MeasureWare lets you obtain data relating to performance characterization, performance trending, capacity planning, workload estimation, and chargeback accounting. Data is obtained over time, and data from different periods can be compared. *MeasureWare* is configured by editing the */var/opt/perf/parm* file.

MeasureWare consists of four programs: *midaemon, scopeux, utility,* and *extract. Midaemon* accesses data from the kernel, massages it, and stores the results in a shared memory segment that is accessed by *scopeux. Scopeux* retrieves the data from the shared memory segment, rejects "uninteresting" data, averages the rest, and stores the results in a circular binary log file.

Utility reports on and can resize the binary log file. *Extract* pulls data from the circular log file and saves it in a binary or ASCII log file. ASCII data can be analyzed via spreadsheet or statistical analysis programs. Binary data is used by the *PerfView* tools, which are described in the next section.

It is very important that the *parm* file be customized appropriately for each system and application environment. The parm file in the directory */var/opt/perf* is the active configuration file used by *scopeux*. It contains a minimally defined configuration, by default. Other example parm files may be found in */opt/perf/newconfig*. The following customizations should be considered.

5.6.1.1 Customizing the ID of the Binary Data File

The ID in the binary data files will default to the official hostname of the system where the data is being collected. You can choose a different name by setting the *id* parameter. Setting a recognizable name for this field is especially important when data is being collected on multiple systems. The reports and graphs will be labelled with this name.

5.6.1.2 Customizing the Log Parameter

Set the *log* parameter to the type(s) of data that are to be collected. The default setting

```
log global application process device=disk,lvm
```

should be sufficient on most systems since it collects all of the available data. However, on busy systems, collecting all of the data will cause the binary files to be overwritten quickly. To minimize the overhead of data collection and storage, *scopeux* averages and saves global and application data every 5 minutes.

Process data is averaged and recorded on disk every minute. Disk and LVM data contains detailed device file names and should always be logged. Otherwise, you may not be able to correlate the per-disk drive data with actual disk devices.

5.6.1.3   Customizing the Data File Size

It is very important to set the *size* parameter appropriately. *MeasureWare* data is collected in a set of binary files of fixed size that are accessed in a wrap-around manner. The files should be large enough to contain a minimum of one week's worth of data, and optimally one to two months worth of data. You may have to set the size by trial and error.

Use the *utility* command to show the current utilization of the files, including the dates that the data covers. As the system grows busier, monitor the utilization so that the files are large enough to accomodate the minimum requirements that you have determined.

The default sizes are:

```
size global=5.0, application=5.0, process=10.0, device=5.0
```

in MB. The *process* file typically fills the fastest; therefore, it should be sized bigger than the other files. The binary data files are are very compact and are stored in the directory */var/opt/perf/datafiles* and are given the names *logappl*, *logdev*, *logglob*, *logindx* and *logproc*. The file called RUN in this same directory is periodically monitored by the *scopeux* process. If you remove this file, *scopeux* will cleanly terminate.

Procedures should be established for extracting and archiving data from these circular binary files so that long-term trends can be analyzed. These files may also be used for performance problem diagnosis to look at the performance of the system before the problem manifested itself.

Use the *extract* command with the *extract* function to save the data in compact binary format for a desired range of dates to another disk file. These extracted files should be archived to tape on a weekly or monthly basis. Make sure that you extract the data before the circular file has wrapped around and overwritten some of the data you need to save.

The *extract* program can also be used to produce ASCII reports that can be analyzed if you like to look at columnar data. These reports can be customized by selecting the desired metrics that are listed in several sample report files, *reptall*, *reptfile*, *repthead* and *repthist* in the directory */var/opt/perf*. Metrics are selected by removing the asterisk at the beginning of the line.

5.6.1.4   Customizing Thresholds

To reduce overhead associated with data collection and disk space utilization, *Measure-Ware* records process data only on what it considers to be interesting processes, as configured in the parm file. By default, the line

```
threshold cpu = 5.0, disk = 5.0
```

causes process data to be recorded for any process that uses at least 5% of CPU utilization *or* does at least 5 disk I/Os per second. Additionally, *MeasureWare* records process data for all process creations and terminations.

You can use process data for performance problem diagnosis or for security auditing purposes, since it records every process that runs on the system. However, it may not produce a record every minute for every process since the threshold parameter limits those processes for which it records data.

See the *MeasureWare* documentation for information on other thresholds that can be defined.

5.6.1.5   Assigning Applications and Users to Application Groups

Each major application and/or group of users should be assigned to a user-defined application group. The group name is arbitrary, but should be recognizable. Applications can be defined based on a combination of:

* Executable program names (not the full path name). Note that an asterisk can be used as a wild card character for the program name.
* User login names

Otherwise, most of the application data will be placed in the OTHER application group. When too much utilization shows up as the application OTHER , the application data is not useful for either charge-back accounting, or for performance management and diagnosis.

The order of applications listed in the parm file is very important. When a process record is analyzed by the scopeux *MeasureWare* process, it scans the parm file from the top looking for the first appropriate application definition. Once it finds a matching application definition, it includes that process data in that application metric. You must carefully look at the application definitions to ensure that if a process can fit into more than one application because of the combination of wild card application names and user names, it will be counted in the application where you really want it counted.

The number of applications listed in the parm file has a direct effect on *MeasureWare* overhead. The more applications listed, the higher the overhead. Make sure that you list the applications in the order of most commonly expected to least expected. That way, *scopeux* will find the correct application sooner, reducing its overhead for searching the parm file.

5.6.1.6   Limitations of Metrics in MeasureWare

MeasureWare does not acquire and record all of the same metrics that are available with *glance* and *gpm*. In some cases, there are additional metrics in *MeasureWare*. However, *MeasureWare* does not acquire and record a very important class of per-processor metrics associated with multiple CPUs on an SMP system. The following is an example.

From Bob's Consulting Log—A client once asked me to help him review some performance data from a system being benchmarked. There did not seem to be any bottlenecks based on simple interactive access. The response time criteria for the benchmark were being met. However, graphs of data from the system showed the following:
- 100% CPU utilization
- Load average of 10
- Multiple processes running as part of the application

The client was perplexed. A load average of 10 coupled with 100% CPU utilization would normally indicate a rather busy system. I looked at the data, asked a few questions to confirm that the benchmark was running properly and getting appropriate results.

Next, I asked whether the system was an SMP system, which it was. I asked further how many CPUs were on the system, and he answered 10. The interpretation of the data now fell into place. A global load average of 10 spread across ten CPUs (processors) leads to a load average of 1 *per processor*, which is much more reasonable, given the satisfactory response times.

Also beware of the metric *gbl_run_queue*. This is misnamed, since in fact it refers to the one-minute load average (described further in Chapter 7), not to the run queue. The actual run queue metric is *gbl_pri_queue*.

5.6.2   PerfView

PerfView is a set of Unix performance management tools that accesses the data collected by MeasureWare, which runs on many vendors' platforms. For general purpose monitoring of HP-UX, the ultimate source of data is the set of counters reported on by *midaemon*, which provides the data through *scopeux*. Data is displayed on the *PerfView* management console, which has a single interface for displaying, analyzing, comparing, and predicting future trends in performance data. Specific *PerfView* components are *PerfView/Analyzer*, *PerfView/Monitor*, and

PerfView/Planner. The *Analyzer* is the central general-purpose display shown in Figure 5-6. A specific example of the graphic display of global disk usage is shown in Figure 5-7.

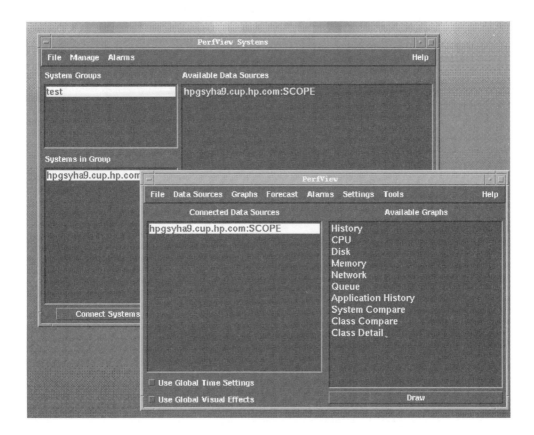

Figure 5-6   *PerfView/Analyzer* Display

The *MeasureWare* agent takes more than a single system view. Because *PerfView's* tools operate in a networked environment, they permit comparison of data from a multitude of data sources among distributed systems, and from different platforms. Additionally, specialized modules are available for collecting performance data from a variety of major databases. Other modules obtain health and performance data from network operating systems including *Novell NetWare* and *Windows NT.*

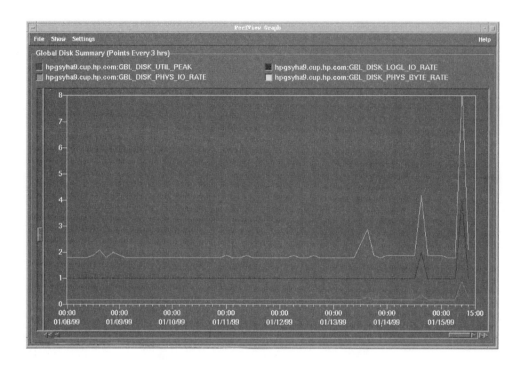

Figure 5-7   Global Disk Usage in *PerfView*

5.6.3   PerfView/Analyzer

The detailed information provided by *PerfView/Analyzer* is useful for obtaining a solid baseline of performance at three levels: process, application, and global resources. *Analyzer* is a Motif-based program that can produce standard and custom graphs from the data of one or more systems. It is used to analyze *MeasureWare* data in non-real time.

Recall that *MeasureWare* records process data every minute and global and application data every five minutes. Therefore, you must wait at least that long after starting *MeasureWare,* or after an event of interest occurs before that data is accessible by *PerfView/Analyzer.*

Analyzer can access the data from the log files in the */var/opt/perf/ datafiles* directory from one or more systems. It can access these files locally, on the same system where it is running, or remotely via NFS mounts.

Be very careful when analyzing data that is averaged over long periods of time such as one or more hours. Averages tend to flatten out spikes and dips in the data, and important events or trends can be missed if the "Points every" setting is too long.

Analyzer is an extremely flexible tool that will allow you to create graphs of performance metric data. Standard graphs are pre-defined and the user can create custom graphs that include any of the supported performance metrics. You can even compare similar data from multiple systems on a single graph.

A very big advantage of *PerfView/Analyzer* and its partners *PerfView/Monitor* and *PerfView/Planner* is the online help system. Not only does the help system give information about using the tool; it also gives detailed information about the meaning of each of the metrics that are available.

5.6.4 PerfView/Monitor

PerfView/Monitor is a Motif-based management tool that receives performance alarms from one or more systems running *MeasureWare*. The emphasis is on getting the information to operators who can take action. Setting the trigger points for alarms depends on your understanding what is normal and what is abnormal performance in a process, application, or system. Alarm thresholds are defined in the */var/opt/perf/alarmdefs* file. Alarms are sent to the central monitoring system, where an operator can receive the alert, analyze the cause and take appropriate action.

When an alarm is received by the central performance monitoring workstation, *PerfView/Monitor* can easily access detailed data stored in the *MeasureWare* binary log files for all the systems for which it is configured to monitor. It accesses these log files via a socket connection over the network. No NFS mount of the remote file systems is necessary. *Monitor* can also easily invoke an instance of *glance* or *gpm* that runs on the remote system where the alarm occurred but is displayed on the central performance monitoring workstation.

5.6.5 PerfView/Planner

PerfView/Planner is a Motif-based add-on module that can be used to predict when a system resource is expected to be exhausted. Requiring at least three months of historical data, it creates a forecast using one of several statistical methods. Data from the forecast may be used to plan for hardware upgrades to the system.

Planner lets you project future performance trends based on the kinds of data displayed above in *PerfView/Analyzer*. Their displays use graphs that are similar to each other.

5.6.6 sar and sadc

As mentioned above, *sar* was designed to log data in the background to a binary-format disk file using the program */usr/lib/sa/sadc*. Therefore, *sar* and *sadc* are useful when collecting data over long periods of time, for baselines or general performance characterization.

5.7 Process Accounting Tools

There are various system programs that provide accounting data. Among these are *acct* and *diskusg*.

5.7.1 acct

/usr/sbin/acct (HP-UX 10.0 and later systems) contains the accounting data that is generated after accounting is enabled with the command

```
turnacct on
```

The man page for *acctsh* describes a number of accounting commands and procedures.

5.7.2 diskusg

A second process accounting tool, *diskusg,* generates disk accounting information and outputs one line per user in the following format:

```
uid login #blocks
```

5.8 Application Optimization Tools

The following tools are available for optimizing applications:

5.8.1 CXperf

CXperf is an interactive runtime performance analyzer for programs compiled with Hewlett-Packard Fortran 90, ANSI C++, and ANSI C compilers. More information about *CXperf* is provided in Chapter 13, "Application Profiling."

5.8.2 dpat (Distributed Performance Analysis Tool)

Dpat is an interactive, X/Windows-based utility for profiling application programs. Ported to HP-UX from the Apollo Domain Operating System, *dpat* has been replaced (since HP-UX 10.20) with *puma*, which is described in Chapter 13, "Application Profiling."

5.8.3 hpc (Histogram Program Counter)

Ported to HP-UX from the Apollo Domain Operating System, *hpc* is a real-time character-mode utility for profiling application programs. *Hpc* has been replaced (since HP-UX 10.20) with *puma*, which is described in Chapter 13, "Application Profiling."

5.8.4 gprof/gprof++

Gprof is the Berkeley Unix version of *prof*, an application profiling tool. On pure Berkeley operating systems like SunOS 4.X, it is named *prof*. Since HP-UX supports both the Berkeley and System V versions, HP decided to rename the Berkeley version *gprof*. *Gprof++* is used for programs written in C++. On HP-UX, *gprof* is part of the Programming Environment and *gprof++* comes with the C++ compiler. *Gprof* performs all the functions that *prof* performs, and then adds call-graph functionality. The use of *gprof* is detailed in Chapter 13, "Application Profiling."

5.8.5   prof

Used as the basic System V profiling tool, *prof* produces the same output as *gprof* (above), but does not produce the call graph. Since *gprof* is the more useful of the two, the authors do not recommend the use of *prof*.

5.8.6   Puma

Available in the HP Performance Analysis Kit (HP PAK), *Puma* monitors the program counter, the call/return stack, and other performance statistics. Data are stored in a file that can be viewed in a number of ways. *Puma* replaces *dpat* and *hpc* at HP-UX 10.20. The use of *Puma* is detailed in Chapter 13, "Application Profiling."

5.8.7   TTV (Thread Trace Visualizer)

TTV is a tool for threaded applications. It uses a graphical format to display trace files produced by the instrumented thread library (*libpthread_tr.sl*). *TTV* lets you see how threads are interacting, and discover threads that are blocked on resources.

5.9   Network Diagnostic Tools

The following diagnostic tools are available to help answer your questions about network performance.

5.9.1   netstat

Netstat provides a wealth of metrics on network activity. It reports packet in-and-out metrics, collisions (Ethernet only), and errors, as well as memory consumed by the network portion of the kernel for network buffers.

Providing statistics for network interfaces and protocols, *netstat* also reports the contents of various network-related data structures. The output format varies according to the options selected. The following is a partial example of the output for *netstat -aAn*, which displays a list of active sockets. Internet connections are listed first, followed by Unix domain connections:

```
Active Internet connections (including servers)
PCB        Proto Recv-Q Send-Q  Local Address      Foreign Address      (state)
114af00 tcp       0      0  127.0.0.1.1383     127.0.0.1.5304    TIME_WAIT
11c2000 tcp       0      0  127.0.0.1.1382     127.0.0.1.5304    TIME_WAIT
1141800 tcp       0      0  127.0.0.1.1381     127.0.0.1.5304    TIME_WAIT
 e39a00 tcp       0      0  127.0.0.1.1380     127.0.0.1.5304    TIME_WAIT
10bb300 tcp       0      0  127.0.0.1.1379     127.0.0.1.5304    TIME_WAIT
11c2c00 tcp       0      0  127.0.0.1.1378     127.0.0.1.5304    TIME_WAIT
 d51e00 tcp       0      0  127.0.0.1.1377     127.0.0.1.5304    TIME_WAIT
1240a00 tcp       0      0  127.0.0.1.1376     127.0.0.1.5304    TIME_WAIT
11c2700 tcp       0      0  127.0.0.1.1373     127.0.0.1.5304    TIME_WAIT
1140a80 udp       0      0  192.3.0.1.5301     *.*
1140a00 udp       0      0  15.13.172.229.5301 *.*
1123780 udp       0      0  192.3.0.1.5300     *.*
 10da80 udp       0      0  15.13.172.229.5300 *.*
 126880 udp       0      0  *.4760             *.*
 126800 udp       0      0  127.0.0.1.4755     *.*
10c1c80 udp       0      0  *.177              *.*
110d780 udp       0      0  *.*                *.*
110d700 udp       0      0  *.*                *.* (Continued Next Page)
```

```
Active Unix domain sockets
Address  Type    Recv-Q Send-Q   Inode    Conn   Refs  Nextref Addr
10ca400 stream      0      0        0   fa05c0     0        0
 f12e00 stream      0      0   87c64c        0     0        0 /etc/vx/vold_diag/socket
 f12f00 stream      0      0   87ca3c        0     0        0 /etc/vx/vold_requ/socket
108a800 stream      0      0        0   fa0300     0        0
105f700 stream      0      0        0   fa0140     0        0 /tmp/.AgentSockets/A
105c700 stream      0      0        0   fa0340     0        0
108a900 stream      0      0        0   fa02c0     0        0 /tmp/.AgentSockets/A
```

5.9.2   nettune (HP-UX 10.x) and ndd (HP-UX 11.0 and Later)

The *nettune* and *ndd* commands permit examination and modification of several items that affect networking. The following example gets the value of the *tcp_send* object (socket send buffer size):

```
$ nettune tcp_send
32768
```

5.9.3   nfsstat

The *nfsstat* command reports information about the Network File System (NFS) and Remote Procedure Call (RPC) interfaces to the kernel, and can also reinitialize this information. If no options are given, the default is

```
nfsstat -cnrs /stand/vmunix
```

which means: display everything but modify nothing. Typical output appears as follows:

```
/opt/IRuser from irma:/opt/IRuser (Addr 15.0.69.57)
 Flags:    hard,int,dynamic, read size=8192, write size=8192,  count = 4
 Lookups: srtt=  8 ( 20ms), dev=  4 ( 20ms), cur=  3 ( 60ms)
 Reads:   srtt=  6 ( 15ms), dev=  3 ( 15ms), cur=  2 ( 40ms)
 All:     srtt=  8 ( 20ms), dev=  4 ( 20ms), cur=  3 ( 60ms)

/opt/acrobat3 from hoffman:/opt/acrobat3 (Addr 15.13.169.233)
 Flags:    soft,int, read size=8192, write size=8192,  count = 4
 Lookups: srtt= 10 ( 25ms), dev=  6 ( 30ms), cur=  4 ( 80ms)
 Reads:   srtt=  7 ( 17ms), dev=  3 ( 15ms), cur=  2 ( 40ms)
 All:     srtt= 10 ( 25ms), dev=  6 ( 30ms), cur=  4 ( 80ms)

/opt/acrordr3 from hoffman:/opt/acrordr3 (Addr 15.13.169.233)
 Flags:    soft,int, read size=8192, write size=8192,  count = 4
 Lookups: srtt=  7 ( 17ms), dev=  4 ( 20ms), cur=  2 ( 40ms)
 Reads:   srtt= 23 ( 57ms), dev=  3 ( 15ms), cur=  4 ( 80ms)
 All:     srtt= 10 ( 25ms), dev=  5 ( 25ms), cur=  3 ( 60ms)
```

GlancePlus and *gpm* provide these and additional metrics, and present them in a much more useable way.

5.10 Capacity Planning Tools

Capacity planning deals with "What if" questions, such as: "Will I have enough capacity to add an additional 20 users," or "What will happen to response time if I add 256 MB of memory or upgrade from a D580 to a V2500?" A capacity plan is based on one or more characteristic workloads, each of which yields data for short time periods. For example, you might do separate capacity plans for OLTP 9-5, for End of Month, and for Overnight Batch processing.

Various vendors offer capacity planning tools and solutions. Further explanation of capacity planning is outside the scope of this book.

Performance Tools Alphabetical Reference

This chapter contains a complete alphabetized listing of all the performance tools discussed in this book. Each tool will be presented in a chart with a standard format that summarizes the major points about the tool, and highlights unique metrics.

Unix performance tools come from many sources:

- **System V**. System V tools concentrate on the three major system resources: CPU, memory and disk. While most provide only global performance information, several do provide limited per-process information.
- **BSD**. As with the System V tools, tools from Berkeley concentrate on CPU, memory and disk resources, and display mostly global metrics.
- **Hewlett-Packard**. HP has provided a variety of tools for HP-UX and other Unix variants, including Solaris and AIX.
- **Other Sources**. Tools from other sources include nfsstat and xload. The purpose of these tools is very specific, and the information they provide is global in nature.

6.1 System V Tools

The System V tools include the following:

- df
- ipcs
- Process Accounting
- prof
- ps
- sar

- size
- *time* and *timex*

6.2 Berkeley Tools

Tools from Berkeley and related organizations include:

- df (called bdf on HP-UX systems)
- gprof
- iostat
- netstat
- ps
- size
- time
- top
- uptime
- vmstat

6.3 HP-UX Tools

HP tools include:

- CXperf
- dpat (HP-UX only)
- GlancePlus (glance and gpm)
- hpc (HP-UX only)
- midaemon (HP-UX only)
- Perf/RX (HP-UX only)
- PerfView
- MeasureWare

6.4 Other Tools

The remaining tools discussed in this book come from various sources:

- nettune and netdd
- nfsstat
- xload

6.5 Headings in the Summary Chart

The summary chart for each tool is organized as follows:

- **Tool Source**. This lists the original author of the tool, such as System V Unix, BSD 4.X Unix, or Hewlett-Packard Company.
- **Documentation**. Documentation for the tool may come in the form of a man page, manual, online help and/or kernel source code. Some tools are much better documented than others. In a few cases, it is necessary to review the kernel source code in order to understand the intent of a particular metric. The value of the tool increases with the quality of the documentation. In other words, if you don't understand what the metric means, you can't use it to decide when and how to tune the system.
- **Common Uses and Tasks**. The main purpose of the tool in managing performance is listed first: either Performance Management or Crisis Management. Some tools are better at making short-term, frequent measurements viewed in real-time for problem diagnosis. Others are better at making less frequent, long-term measurements for baseline or characterization purposes. Then, categories applicable to the tool are listed:

  - **Application Optimization** is of concern chiefly to application designers. These tools profile the application for CPU utilization, or provide an indication of resource utilization by that application.
  - **Baseline measurements** are made when the system is running normally. They are compared with current measurements to highlight changes in system performance.
  - **Benchmarking** requires real-time measurement and analysis for short-duration benchmarks, or the ability to store measurements in a form that is easy to analyze. Tools that are commonly used or lend themselves to benchmarking are listed in this category.
  - **Capacity planning** requires long-term averages over weeks or months that measure CPU, memory, disk, and network utilization and provide response time or throughput measurements. It does not require real-time measurements. A tool's ability to group resource utilization by various applications is advantageous for capacity planning.
  - **Casual monitoring** is provided by a few tools that show limited information on a real-time basis; for example, the list of currently running processes.
  - **Chargeback accounting** requires detailed listing of resource utilization by user or groups of users, and may include grouping by application or process.
  - **Performance characterization** results in long-term measurements detailing major resource utilization and possible response-time measurements. Useful tools of this type provide an easy way to store and analyze large amounts of data.
  - **Problem diagnosis** requires great detail and frequent, short-duration measurements. When the problem only happens occasionally, easy measurement storage and analy-

sis are an advantage.

- **Resource utilization** is useful both to the System Administrator for system tuning, and to the Application Designer for sizing and utilization.

- **Interval of Presentation**. Measurements that can be displayed as frequently as every second are especially useful for Crisis Management at the cost of higher overhead. Performance Management tasks use measurements that are of longer duration than the measurements obtained in a crisis.
- **Data Source**. The source of the data—*/dev/kmem* or the Kernel Instrumentation and Measurement Interface—is important in determining data accuracy.
- **Kernel Data Collection**. Data collection may be continuous, or it may be turned on and off by a particular user process.
- **Type of Data**. This category lists whether or not the data is available at the Global, Application, Process, and/or Procedure levels.
- **Metrics**. The major categories of metrics are shown by kernel subsystem (such as CPU or Network) in this row of the table.
- **Summarization**. This category indicates what type of summary the tool provides. For example, some tools display an average of all of the samples at the end of the output. Other tools provide interval, average, and high values for certain metrics only.
- **Logging**. Some tools only write to the standard output, and can be redirected to a file. Other tools use screen addressing, and their output cannot be redirected to a file. These tools often provide a logging feature to log a screen of data to a file or to a printer.
- **Overhead Dependencies**. This category lists the factors that affect how much overhead is consumed by the tool.
- **Advantages**.
- **Disadvantages**.

6.6 Tool Reference Tables

The remainder of this chapter presents reference tables for the performance tools.

6.6.1 bdf

Tool Source	BSD 4.X Unix
Documentation	*Man* page
Common Uses and Tasks	Performance and crisis management
	• Problem diagnosis • Resource utilization
Interval of Presentation	On demand
Presentation Method	Tabular data
Data Source	On-disk file system
Kernel Data Collection	None
Type of Data	Global
Metrics	• File system utilization (capacity) • Inode utilization (capacity) • File system swap utilization
Summarization	By file system
Logging	Redirect standard out to a file
Overhead Dependencies	Number of file systems
Advantages	Shows on-disk HFS inode utilization
Disadvantages	• Does not show JFS inode utilization • Causes a sync of file systems, which can cause momentary performance degradation

6.6.2 CXperf (HP-UX 11.0 (9806) and later)

Tool Source	Hewlett-Packard
Documentation	User's manual
Common Uses and Tasks	Performance management
	Application optimization
Interval of Presentation	
Presentation Method	Graphical data
Data Source	Kernel
Kernel Data Collection	Turned on by instrumenting the application and running the *CXperf* tool
Type of Data	Process
Metrics	• Procedure execution counts • CPU time • Wallclock time • Instruction counts • Instruction and Data TLB misses • Instruction and data cache hits and misses • Context switches • Thread CPU switches
Summarization	Detailed information by procedure
Logging	To data file
Overhead Dependencies	Particular metrics chosen for data collection
Advantages	• Works with applications in ANSI C, ANSI C++, Fortran 77 and 90, and Assembler • Works with threaded applications • Is the only tool that reports TLB misses and hardware cache hits and misses • Provides call graph information
Disadvantages	• Supported only on HP-UX 11.0 • Supported only on D-, K-, N-, and V-class systems • Overhead can be quite large

6.6.3 dpat (replaced in later releases by Puma)

Tool Source	Hewlett-Packard Company
Documentation	Manual, *man* page
Common Uses and Tasks	Performance Management
	Application Optimization
Interval of Presentation	One or more seconds
Presentation Method	Procedure histogram and flow graph to X/Window
Data Source	The individual process
Kernel Data Collection	None
Type of Data	Procedure
Metrics	CPU (by procedure) procedure flow
Summarization	Sample interval
Logging	None
Overhead Dependencies	Sampling frequency
Advantages	• Histogram presentation is easy to assimilate • Does not require special compilation • Provides playback of flow graph • Works well for compute-bound programs
Disadvantages	• Histogram presented only while process executes (cannot be saved or printed) • Sampling method does not capture system call time

6.6.4 GlancePlus/UX

Tool Source	Hewlett-Packard Company
Documentation	*Man* page, manual, online help
Common Uses and Tasks	Performance and crisis management
	• Problem diagnosis • Performance characterization • Benchmarking • Resource utilization
Interval of Presentation	Two or more seconds
Presentation Method	Tabular, multi-screen
Data Source	*/dev/kmem* and KI/MI
Kernel Data Collection	Turned on by *midaemon*
Type of Data	• Global • Process
Metrics	• CPU (global and process) • Memory (global and process • Disk (global and process) • Kernel Resources (global) • Network (LAN - global) • Network (NFS - global)
Summarization	• Internal average • Average and high value since start-up
Logging	• Optional screen logging to a file • Optional screen print
Overhead Dependencies	• Number of processes • Presentation interval
Advantages	• Extensive per-process info • Extensive online help • Process filtering • Available for HP-UX, Solaris, AIX
Disadvantages	• Terminal version uses *curses* • Relatively slow start-up • Not bundled with OS

6.6.5 gpm (GlancePlus/Motif)

Tool Source	Hewlett-Packard Company
Documentation	*Man* page, manual, online help
Common Uses and Tasks	Performance and crisis management
	• Problem diagnosis • Performance characterization • Benchmarking • Resource utilization
Interval of Presentation	One or more seconds
Presentation Method	Tables & color graphs Tabular data with sortable columns
Data Source	*/dev/kmem* and KI/MI
Kernel Data Collection	Turned on by *midaemon*
Type of Data	• Global • Process
Metrics	• CPU (global and process) • Memory (global and process) • Disk (global and process) • Kernel Resources (global) • Network (LAN - global) • Network (NFS - global)
Summarization	• Interval average • Average and high value since start-up
Logging	Printing only through Adviser
Overhead Dependencies	• Number of processes • System call rate • Presentation interval
Advantages	• Color graphical presentation • Extensive per-process info • Extensive online help • Extensive process filtering • Customizable alarms and advice • Available for HP-UX, AIX, and Solaris
Disadvantages	• Relatively slow start-up • Not bundled with OS • Very limited logging capability

6.6.6 gprof / gprof++

Tool Source	BSD 4.X Unix
Documentation	*Man* page
Common Uses and Tasks	Performance Management
	Application Optimization
Interval of Presentation	Process completion
Presentation Method	Tabular data and call graph
Data Source	Individual process
Kernel Data Collection	Turned on when process starts
Type of Data	Procedure
Metrics	• CPU (by procedure) • Tabular procedure call graph • Call counts
Summarization	Process completion
Logging	Binary data file
Overhead Dependencies	None
Advantages	• Procedure call graph shows parent and child relationships • Shows where a process is spending the most time • Follows the program as it executes system calls
Disadvantages	• Requires special compilation (-G) • Process must terminate normally • Accuracy affected by multi-tasking • Does not work with shared libraries • Does not profile all system libraries

6.6.7 hpc—Histogram Program Counter (replaced in later releases by Puma)

Tool Source	Hewlett-Packard Company
Documentation	Manual and *man* page
Common Uses and Tasks	Performance Management
	Application Optimization
Interval of Presentation	One or more seconds
Presentation Method	Tabular histogram
Data Source	Process
Kernel Data Collection	None
Type of Data	Procedure
Metrics	CPU (by procedure and source line within procedure)
Summarization	Interval and process completion
Logging	None
Overhead Dependencies	Debug information
Advantages	• Shows where a process is spending its time down to the source code line • Works well for compute-bound programs • Histogram is easy to assimilate
Disadvantages	• Requires special compilation (-G) • No call-graph information • Accuracy affected by multi-tasking • Sampling method does not capture system call time

6.6.8 iostat (IO Statistics)

Tool Source	BSD 4.X Unix
Documentation	*Man* page and kernel source
Common Uses and Tasks	Crisis management
	Problem diagnosis
Interval of Presentation	One or more seconds
Presentation Method	Tabular data
Data Source	*/dev/kmem* counters
Kernel Data Collection	Always turned on
Type of Data	Global
Metrics	Disk (physical) Terminal I/O (optional)
Summarization	None
Logging	Redirect standard output to a file
Overhead Dependencies	Presentation interval
Advantages	• Statistics by disk drive • Fast start up
Disadvantages	• Many lines per interval • Limited statistics

6.6.9 ipcs and ipcrm

Tool Source	System V Unix
Documentation	*Man* pages
Common Uses and Tasks	Performance and crisis management
	• Problem diagnosis • Application optimization
Interval of Presentation	On demand
Presentation Method	Tabular data
Data Source	*/dev/kmem*
Kernel Data Collection	Always turned on
Type of Data	• Global • Process (limited)

Metrics	Kernel resource utilization for:
	  • Semaphores
	  • Message queues
	  • Shared memory

Summarization	None
Logging	Redirect standard out to a file
Overhead Dependencies	Number of IPC resources in use
Advantages	• Can detect and remove IPC entries flagged in use where the owners have terminated • Can detect current size of message queues and shared memory segments
Disadvantages	Process information limited to owner and last process to use the resource

6.6.10 MeasureWare

Tool Source	Hewlett-Packard Company
Documentation	*Man* pages, manual, online help
Common Uses and Tasks	Performance management
	• Performance characterization • Performance trending • Capacity planning • Workload estimation • Chargeback accounting
Interval of Presentation	One minute and 5 minute
Presentation Method	Tabular data suitable for import by another tool
Data Source	*/dev/kmem* and KI/MI
Kernel Data Collection	Turned on by *scopeux*
Type of Data	Global, process, and application
Metrics	• CPU (global, process, application) • Memory (global, process, application) • Disk (global, process) • Network (global)
Summarization	None
Logging	• To binary logfile • Converted to ASCII for export
Overhead Dependencies	• Number of processes • System call rate • Number and extent of application definitions
Advantages	• Compact logfiles • Extensive per-process information • Easy to maintain historical data • Easy to export data to other tools • Available for HP-UX, Solaris, AIX
Disadvantages	• Most useful in conjunction with another tool • Not bundled with OS

6.6.11 midaemon (Measurement Interface Daemon)

Tool Source	Hewlett-Packard Company
Documentation	Manual, *man* page
Common Uses and Tasks	Not applicable
Interval of Presentation	Not applicable
Presentation Method	Not applicable
Data Source	*pstat* and KI/MI
Kernel Data Collection	Turned on by *midaemon*
Type of Data	• Global • Process
Metrics	Numerous—used by *glance, gpm,* and *scopeux*
Summarization	Not applicable
Logging	To shared memory segment
Overhead Dependencies	• Number of running process • System call and context switch rates
Advantages	• Data is much more accurate than normal */dev/kmem* data • Consistent mechanism for data collection • Overhead of collection can be measured
Disadvantages	Additional overhead

6.6.12 PerfView

Tool Source	Hewlett-Packard Company
Documentation	*Man* page, manual, online help
Common Uses and Tasks	Performance and crisis management
	Problem diagnosis
Interval of Presentation	On demand
Presentation Method	Color graphics
Data Source	*/dev/kmem* & KI/MI
Kernel Data Collection	Turned on by *pv_alarmd*
Type of Data	• Global • Process
Metrics	• CPU (global and process) • Memory (global and process) • Disk (global) • Network (global LAN and NFS)
Summarization	One minute, five minutes and hourly
Logging	• To binary logfile • Alarms sent to central monitoring system
Overhead Dependencies	• Number of running processes • System call rate
Advantages	• Centralized and automated monitoring of the performance of a network of systems • Can be used with *GlancePlus/UX* and *PerfView/Analyzer* for more detailed investigation
Disadvantages	• Requires other tools for more detail • Minimum sample time is 5 minutes for some metrics and 15 minutes for others

6.6.13 Process Accounting

Tool Source	System V Unix
Documentation	*Man* pages, manual
Common Uses and Tasks	Performance management
	• Resource utilization • Chargeback accounting • Problem diagnosis
Interval of Presentation	On demand
Presentation Method	Tabular data
Data Source	*/dev/kmem*
Kernel Data Collection	Turned on by */usr/lib/acct/turnacct on*
Type of Data	Process
Metrics	CPU (process) Disk space utilization (user)
Summarization	By user
Logging	To binary disk file
Overhead Dependencies	• Number of active processes • Frequency of report generation
Advantages	• Summarizes CPU and Disk space utilization by user • Customizable reports
Disadvantages	Consumes significant amount of CPU to collect and record the data

6.6.14 prof

Tool Source	System V Unix
Documentation	*Man* page
Common Uses and Tasks	Performance Management
	Application Optimization
Interval of Presentation	Process completion
Presentation Method	Tabular data
Data Source	• Kernel sampling • Call to counting procedure inserted into code
Kernel Data Collection	Turned on when process starts
Type of Data	Procedure
Metrics	• CPU (by procedure) • Call counts
Summarization	At process termination
Logging	To binary disk file
Overhead Dependencies	None
Advantages	Shows where a process is spending its time
Disadvantages	• Requires special compilation (-p) • No call graph information • Process must terminate normally • Accuracy affected by multi-tasking • Does not work with shared libraries

6.6.15 ps (process status)

Tool Source	System V Unix
Documentation	*Man* page and kernel source
Common Uses and Tasks	Crisis management
	• Problem diagnosis • Benchmarking • Casual monitoring
Interval of Presentation	On demand
Presentation Method	Tabular data
Data Source	*/dev/kmem*
Kernel Data Collection	Always turned on
Type of Data	Process
Metrics	• Current state • Current priority • Nice value • Start time • Cumulative execution time • PID, PPID
Summarization	None
Logging	Redirect standard output to a file
Overhead Dependencies	Number of running processes
Advantages	• Familiarity • Filters for limiting output
Disadvantages	• Minimal information • No averaging or summarization

6.6.16 sar (System Activity Reporter)

Tool Source	System V Unix
Documentation	*Man* page and kernel source
Common Uses and Tasks	Performance and crisis management
	• Baselines • Problem diagnosis • Benchmarking • Resource utilization
Interval of Presentation	One or more seconds
Presentation Method	Tabular data
Data Source	*pstat*
Kernel Data Collection	Always turned on
Type of Data	Global
Metrics	• CPU • Memory • Disk (physical and logical) • Kernel Resources
Summarization	Averages the samples at the end
Logging	• Binary data to disk (optional) • ASCII data to disk (optional)
Overhead Dependencies	Presentation interval
Advantages	• Lots of data • Familiarity with the tool • Kernel resource overflow statistics • Ipc usage rate statistics
Disadvantages	• No VM paging information • Rudimentary summarization • No graphics or data reformatting • Many lines per interval

6.6.17 scopeux

Tool Source	Hewlett-Packard Company
Documentation	*Man* page
Common Uses and Tasks	Performance and crisis management
	• Baselines • Problem diagnosis • Benchmarking • Resource utilization
Interval of Presentation	One and five minutes
Presentation Method	Counters
Data Source	*midaemon* (Measurement Interface)
Kernel Data Collection	Turned on by *midaemon*
Type of Data	• Global • Application • Process
Metrics	• CPU • Memory • Disk • Kernel Resources • Network
Summarization	One and five minutes
Logging	Binary data to disk
Overhead Dependencies	• Number and extent of application definitions • Number of running processes
Advantages	Method for collecting and consolidating data
Disadvantages	Needs another tool to interpret the data

6.6.18 size

Tool Source	System V Unix
Documentation	*Man* page
Common Uses and Tasks	Performance and crisis management
	Problem diagnosis
Interval of Presentation	On demand
Presentation Method	One line of data
Data Source	*a.out* file
Kernel Data Collection	None
Type of Data	Process
Metrics	Static size of process (text, data, BSS)
Summarization	None
Logging	None
Overhead Dependencies	None
Advantages	Quick look at static process size for resource utilization planning
Disadvantages	Does not include dynamically allocated memory, shared memory, or shared libraries

6.6.19 swapinfo (Swap space Information)

Tool Source	Hewlett-Packard Company
Documentation	*Man* page
Common Uses and Tasks	Performance and crisis management
	• Problem diagnosis • Resource utilization
Interval of Presentation	On demand
Presentation Method	Tabular data
Data Source	*/dev/kmem*
Kernel Data Collection	Always turned on
Type of Data	Global
Metrics	Swap device space reservation and utilization
Summarization	By swap device
Logging	None
Overhead Dependencies	• Number of swap devices & file systems • Number of processes on swap devices
Advantages	Quick look at swap space utilization
Disadvantages	Limited information

6.6.20 time, timex

Tool Source	System V Unix
Documentation	*Man* page
Common Uses and Tasks	Crisis management
	• Problem diagnosis • Benchmarking • Application optimization
Interval of Presentation	Process completion
Presentation Method	Tabular data
Data Source	*/dev/kmem*
Kernel Data Collection	Always turned on
Type of Data	Process
Metrics	CPU (user, system, and elapsed times). *Timex* optionally includes *sar* and process-accounting information
Summarization	None
Logging	Redirect standard error to a file
Overhead Dependencies	None
Advantages	Minimal overhead
Disadvantages	Minimal information. *Timex* requires *sadc* to be running in some versions

6.6.21 top

Tool Source	BSD 4.X Unix
Documentation	*Man* page
Common Uses and Tasks	Performance and crisis management
	• Problem diagnosis • Performance characterization • Benchmarking
Interval of Presentation	One or more seconds
Presentation Method	Screen tabular data
Data Source	*pstat*
Kernel Data Collection	Always turned on
Type of Data	Global Process
Metrics	• CPU (Global and Process) • Memory (Global and Process)
Summarization	None
Logging	None
Overhead Dependencies	Presentation interval
Advantages	• Quick look at global CPU & process data • Load average per CPU on SMP system
Disadvantages	• Limited statistics • Uses curses for terminal output

6.6.22 uptime

Tool Source	BSD 4.X Unix
Documentation	*Man* page
Common Uses and Tasks	Performance and crisis management
	• Problem diagnosis • Performance characterization
Interval of Presentation	On demand
Presentation Method	Tabular data
Data Source	*/dev/kmem*
Kernel Data Collection	Always turned on
Type of Data	Global
Metrics	• One, five and 15-minute load averages • Number of users
Summarization	None
Logging	None
Overhead Dependencies	None
Advantages	Quick look at CPU load averages
Disadvantages	Limited information

6.6.23 vmstat

Tool Source	BSD 4.X Unix
Documentation	*Man* page, kernel source & include files
Common Uses and Tasks	Crisis management
	Problem diagnosis
Interval of Presentation	One or more seconds
Presentation Method	Columnar data to screen
Data Source	*pstat*
Kernel Data Collection	Always turned on
Type of Data	Global
Metrics	• CPU • Memory
Summarization	First line: average since boot or reset. Otherwise, none
Logging	Redirect standard output to a file
Overhead Dependencies	Presentation interval
Advantages	• Fast start-up • Minimal overhead • One line per interval
Disadvantages	• Poorly documented • Cryptic headings

6.6.24 xload (X/Windows-Based CPU Load)

Tool Source	Massachusetts Institute of Technology
Documentation	*Man* page
Common Uses and Tasks	Performance management
	Casual monitoring
Interval of Presentation	On demand and continuous
Presentation Method	X/Window graph
Data Source	*/dev/kmem*
Kernel Data Collection	Always turned on
Type of Data	Global
Metrics	CPU Load Average
Summarization	One minute
Logging	None
Overhead Dependencies	None
Advantages	Graphic representation
Disadvantages	Minimal information

Performance Bottleneck Analysis

Part 3 discusses performance bottleneck analysis, and presents tuning strategies that use the tools that were discussed in Part 2 to solve problems in the major areas of the operating system. The chapters are:

- Hardware Performance Issues
- CPU Bottlenecks
- Memory Bottlenecks
- Disk Bottlenecks

## CHAPTER 7

Hardware Performance Issues

T he hardware components of Unix systems may be the source of major performance issues. Processor speed is certainly not the only significant variable. Cache size and organization, TLB size and organization, bus structure and speed, I/O characteristics—all these and others are also very important.

This chapter will discuss some performance-related aspects of the major hardware units. Certain terms will be defined, and the architecture of several HP-UX systems will be presented in some detail. Topics are as follows:

- Terminology
- Processor instructions and modules
- Multi-processing
- Cache memory for instructions and data
- Virtual address space
- PA-RISC architectures
- Summary of system attributes

7.1 Terminology

Like other fields, the computer industry has spawned its own special terminology. Knowing some of this terminology is essential to understanding how the design of the computer hardware may affect system performance.

7.1.1   Main Memory

Main memory or *physical memory* is the location where data and executable software reside while the computer is operating. Processors carry out computation by copying instructions and data from main memory into several *registers*, special locations within the processor for data while it is being manipulated. The function of copying data and instructions is known as *fetching objects from main memory.*

Main memory is physically separate from the CPU. Today, it is common to have hundreds of megabytes or several gigabytes of main memory. The size and allocation of physical memory usually have a strong impact on system performance and may affect other system resource utilization as well.

7.1.2   Cache Memory

Cache memory is a form of high-speed memory that is used for storing recently used data and instructions. Cache size and type directly affect performance. Cache memory may be internal and/or external to the CPU chip, but it is always in close proximity to this chip. Caches may range in size from 16 KB to 4MB.

Caches are made from chips that are much faster and more expensive than those used for main memory. Therefore, caches are much smaller than main memory, but they run much closer to the speed of the CPU itself. Instructions and data are moved in blocks (called lines); more is moved than is immediately requested in the hope that future references will be sequential.

7.1.3   Input/Output Devices (I/O Devices)

Input/Output devices or *I/O devices* are components that provide an external interface for the computer. Typical devices include disks, monitors, tape and CD drives, and networking hardware. Each I/O device has its own performance characteristics, and the link to which it is attached has distinct attributes that affect performance.

One important class of I/O devices is called *peripherals.* This is because they frequently stand apart from the computer chassis itself, and often operate at the periphery of the flow of data—that is, they provide the first input to the computer, or receive the last output (a disk write or a display update, for example).

7.1.4   Buses

A *bus* is a data conduit through which data moves as it goes from memory to a processor's registers, or from memory to an external device like a disk or printer. Buses are of various types and speeds, and their speed is a fundamental aspect of performance.

Buses are used for intercommunication among the major components of the computer: between the processors and memory, between memory and I/O devices, and so forth. Occasionally a computer system can use different buses running at different speeds. In these cases, a bus converter or adapter may be necessary.

Buses may be proprietary, or they may conform to various standards. SCSI buses used for I/O devices, for example, use the ISO standard SCSI protocol. They are said to be compliant with SCSI standards, including SCSI II, and Fast/Wide SCSI.

7.1.5   Graphics Devices

Graphics devices deserve special mention because they often require large quantities of memory and processor activity to provide the needed functionality for an application, including transformation and conversion of bitmap data. The high-resolution graphics display needed for CAD applications frequently requires specialized supporting hardware within the computer, as well as additional memory and high speed transmission of data.

As more and more applications follow the client/server model, and as graphics-intensive applications on the Internet become the norm rather than the exceptional case, these performance issues will increase in frequency and importance.

7.2   Processor Instructions and Modules

Many current Unix systems, including those of Hewlett-Packard, use instructions that are defined for Reduced Instruction Set Computing (RISC). The following sections describe how instructions operate on different hardware platforms running HP-UX.

7.2.1   Instruction Types

The CPU evaluates various *instruction types* by using one or more functional units. Instructions are of two major types: *integer* and *floating point*. Integer instructions include loads, stores, addition, subtraction, shift, rotate, bit manipulation, and branch. Floating point instructions include the following:

- Floating point addition, subtraction, and conversion. These may require two to three CPU cycles to complete, and are executed on the floating point arithmetic logical unit (ALU).

- Multiplications, requiring two to three cycles, are executed on the multiplier unit (MPY).

- Divisions and square root operations may require up to nine cycles for single precision (32-bit) or 15 cycles for double precision. They are executed on the divider unit (DIV).

It is important to understand that different instructions may be executed on different functional units. Therefore, different classes of instructions may execute concurrently. This is especially important for engineering and scientific applications. Since the organization of functional units may differ from one computer chip implementation to another, these types of applications must be recompiled to fully take advantage of a particular architecture. Business-oriented applications do not benefit as much from this type of recompilation.

7.2.2   Scalar versus Superscalar

Processors are implemented with multiple *modules*, each one of which can execute independently. Different modules execute different types of instructions. Examples of modules are integer units, arithmetic logic units (ALUs), and co-processors such as the floating-point co-processor.

Scalar processors have the ability to start one instruction per cycle; *superscalar* processors can start multiple instructions per cycle. Superscalar processing depends on having a wide enough instruction path to obtain two or more instructions in one fetch.

Applications must be recompiled to take advantage of a superscalar architecture. Business applications execute integer instructions almost exclusively, and may benefit greatly from recompilation to take advantage of superscalar architecture. Engineering and scientific applications generally see significantly improved performance from recompilation for a specific superscalar architecture for both integer and floating point instructions.

Hewlett-Packard Precision Architecture (PA-RISC) systems have different scalar attributes. The newest versions can execute six or more RISC instructions concurrently. Table 7-1, "Scalar and Superscalar CPUs," on page 128 shows the level for a variety of PA-RISC systems that are commonly used today.

Table 7-1   Scalar and Superscalar CPUs

PA-RISC Version	Models	Characteristics
PA 1.0	PN5, PN10, PCX	• Scalar implementation • One integer *or* one floating point instruction per cycle • 32 bit instruction path
PA 1.1a	PA7000, PCX/S	• Scalar implementation • One integer *or* one floating point instruction per cycle • 32 bit instruction path
PA 1.1b	PA7100, PA7150, PCX/T	• Limited superscalar implementation • One integer *and* one floating point instruction per cycle for floating point; ALU and MPY instructions alternate • 64 bit instruction path (two instructions in one fetch)
PA 1.1c	PA7100L, PCX/L	• Superscalar implementation • Two integer *or* one integer and one floating point instruction per cycle • 64 bit instruction path

Table 7-1   Scalar and Superscalar CPUs (Continued)

PA-RISC Version	Models	Characteristics
PA 1.2	PA 7200, PCX/T	• Limited superscalar implementation • One integer and one floating point instruction per cycle for floating point; ALU and MPY instructions alternate • 64-bit instruction path (two instructions in one fetch)
PA 2.0	PA 8000, 8200	• Superscalar implementation with out of order execution • Two integer and two floating point and two loads or two stores • 64-bit extensions • 128-bit instruction and data paths

7.2.3   Vectorization

Vectorization is a technique for looking at loops and changing how the loop is executed. Loops may be replaced with calls to a vector routine that is hand-coded in assembly language. This takes advantage of the parallel CPU components such as co-processors and superscalar modules. Vectorization does not have anything to do with multi-processing.

7.2.4   Parallelization

Parallelization is the attempt to make different pieces of a single process run on different CPUs. The application typically has to be designed for parallelization, and compiler technology can facilitate this somewhat. Kernel threads make this type of manipulation easier, because different threads can run on different processors, but *only if the application is designed with threads in mind*.

There can also be process level parallelization if it is designed into the application. For example, a database might be designed with multiple back-end processes, each of which runs on a different CPU. These may or may not be able to do parallel work, depending on how users access the application.

Parallelization may also result in pieces of the application running on completely separate computer systems. For instance, an application may interact with the user on one system, use another system for the compute-bound portion, and display intensive graphical results on a third system.

7.3 Multi-Processing

Computer systems started out as *single processor systems* having a single Central Processing Unit (CPU). Single processor systems evolved into *multi-processor systems*. Today, multi-CPU systems contain in the order of tens of processors. Typical multi-processor implementations vary from a maximum of four to a maximum of 32, 64 or 128 CPUs. Various types of implementations have been created using multiple CPUs.

7.3.1 Master/Slave Implementation

The earliest multi-processor system used a *master/slave* implementation. In this type of system, the operating system (OS) ran on only one processor, the master processor. Other CPUs were reserved for user processes.

The master/slave arrangement made it easy for the writers of the operating system, because specialized multi-processing code was not required. Performance was usually very good for compute-bound applications. Applications that were I/O-intensive would compete for the operating system, which ran only on the master CPU. Adding CPUs usually would not improve performance for I/O-intensive applications.

7.3.2 Asymmetric Implementation

Like the master/slave multi-processor, the *asymmetric implementation* allowed the OS to run on a single CPU at a time, but it could be any of the CPUs in the system. This implementation was an improvement on the master/slave model, since the operating system could run on the same processor as the user process, therefore taking advantage of the built-up *context* (cached data) from the user process.

7.3.3 Symmetric Multi-Processing Implementation

The *symmetric multi-processing (SMP)* implementation allowed the OS to run on any processor, and now allowed different parts of the OS to run on different processors at the same time. To accomplish this, the operating system can be modified in either of two ways. First, different sections of code may be designated as able to run concurrently. For example, multiple I/O's can be processed using different device drivers. Alternatively, the data itself may be the differentiator. For example, multiple processors may be executing System V semaphore lock/unlock code but only acting on different semaphore sets.

The HP-UX kernel has supported symmetric multi-processing beginning with HP-UX version 8.06. The OS uses several locking mechanisms—spinlocks and kernel semaphores—to ensure that multiple processes do not modify the same data at the same time.

Symmetric multi-processing also allows for various granularities in the unit of execution, at either the process or the thread level. To take advantage of this, the operating system itself must be designed to run in a multi-threaded environment. The HP-UX operating system has been designed to run in this fashion beginning with HP-UX version 11.0.

7.3.4 Massively Parallel Processing Implementation

Systems that use a *massively parallel processing (MPP) implementation* typically include hundreds of processors, not tens of processors. The OS has to be different, and the application must be designed to take advantage of the MPP system. You can't just take an application off the shelf and implement in this environment without customization.

In an MPP machine, each processor may have its own memory, or multiple processors may share the same memory.

7.3.5   CPU Pipelines

In modern processors, the *CPU pipeline* is employed to execute instructions in steps or stages. Multiple instructions may be overlapped in the same processor, each in a different stage of execution, thus operating in parallel. (This is not the same as superscalar architecture, which allows the computer to start multiple instructions at the same time.) The goal in this type of design is to reduce cycle time, and thus increase the rate of instruction execution. Cycle time is the reciprocal of the clock speed (often measured in MegaHertz) of a CPU chip. The number of stages is the number of instructions that must be executed before the CPU is operating at full efficiency.

Pipeline length has evolved with the development of processor technology.

Table 7-2   Pipeline Length

Architecture	Stages
Early PA-RISC 1.0	3 stages
Modern PA-RISC 1.X	5+ stages. (This means 5 stages plus some additional operations)
PA-RISC 2.0 and later	Variable, because of out-of-order execution with a completion queue. Number of stages is not relevant here.

Figure 7-1 shows a simple CPU pipeline with three stages.

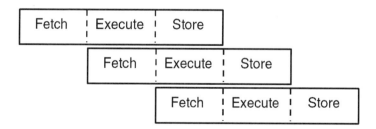

Figure 7-1   Simple CPU Pipeline

As soon as three instructions are executing concurrently, the processor has reached its most efficient operation, starting a new instruction with every CPU cycle. "Fetch" means "go get the instruction"; "execute" means "evaluate its type"; and "store" means "complete the intent of the instruction."

Figure 7-2 shows a more complex CPU pipeline with five stages. In this example, the Execute phase can be either an ALU operation or the computation of the effective address of a branch. In this case, as soon as five instructions are executing concurrently, the processor has

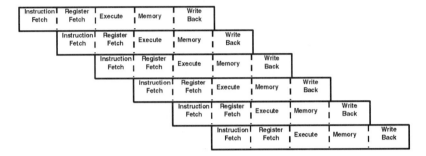

Figure 7-2   More Complex CPU Pipeline

reached its most efficient operation.

7.3.6   Problems with Pipelined Architectures

Several categories of problems peculiar to pipelined architectures may occur during instruction execution. The optimization phase of program compilation attempts to make these problems happen less frequently.

7.3.6.1   Register Interlock

Register interlock occurs within a pipelined machine because certain instructions such as loads and stores may be multi-cycle, requiring several cycles to complete execution. When register interlock occurs, the CPU is forced to wait on an instruction that takes more than one cycle to complete while the next instruction references the same register. In PA-RISC systems, this can result in CPU stalls; the situation becomes more serious if there is a cache miss, that is, if necessary data or instructions are not in cache memory.

Here is an example in simplified assembly code (LDW = Load Word, STW = Store Word):

```
LDW R1
LDW R2
ADD R1, R2, R3    --- Probable Interlock
STW R3            --- Possible interlock
LDW R5
LDW R6
```

Compiler optimization attempts to prevent these situations by re-ordering instructions so that multi-cycle instructions that reference the same register are separated. After optimization, the code might look like the following:

```
LDW R1
LDW R2
LDW R5
ADD R1,R2,R3
LDW R6
STW R3
```

The optimizer must know how many cycles instructions take to complete for a given architecture.

7.3.6.2   Branching

Branching is the source of additional problems. Branches on PA-RISC and on many other processors always take two instruction cycles. The instruction immediately following the branch is called the "delay slot," which is executed while the branch is completing. If the application is not optimized, the delay slot is filled with a no-op instruction, thus wasting an entire instruction cycle. Compiler optimization can make use of the delay slot to reduce the impact by placing a non-dependent instruction after the branch.

Branching also can result in flushing the pipeline. In pipelining, the next instruction will be started as soon as the current one is underway. But if the current instruction results in a branch, the next several instructions that were already in the pipeline must be flushed, since the sequence of instruction execution has changed to the target of the branch. Flushing the pipeline wastes two or more machine cycles depending on the size of the pipeline. Here is an example (COMBT = Compare and Branch if True):

```
LDW R1
COMBT <,R1,R0,<somewhere>
STW R5 --- Delay Slot
ADD R1,R9,R10 --- Flushed from the pipeline if branch taken
```

The bigger the pipeline, the more information gets lost in this branching situation.

7.3.7   Very Large Instruction Word (VLIW)

The *very large instruction word* (VLIW) is a design that predates RISC technology. An instruction field requiring multiple bits is encoded for each unit in the CPU. When CPU's are built with many functional units, more than 32 bits may be needed to fully encode the instruction.

The VLIW concept has been modified and used in the PA-RISC 2.0 design to improve performance. The modified design is called Out-of-Order Execution. Figure 7-3 shows a conceptual view of the VLIW.

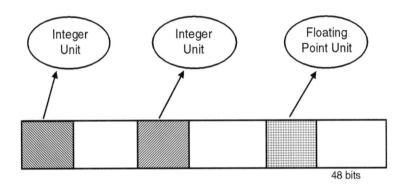

Figure 7-3   Very Large Instruction Word

7.3.8   Out-of-Order Execution

With out-of-order execution, each instruction remains 32 bits in size. The compiler organizes non-dependent instructions into instruction bundles that can be executed by the hardware in whatever order is most efficient. The CPU executes the instructions on the various functional units that are available. Instructions are then retired (completed) in the same order as specified in the program code, then placed in the completion queue. This preserves the sequential execution order of the application. If an instruction traps, the completion queue is flushed; this may involve as many as 28 entries on the PA 8000.

One advantage of using out-of-order execution is that functional unit and scheduling differences among processors do not require recompilation of the application to improve efficiency. Instead, the CPU executes the instructions in the instruction bundle in the most beneficial way according to its particular design. This is yet another example of the importance of using compiler optimization and profile-based optimization in improving application performance. See Part 4 for approaches to application performance.

7.4   Cache Memory for Instructions and Data

The caches used for data and instructions are another source of performance issues. *Cache memory* is a form of high speed memory that holds recently accessed instructions and data in the hope that they will soon be accessed again. Caches may be located on the same chip as the CPU, or they may be off-chip but in close proximity to the CPU. Sometimes there are two caches, one on-chip and the other off-chip. In this case, the on-chip cache is called a level 2 cache.

Caches may be used specifically to store data that is read in with the expectation that it will be needed again soon by the CPU. In a multi-tasking environment, the cache contains entries belonging to many different processes, in the hope that the processes will execute again before needed locations are flushed by other processes.

Caches may be unified (that is, data and instructions may share a single cache) or split (separate caches). There may also be direct mapped or n-way set associative caches. In direct mapping, an address in memory is found at a hashed (computed) address in the cache. If another address also hashes to this number, and the cache slot is already filled, then the processor has to flush the cache slot and read the new data from physical memory, which takes more time.

In two-way set associative mapping, a set of alternate slots may be used when more than one memory address hashes to the same slot in the cache. This is a more expensive but better-performing design.

Caches may be of varying size. Since they are made from higher speed components than is main memory, they are expensive. Larger caches can significantly improve system performance but also increase the cost of the system. They can improve the performance of commercial applications, because many recently accessed main memory locations belonging to different processes can be cached. Larger caches can also improve the performance of scientific or engineering applications by holding more data that can be operated on without accessing main memory, or by holding the instructions that, for example, belong to a large loop and are executed many times. Figure 7-4 shows some examples of instruction and data caches.

7.4.1   Cache Performance Issues

All of the following attributes of cache design have performance issues. Designers must trade off price against optimal design, which is expensive. Here is the list:

- Write-back or write-through design. (All PA-RISC caches are write-back.)
- Speed of access to the cache by the CPU. An access may require multiple cycles.
- Speed of access between main memory and cache. This depends on the actual implementation, and varies from 20 to 100 cycles or more.
- Size of instruction and data caches
- Organization of cache (associativity)
- Whether cache is internal (on-chip) or external to the CPU (off-chip)
- Whether the virtual address space is flat or aliased
- Whether unified or separate caches are implemented
- Virtual address to cache line number indexing method
- Access patterns by the workload (cache hit/miss rate). This is where compiler optimization helps.

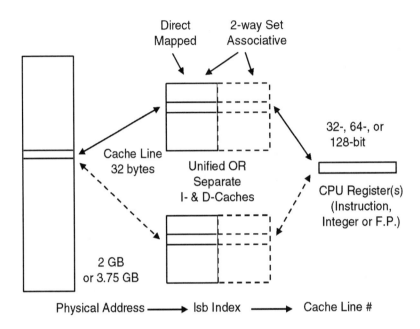

Figure 7-4   Instruction and Data Caches

7.4.2   Visible Cache Problems

Cache problems become visible as overuse of user or system CPU resources. You can see this in CPU utilization metrics, or you can compare performance metrics on systems with different cache sizes or organizations. Unfortunately, it is very difficult to detect cache problems directly. While some high-end systems may provide hardware counters that measure cache performance, there is no general-purpose instrumentation that collects data from these counters. The only tool currently available that collects data from these counters is *CXperf*. See Chapter 13 on "Application Profiling" for a discussion of using *CXperf* to get per-process cache utilization information.

Cache problems may be due to either data or instruction access patterns in a single process, or among multiple processes. How do you solve cache problems? The hardware solution is to switch to a system with:

- A larger cache

- A different cache organization

- A different indexing method (that is, using a different number of bits)

Software solutions include using compiler optimization to change how memory is used, and modifying the application itself to change memory access patterns. It is easy to demonstrate how performance may be dramatically affected by data access patterns.

The following code samples show two very similar calculations; the only difference between them is in the dimension of the array that is varied first in the loops. In Sample Code 1, the outer loop varies the first dimension, then the second, whereas in Sample Code 2, the outer loop varies the second dimension, then the first.

Sample Code 1

```
#define X 1024
#define Y 1024

main()
{

int a[X][Y];
int b,i,j;

for (j=0;j<Y;j++){
    for(i=0;i<X;i++){
        a[i][j]= i+j;
        }
    }

for (j=0;j<Y;j++){
    for(i=0;i<X;i++){
        b = a[i][j]*a[i][j];
        }
    }

}
```

Sample Code 2

```
#define X 1024
#define Y 1024

main()
{

int a[X][Y];
int b,i,j;

for (i=0;i<X;i++){
    for(j=0;j<Y;j++){
        a[i][j]= i+j;
        }
    }

for (i=0;i<X;i++){
    for(j=0;j<Y;j++){
        b = a[i][j]*a[i][j];
        }
    }
}
```

When these programs are compiled using only the -O option, and then executed using the *time* command, the results are as follows. (The execution environment was a lightly loaded HP 9000 Model 782 workstation.)

Timings from Execution of Sample Code 1 and Sample Code 2

```
# time ./c1

real    0m1.37s
user    0m1.28s
sys     0m0.07s

# time ./c2

real    0m0.11s
user    0m0.05s
sys     0m0.06s
```

Why is c2 so much faster? The reason is that c2 accesses the data in the same order in which it is stored in physical memory, thereby taking advantage of transferring a cache line (32 bytes) from memory to the cache in a single transfer. It also benefits from efficient use of the TLB (discussed in the section "Page Directory and Translation Lookaside Buffer" on page 140).

7.4.3   Cache Coherence

In a Symmetric Multi-Processing (SMP) system, each of the multiple CPUs has its own cache. Cache coherence is the requirement that all caches be consistent when modifying memory. Multiple caches may be referencing the same locations, as when a process is switched to a different CPU, or when two processes share data via an IPC mechanism.

A process normally builds up a local context in the cache on the CPU where it is executing. A problem occurs when a process is switched from one CPU to another (which uses a different cache); because of the switch, the context changes and must be built up again. Or, the process may not execute for a certain period of time while it waits for an event. On a busy system, other processes may access the same cache slots using different main memory addresses, causing the cache context from the waiting process to be flushed. When the process starts executing again, it has to rebuild its context in cache.

A similar problem relates to processes that communicate with one another using an interprocess communication method such as semaphores or pipes. The recipient of the data most likely resides on another CPU. This forces the caches to flush to memory, which is a slow operation, and transfer the data to the other cache, where it can be used by the new process. Such cache flushes and transfers may consume up to several hundred CPU cycles, causing the CPU to sit idle for that time.

7.5 Physical Address Space

The amount of physical main memory available on a particular system depends on four criteria:
  • The number of physical slots available for memory boards
  • The density of RAM chips used to build the memory boards
  • The number of bits used to address physical memory
  • The amount of memory supported by the operating system

Today's HP systems may support anywhere from 32 MB to 16 GB of main memory. System performance may vary greatly depending on the amount of main memory, speed of access, caching methods, and address translation hardware (described in the next section).

The operating system supports a much larger amount of memory than is available physically: this is called *virtual memory*. Virtual memory may be located within

  • Physical memory
  • The swap area (raw or file system swap)
  • Executable files
  • A memory mapped file

(The last three of these are known as *backing store*.) To understand how virtual memory is used by the OS, one must first understand virtual address space.

7.6 Virtual Address Space

The *global virtual address space* is a system-wide representation of all virtual memory spaces for all processes. Depending on the HP-UX implementation, the system may use 48 or 64 bits to address memory. The total number of memory locations that can be addressed is thus 2**48 or 2**64. The *page directory table* is an HP-specific data structure that contains one entry for each physical page of memory. It is located in the data space of the operating system, and always resides in physical memory.

Figure 7-5 shows the basic addressing scheme. Pages in the global virtual address space

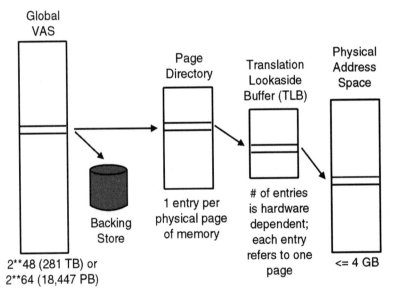

Figure 7-5 Virtual Addressing

are accessed with a virtual page address. This address may map to a location on disk or a location in main memory. If it refers to a location in main memory, an entry in the page directory table provides the translation from virtual to physical address. Recently referenced entries from this table are stored in a special hardware cache on the CPU chip, known as the *Translation Lookaside Buffer* (TLB).

7.6.1   Page Directory and Translation Lookaside Buffer

The page directory contains one entry for every page in physical memory. Page directory and TLB entries contain the following:

- Virtual page number
- Physical page number
- Access rights: read, write, execute on this page
- Protection id: who owns the page
- Recently referenced bit (in the page directory only)

Two kinds of TLBs may be implemented: direct-mapped and fully associative. A direct-mapped TLB takes a page number and runs it through an indexing scheme, which returns a slot ID. With the fully associative TLB, which has content-addressable memory, a translation can go anywhere in the TLB. Fully associative TLBs are smaller; direct-mapped TLB's may be as large as 16 K or more. Special TLB entries are used to improve system performance. The TLB does not need to be flushed.

7.6.2   TLB Performance Issues

TLB issues include the following:

- Coexistence of entries from many processes
- Size of the TLB
- Organization of the TLB
- Whether unified or separate TLBs are implemented
- Whether hardware assist miss handling is present
- Page address to TLB entry number indexing method (except for fully associative TLBs)
- Replacement algorithm (for fully associative TLBs)
- Access patterns by the workload (TLB hit/miss rate)

7.6.3   TLB Problems

TLB issues show up as CPU overhead caused by extra context switches and TLB mainte-nance. Metrics include CPU utilization and, indirectly, context switch and page-fault rates. Prob-lems may be visible through comparison with systems that have different TLB sizes or organizations. Hardware counters may also provide useful information, although only *CXperf* has access to these counters.

In PA-RISC, address space is flat rather than aliased. This means that cache and TLB entries do not need a PID tag, which would require additional hardware complexity with result-ing additional overhead. (A *flat address space* is one in which one and only one virtual address maps to a particular physical address. An *aliased* address space allows multiple (different) vir-tual addresses to map to the same physical address.)

7.7   PA-RISC Architectures

The designs of specific versions of PA-RISC architecture can have particular effects on performance. This section reviews the major groups of PA-RISC architecture at a high level. For complete information, refer to the detailed documentation for a specific architecture.

7.7.1   Early Models

Figure 7-6 shows an early type of architecture: the HP-PB-based Series 800 Models F, G, H, and I. (HP-PB stands for HP Precision Bus architecture.)

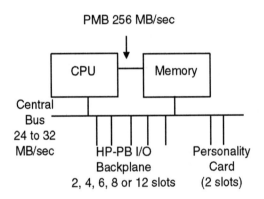

Figure 7-6   Early PA-RISC Systems

The original HP-PB systems used a single backplane to which everything was connected. Later HP-PB systems also included a private memory bus (PMB) between the CPU and memory, since the I/O backplane was relatively slow.

7.7.2   E-Series

Figure 7-7 shows E-Series architecture using the HP-PB bus with 20 MB/sec sustained speed and a 32 MB/sec peak.

This more complex system uses bus adapters, which convert between protocols, and bus converters, which match speed. The GSC bus was much faster than the HP-PB bus.

7.7.3   700 Series

Figure 7-8 shows some of the 700 Series architectures. Note the existence of different types of buses; this variety allows for very flexible design, but applications may run differently when executed on systems with different buses.

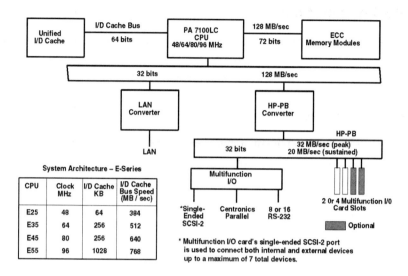

E-Series

Figure 7-7 E-Series Architecture

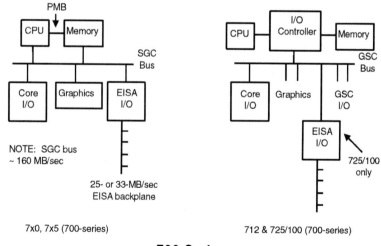

700-Series

Figure 7-8 700-Series Architecture

7.7.4   890 and T500

Figure 7-9 shows 890 and T500 architecture. BIU stands for Bus Interface Unit; there is some inefficiency here because of sharing by CPUs. The main bus speed is quite fast (1 GB per second), and the large number of I/O slots (112) allows for wide distribution of the I/O.

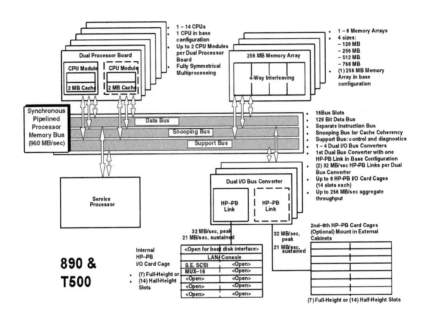

Figure 7-9   890 and T500 Architecture

7.7.5   T600

Figure 7-10 shows T600 architecture.

7.7.6   K-Series

Figure 7-11 shows generic K-Series architecture. The HSC buses, which run at 80–128 MB/second, are much faster than PB buses (32 MB/second peak). The runway bus is slower than the 1 GB on the T500, but in reality, the T500 is only using half its speed, so the K-Series is actually faster in I/O.

Figures 7-12 through 7-15 show the architecture of specific K models.

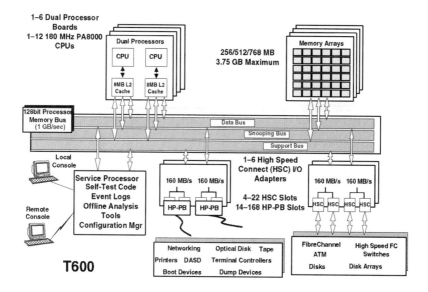

Figure 7-10   T600 Architecture

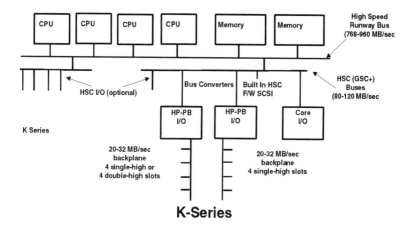

Figure 7-11   K-Series Architecture

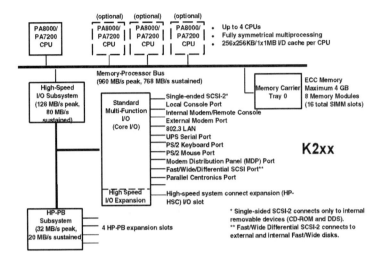

Figure 7-12 K2xx Architecture

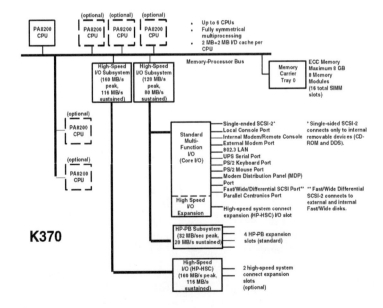

Figure 7-13 K370 Architecture

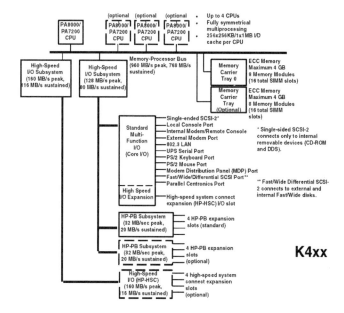

Figure 7-14   K4xx Architecture

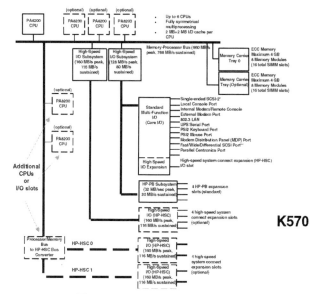

Figure 7-15   K570 Architecture

7.7.7   V-Series

Figure 7-16 shows V-Series architecture.

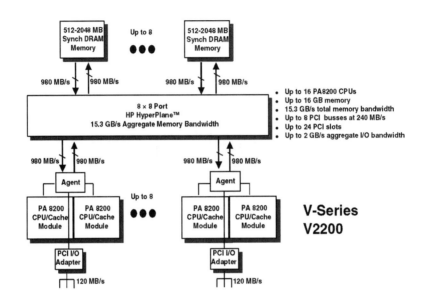

Figure 7-16   V2200 Architecture

7.7.8   D-Series

Figure 7-17 shows a generic D-Series. Figures 7-18 through 7-23 show some specific D models.

7.7.9   N-Series

Figure 7-24 shows N-Series architecture.

7.7.10   IO Performance Issues

I/O performance is affected by the following factors:

• System bus speed
• I/O backplane bandwidth
• Number of I/O backplanes
• Number of host adapters
• Host adapter speed

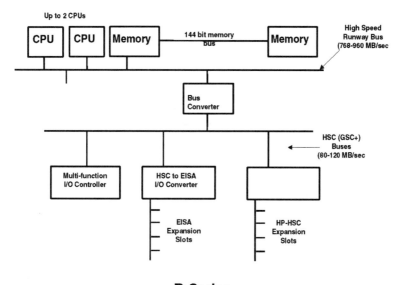

D-Series

Figure 7-17 D-Series Architecture

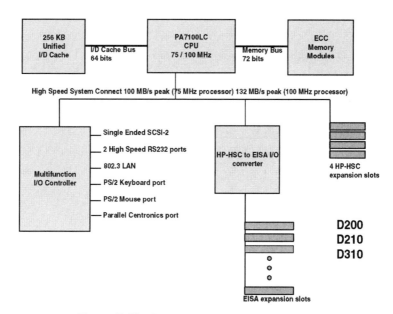

Figure 7-18 D200, D210, D310 Architecture

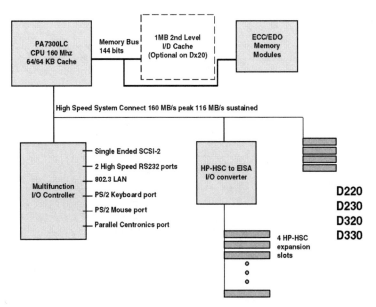

Figure 7-19   D220, D230, D320, D330 Architecture

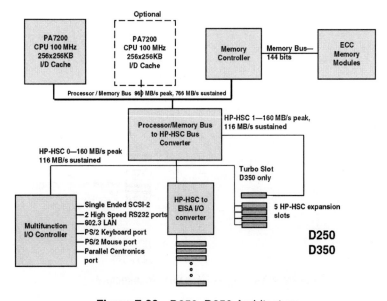

Figure 7-20   D250, D350 Architecture

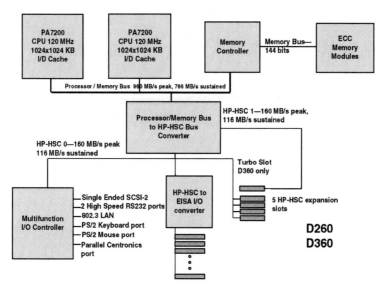

Figure 7-21   D260, D360 Architecture

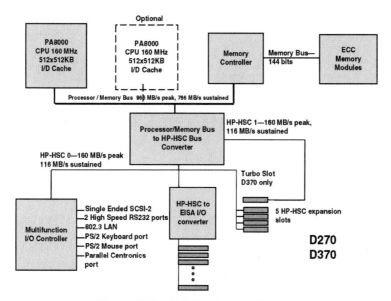

Figure 7-22   D270, D370 Architecture

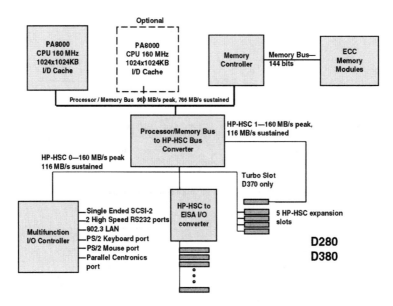

Figure 7-23   D280, D380 Architecture

I/O throughput is itself constrained by the speed of the system Main Bus, to which the CPU, memory and I/O backplanes are usually attached. I/O throughput is limited by the "weakest link" in the chain of components.

Backplane bandwidth is determined by the hardware design. This includes the length of the backplane, width (number of parallel lines), the speed of components, and the protocol employed in accessing the backplane. Hardware designers constantly strive to improve backplane bandwidth.

The number of I/O backplanes in a system determines how widely distributed the I/O can be. If there is only one backplane, all I/O is constrained by the bandwidth of that backplane. Multiple backplanes allow the administrator to spread out the I/Os for the same or different I/O types (SCSI, FibreChannel, Ethernet, for example), thus increasing total I/O throughput.

Finally, I/O throughput is constrained by the number and speed of individual host adapters, such as Fast/Wide SCSI or FibreChannel. For instance, a F/W SCSI host adapter supports up to 15 disk targets. Although each disk may be able to transfer data at a sustained rate of 5 MB per second, the host adapter is limited to a peak aggregate rate of 20 MB per second. Therefore, adding disk drives may require additional host adapters and I/O backplanes to maintain adequate performance.

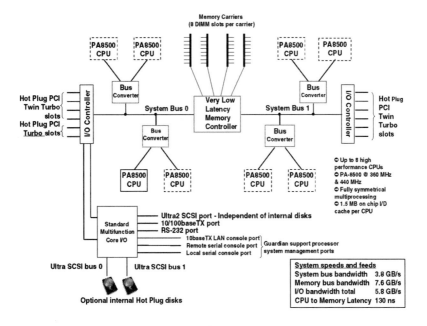

Figure 7-24   N-Series Architecture

7.7.11 I/O Problem Solving

How do I/O problems manifest? It is extremely difficult to decide whether slow I/O per-formance is due to backplane, bus and host adapter saturation, or data distribution and layout. The I/O performance of disks and networks is of greatest concern. Performance can often be improved by distributing network or disk I/Os across multiple host adapters. However, adding host adapters will not improve performance if the I/O backplane is saturated. Deducing the source of the I/O problem is extremely difficult, and generally may only be inferred indirectly. Sometimes it is easiest to use a trial-and-error approach by adding host adapters. The best results occur only on systems that have multiple I/O backplanes.

7.8 Summary Data

The following tables summarize the attributes of the PA-RISC systems over time. Some cells are left blank because we did not have this information at press time.

Table 7-3   Summary of System Attributes (Part I)

	PA 1.0	PA 1.0 (870)	PA 1.0 (890)	PA 1.1b (T500)
Scalar Type	scalar	scalar	scalar	superscalar integer + FP
Clock Speed	8-32 MHZ	50 MHZ	60 MHZ	90 MHZ
Memory Bus	central bus		SMB	SMB
HW Page Size	2KB	2KB	2KB	4KB
Cache Organization	unified	split	split	split
Cache Sizes	4 KB- 256 KB	2 x 512 KB	2 x 2 MB	2 x 1 MB
Cache Associativity	direct or 2-way	2-way	2-way	direct
Models	840/50/55/60/65; 825/ 35/45; 808/815; 822/ 32/42/52	870	890	T500 (891)
Bus Speeds	220 MB/sec; 1-2 x 5 MB/sec or 24 MB/sec	256 MB/sec 2 x 20 MB/sec 8 x 5 MB/sec	1 GB/sec 8 x 32 MB/ sec	1 GB/sec 8 x 32 MB/sec
TLB Organization	unfied	unified and split	unified and split	unified
TLB Sizes	4K to 16 K	64 2-way 2 x 4K direct	64 2-way 2 x 16K direct	120
TLB Associativity	direct	direct internal, 2-way internal	direct inter- nal, 2-way external	fully associative
TLB Miss Handling	software	software	software	hardware and soft- ware
Block TLB	no	no	no	yes—16
FP Registers	16	16	16	32
VAS	2**48 (except 842/ 852)	2**64	2**64	2**48
I/O Type	CIO; 8 x 2 = HP-PB	CIO	HP-PB	HP-PB
Slots	8 - ??	20 + 32	14–112	14–112

Table 7-4   Summary of System Attributes (Part II)

	PA 1.1a (800)	PA 1.1a (700)	PA 1.1b (890)	PA 1.1b (700)
Scalar Type	limited FP parallelism	limited FP parallelism	superscalar integer + FP	superscalar integer + FP
Clock Speed	32/48/64 MHZ	50/66 MHZ	96 MHZ	99/125 MHZ;33/ 50/75 MHZ
Memory Bus	HP-PB	SGC	PMB	SGC
HW Page Size	4KB	4KB	4KB	4KB
Cache Organization	Split	Split	Split	Split
Cache Sizes	2 x 32 KB to 2 x 256 KB	2 x 64 KB to 128 KB (I) + 256 KB (D)	2 x 256 KB (except T500)	2 x 64 KB to 2 x 256 KB
Cache Associativity	direct	direct	direct	direct
Models	827-877 F/G/H/I 20-40	720/30/50	887/897 G/H/I 50 T500	715/33,50,75,725/ 50,75,100 735/99,125 755/99, 125
Bus Speeds	256 MB/sec 32 MB/sec	25-33 MB/sec	256 MB/sec pk 32 MB/sec pk	?? MB/sec 33 MB/sec
TLB Organization	split	split	unified	unified
TLB Sizes	2 x 96	2 x 96	120	120
TLB Associativity	fully associative	fully associative	fully associative	fully associative
TLB Miss Handling	software	software	hardware and software	hardware and software
Block TLB	yes—4 each	yes—4 each	yes—16	yes—16
FP Registers	32	32	32	32
VAS	2**48	2**48	2**48	2**48
I/O Type	HP-PB	Core, SGC, EISA	HP-PB	Core, SGC, EISA
Slots	2/4/6/8/12	0/1/4	2/4/6/8/12	0/1/4

Table 7-5   Summary of System Attributes (Part III)

	PA 1.1c (800)	PA 1.1c (700)	PA 1.1d (7200)	PA 1.1e (7300)
Scalar Type	superscalar 2 Int + 1 FP	superscalar 2 Int + 1 FP	superscalar 1 Int + 1 FP	superscalar
Clock Speed	48/64/80/96 MHZ	60/80/100 MHZ	100/120 MHZ	132/160 MHZ
Memory Bus	GSC	GSC	Runway	HSC
HW Page Size	4KB	4KB	4KB	4KB
Cache Organization	unified	unified	split	split
Cache Sizes	64 or 256 KB or 1 MB	64 or 256 KB 1 MB for XC	2 x 256 KB 2 x 1 MB	2 x 256 KB Opt 1 MB L2 (unified)
Cache Associativity	direct	direct	direct	
Models	E25/35/45/55	712/60,80,100 715/64,80,100 715/100XC	K100/200/210/ 220/230/400/ 410/420/D250/ 260/350/360	D220/230/320/330
Bus Speeds	128 MB/sec pk 32 MB/sec pk		960 MB/sec pk 128 MB/sec pk 32 MB/sec pk	PMB; 160 MB/sec pk EISA
TLB Organization	split	split	unified	
TLB Sizes	2 x 64	2 x 64	120	
TLB Associativity	fully associative	fully associative	fully associative	
TLB Miss Handling			hardware and software	
Block TLB			yes—16	
FP Registers	32	32	32	
VAS	2**48	2**48	2**48	
I/O Type	HP-PB	HSC, EISA	HSC& HP-PB or EISA	HSC, EISA
Slots	2 or 4	1 HSC or EISA	5 HSC 4 + 4 HP-PB	6 HSC 4 EISA

Table 7-6 Summary of System Attributes (Part IV)

	PA 2.0 (8000)	PA 2.0 (8200)	PA 2.x (8000)	PA 2.x (8200)
Scalar Type	superscalar	superscalar	superscalar	superscalar
Clock Speed	160/180 MHZ	200 MHZ	180 MHZ	200 MHZ
Memory Bus	runway			
HW Page Size	4KB	4KB	4KB	
Cache Organization	split	unified	split	split
Cache Sizes	2 x 1MB	2 x 2MB	2 x 2MB 8 MB L2 (unified)	2 x 2MB
Cache Associativity	direct			
Models	D270/280/K250/ 260/450/460	K370/570	T600	V2200
Bus Speeds	968 MB/sec pk 128 MB/sec pk 32 MB/sec pk	PMB 128/160 MB/sec 32 MB/sec pk	1 GB/sec pk 160 MB/sec pk 32 MB/sec pk	8/8 x 980 MB/sec 120/240 MB PCI
TLB Organization				
TLB Sizes				
TLB Associativity				
TLB Miss Handling				
Block TLB				
FP Registers				
VAS				
I/O Type	HP-PB, HSC, EISA	HP-PB,HSC	HP-PB, HSC	PCI
Slots	2–4 HP-PB (K) 1–5 HSC 4 EISA (D)	2 HP-PB 1–9 HSC	14–168 HP-PB 2 -2 4 HSC	24

CPU Bottlenecks

T his chapter describes major CPU bottlenecks, gives typical symptoms and techniques for diagnosis, and presents many of the metrics relating to CPU. It also describes some methods for tuning.

Topics covered in Chapter 8 are:

- Processes and scheduling
- Real-time scheduling
- Time-share scheduling
- Context switches
- SMP scheduling issues
- Processor affinity
- Traps and protection violations
- Global CPU metrics
- Typical metric values
- Symptoms of a CPU bottleneck
- CPU use and performance tools
- Tuning CPU bottlenecks

8.1   Processes and Scheduling

Scheduling is the assignment by the operating system of CPU resources to individual processes and/or threads (starting in HP-UX 11.0). HP-UX assigns a priority to each process or thread, and the scheduler enforces this priority by allowing the process the appropriate amount of CPU. Three types of priorities are in use in HP-UX: the Posix *rtsched* real time priority; the HP-UX *rtprio* real time priority; and the default HP-UX time-share priorities for normal system and user processes.

The different types of priorities are shown in Figure 8-1.

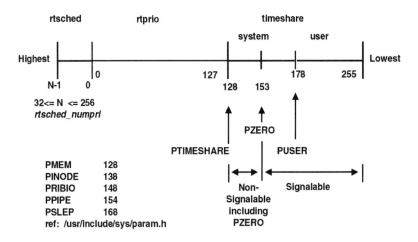

Figure 8-1   Process Priorities

8.2   Real-Time Scheduling

Real-time schedulers provide the means of establishing a category of higher precedence than the default for processes that need it. A well behaved real-time process:

• Is important
• Consumes a small amount of memory
• Locks itself into memory to minimize startup overhead
• Executes quickly
• Passes heavy processing to a time-share process
• Has been thoroughly debugged
• Runs relatively infrequently
• Is linked with archive libraries

Unix systems employ a variety of real-time schedulers to manage these processes.

8.2.1 HP-UX Rtprio Real-Time Scheduler

The HP-UX real-time scheduler defines HP-UX real-time processes as those running with priority ranges from 0 (highest priority) to 127 (lowest priority). These processes have precedence over the HP-UX time-share priority processes. Moreover, priority does not degrade or improve as the process executes, but remains constant.

Rtprio real-time has been available in HP-UX since 1986. Programs assigned an *rtprio* priority have precedence over all time-share processes, but have less precedence than programs with a Posix real-time priority. Only processes at the same HP-UX real-time priority are timesliced. Otherwise, an HP-UX real-time process receives as much CPU as it requires unless a process of a higher priority, including Posix real-time, wants to run.

8.2.2 Posix Rtsched Real-Time Scheduler

The Posix real-time scheduler uses three scheduling algorithms: SCHED_FIFO, in which the queue is ordered by the amount of time processes have been in the list; SCHED_RR, in which each priority queue is timesliced; and SCHED_RR2, in which the timeslice interval depends on priority. The *rtsched* man page contains details about these algorithms.

The Posix *Rtsched* real-time priorities are defined by the Posix 1003.4 standard. The man page states that priorities are assigned as positive numbers from 0 to 31; however, the priorities are actually presented in reports as negative numbers from -1 through -32. Also, the maximum real time priority can be set as high as 255 by setting the tunable kernel parameter *rtsched_numpri*.

8.3 Time-Share Scheduling

Time-share priority, which is the default for most processes, is more complicated, because it is divided into system and user priorities, as well as signalable and non-signalable priorities. User processes occupy priorities 178–255, with 255 as the lowest priority. System priorities occupy 128–177. Two types of time-share schedulers are described in the following sections: the normal HP-UX time-share scheduler, and PRM, or Process Resource Manager.

8.3.1 Normal Time-Share Scheduler

The behavior of the normal time-share scheduler needs to be understood when determining whether priority is the cause of a bottleneck. Each CPU in an SMP system has a queue of runnable processes or threads which are run and halted depending on the current priority that the operating system has assigned to them. The highest priority runnable process in the CPU's queue is dispatched. All the threads of a particular process might not have the same priority.

The scheduler assumes by default that all processes have equal importance, and that all recent CPU usage is remembered. As each process consumes CPU time, its priority degrades linearly. When another process's priority exceeds that of the process whose priority is degrading, the current process is put to sleep and the other process starts. As each process waits, its priority improves exponentially. Equal priority processes are timesliced.

When ordinary user processes are awaiting system resources, they are not runnable. During this time, they are assigned a system priority. For example, if a process is set to sleep for 30 seconds by calling the *sleep()* system call, it will be assigned a system priority of PSLEP, or 168. Blocked processes are assigned high priority at the system level so that they will get CPU time long enough to release critical system resources. They will then return to their user priority.

Processes are also categorized as *signalable* or *non-signalable*. During I/O operations, the operating system might change the priority of a process from signalable to non-signalable so that it cannot be interrupted until the I/O is finished.

NOTE: You may have tried to kill a process and found that it would not terminate. This was probably due to its being blocked on a resource that required a non-signalable priority. The kill signal would have resulted in the deallocation of the pages assigned to the process. Therefore, the operating system prevents the process from being killed and having its pages deallocated during these asynchronous operations by giving the process a non-signalable priority.

8.3.1.1   Nice Values

One interesting feature of the normal time-share scheduler is that priorities can be influenced by assigning a value to them using the *nice(1m)* command. *Nice* values of 21 to 39 degrade priority, while *nice* values of 0 to 19 improve it. These latter *nice* values (sometimes called *nasty* values!) require superuser access. Starting in HP-UX 10.0, the *nice* value also affects the likelihood of a process's pages being selected for pageout under memory pressure.

NOTE: Some shells "nice" background processes by default. The K shell, for example, sets the shell variable *bgnice* to 4 by default, which sets the *nice* value to 24.

8.3.1.2   Algorithms for Modifying Priority

Every clock tick (10 milliseconds), CPU time is accumulated for the currently running process, whether or not it used the CPU for the entire tick. Every 4 clock ticks (40 milliseconds), the priority of the currently running process is degraded based on the amount of CPU time consumed during the last 4 ticks. Every 10 ticks (100 milliseconds), the newly calculated priorities take effect. A forced context switch may occur to run the highest priority process if the currently running process no longer has the highest priority.

NOTE: This 100 millisecond interval can be changed by setting the tunable kernel parameter *timeslice*.

Although processors have become much faster, the clock tick is still set at 10 msec. Many processes may run, block, and run again within the tick period, which is why this method has become less accurate as a means of calculating CPU utilization.

Although global CPU utilization is still calculated based on what is happening at the time of the tick, per-process CPU utilitization has been made much more accurate. A timestamp is recorded when the process is dispatched, and again when it is context-switched out. The difference is added to the current sum, and is used to accumulate total CPU utilization for that process. Priority calculations are still based upon the old sampling method, however.

8.3.2   Process Resource Manager (PRM)

HP's Process Resource Manager product (HP PRM) provides an alternative mechanism for scheduling. This product is based on the earlier *Fair Share Scheduler*, although it does not maintain a history of priorities. PRM gives the CPU to groups of processes based on percentage allocations assigned by the system administrator. PRM honors processor affinity (defined later) on SMP systems.

8.3.2.1   Advantages of PRM

PRM can be switched on and off, and replaces the standard scheduler when it is turned on. With PRM, processes are assigned to groups, which are guaranteed a minimum percentage of CPU time, and excess CPU is distributed according to the same allocations. Groups are configured by the system administrator, and group membership or percentage allocation can be changed by editing ASCII files. Within a process group, PRM behaves like the standard scheduler. PRM gives the allocated share of the CPU to a process group, not necessarily to a specific process.

CPU allocations are enforced only when the CPU is saturated; that is, if there is no available CPU. Process groups may exceed their allocations unless the CPU cap is configured. PRM can be used to simulate a true batch queue, such as that found on mainframes. A batch process group can be allocated 1% of the CPU, and will receive a larger allocation only when other more important processes are not using the CPU.

8.3.2.2   Process Groups

PRM's process groups are dynamically loadable. You can define up to 48 process groups (16, in earlier versions) according to one of the following models:

- Budget
- Number of users
- Application priority, including service-level agreement

Membership in a process resource group is assigned by user name or by the absolute path name that is to be executed by *prmrun*. Users may belong to more than one process group, and a process may be moved to any group to which the user is assigned.

8.3.2.3   How PRM Works

In PRM, processes are scheduled into slots in an arrangement that resembles a carnival carousel. The "carousel" has 100 slots, each representing one percent. When PRM is configured or reconfigured, process groups are distributed according to their percentage allocations. See Figure 8-2 for an example in which only three groups have been defined.

Once PRM has been enabled, every time the clock ticks, the scheduler chooses the highest priority runnable process in the process group of the current slot. If none of the processes in the process group is runnable, the carousel turns to the next slot. In any case, the carousel turns to the next slot at every clock tick (10 msec). The PRM carousel is shown in Figure 8-2.

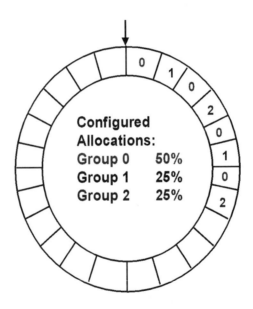

Figure 8-2   PRM Carousel

On an SMP system, each CPU has its own carousel, and the runnable processes in the selected group are distributed across the CPUs. If a selected process is locked by affinity to a particular processor, that processor is skipped for the non-locked processes during that pass of the distribution.

8.3.2.4   Side Effects of PRM

PRM has numerous side effects that derive from its methods of operation. A number of these are described here.

- Processes that bypass login—such as socket applications—are not initially assigned to a user's resource group, but are assigned to the SYSTEM group. This makes PRM less useful for client/server applications such as database systems in which clients access the database across the network.

- Real-time processes can exceed the PRM allocations and can prevent other processes in the same group from ever running at all. In effect, this starves all other processes in a process group.

- High allocations result in short latencies. Applications that need deterministic latencies should be given a higher allocation than they might otherwise need. On the other hand, low allocations might result in long latencies.

- Although a process group may be allocated only one of several percent, that may not be desirable, since processes in that group may wait for relatively long periods for CPU time.

- PRM distributes processes in a process group across CPUs in an SMP system. This *might* result in a greater or smaller number of CPU switches (discussed below), depending on the nature of the processes.

- A process group will receive a smaller amount of CPU than its allocation if there are more CPUs than active processes in a process group. Therefore, groups should be defined so that they typically have at least as many runnable processes as there are CPUs.

- Context switches can occur at every clock tick rather than every timeslice, which is the usual case.

- The user of *su* can cause undesirable effects, such as a process running in a different group than expected. Only when *su-* is used will the process be assigned to the *new* user's group.

- Absolute path name definitions are effective only when the process is run with the *prmrun* command.

8.4 Context Switches

A context switch is an event that takes place as a CPU begins work on a new process. A **voluntary** context switch occurs when a process sleeps, exits, or waits for an event, such as I/O. A **forced** context switch occurs in the following cases:

- At the end of a timeslice when a process with an equal or higher priority is runnable
- When a process returns from a system call or trap and a higher priority process is runnable
- At a clock tick when a higher priority real-time process is runnable
- When a process is stopped with *ptrace(2)*
- When a thread is stopped with *ttrace(2)*

With PRM, a forced context switch most likely occurs at every clock tick (10 milliseconds).

Context switches consume roughly 10,000 CPU cycles needed by the kernel. It follows that a large number of context switches will result in excessive system CPU utilization and poor application performance.

8.5 SMP Scheduling Issues

Traditionally, SMP systems have implemented a scheduling policy with the guiding rule that simplicity produces lower overhead. Here is the algorithm that is used:

- A child process, including the shell, is always initially assigned to the same CPU as the parent process.
- Once every second, if the difference in load averages among the CPUs is greater than .2, the scheduler moves *at most one* process from the most heavily loaded processor to the least heavily loaded processor.
- When a process resumes from a blocked state, the scheduler tries to assign it to the same processor on which it was running before it blocked. If the CPUs are not balanced, it will instead assign the process to the least heavily loaded processor.
- Processor affinity algorithms, described below, modify the above policies.

The SMP scheduling policies just discussed provide an opportunity for additional types of bottlenecks. These bottlenecks may include resource contention, overhead for maintaining cache coherency, TLB misses, run queue priorities, assumptions about order of execution, and serialization.

8.5.1 Resource Contention

The kernel uses locks to protect kernel data and/or code from being modified or executed at exactly the same moment on different CPUs. These locks are either spinlocks, which are non-blocking, or kernel semaphores, which cause blocking. Spinlocks consume system CPU and may result in poor application performance when there is contention for the same resources among processors. Spinlocks are used when it is expected that resources will be held for relatively short periods of time.

Kernel semaphores are used when resources are expected to be held for long periods of time. However, locking a kernel semaphore is an expensive operation, since it results in a context switch of the user process requesting a non-available resource.

8.5.2 Cache Coherency and CPU Switches

In SMP systems, each CPU has its own hardware cache, and these must be synchronized. This can be a significant problem when a process moves from one CPU to another during the course of execution. A running process builds up a context in the cache of the CPU on which it is running. If a process is switched to another CPU, its cache content may need to be copied to another cache and flushed to main memory. Copying cache data or flushing caches to main memory are expensive operations, because the CPU remains idle while this is occurring.

8.5.3 Run Queue Prioritites

Because each CPU has its own run queue, not all the highest priority processes *system wide* may be running. Example:

CPU 1: priorities 181, 183, 221
CPU 2: priorities 185, 208

One would normally expect processes with priorities 181 and 183 to be dispatched. In this example, the priority 183 process was unluckily assigned to the wrong CPU. The process with priority 185 was dispatched instead, because it was the highest priority runnable process on its CPU.

8.5.4 Order of Execution

On a uniprocessor system, it may be safely assumed that a real-time priority process will execute before a time-share process. On an SMP system, however, both processes may run concurrently, which may result in unexpected behavior if the programmer did not plan for it. Here is an example:

Process A has a real-time priority. Process B has a time-share priority. On a uni-processor system, process A is guaranteed to use as much of the CPU as it wants before process B can run. On an SMP system, they may run concurrently on different processors. If they are cooperating processes, it is likely there will be a data synchronization problem on the SMP system.

8.5.5 Serialization

Another type of problem may occur when processes executing on different CPUs are serialized on a shared resource. Serialization problems could occur on a uniprocessor system; however, this is fairly unlikely. The impact of a serialization problem is much greater on an SMP system. So is the probability of its occurrence. Example:

Processes A and B both lock semaphore S before doing certain critical work. If process A holds the lock, process B will sleep when it tries to acquire the lock. On a uniprocessor system, this is normally not a problem since process A will be doing useful work on the only CPU in the system. On a two-CPU SMP system, if there are no other processes wanting to use the CPU, one CPU will remain idle since process B cannot run because it is blocked waiting to lock the semaphore which has been locked by process A. Therefore, less work will be done than what was expected. This is a major reason that some applications do not scale well in an SMP system.

8.5.6   Deadlocks

Deadlocks (also called *deadly embraces*) occur when multiple processes try to access resources at the same time, but probably in a different order. Although deadlocks can occur on a uni-processor system, they are much more likely to occur on an SMP system where multiple processes can execute concurrently on different CPUs. Here is an example:

> Process A, executing on CPU 0 locks semaphore S1. Process B, executing on CPU 1 locks semaphore S2. Process A tries to lock semaphore S2 but blocks, since this semaphore is already locked by Process B. Process B attempts to lock semaphore S1 but blocks, since that semaphore is already locked by process A. One possible solution to this problem is to require programmers to lock semaphores only in a pre-defined order.

8.6 Processor Affinity

Processor affinity is a method used on some SMP systems to lock a process to a particular CPU. It is usually used with processes that communicate with each other by some IPC mechanism to minimize cache coherency problems. The interface (defined in *<sys/mpctl.h>*) is supported in HP-UX 10.20 and later, on SMP systems, and is documented in the *mpctl(2)* man page.

While processor affinity can lock a process to a CPU, it *cannot* do the following:

- Exclude processes from processors
- Assign processes to a group of processors
- Reserve processors for locked processes only
- Flag processes to be moved as a group

A new capability called the *gang scheduler,* available on HP-UX 11.0 (9812) and later, allows a group of processes to be assigned to a group of processors.

Here is an example of a piece of code that will lock the calling process to CPU #3:

```
#include <sys/mpctl.h>
err = mpctl(MPC_SETPROCESS_FORCE,(sput)3,MPC_SELFPID);
```

A similar call can be used to lock a process other than the calling process. To unlock a process, code similar to the following can be used:

```
#include <sys/mctl.h>
err = mpctl(MPC_SETPROCESS,MPC_SPUFLOAT,MPC_SELFPID);
```

There are also parameters to specify particular threads (HP-UX 11.0 and later), rather than the entire process. Processor affinity may be used to improve the performance of applications that have multiple processes that communicate via IPC.

Care should be taken when using processor affinity to lock different threads to different CPUs, or different processes that use inter-process communication, because these techniques can result in cache coherency problems.

Another type of application that may benefit from processor affinity is one in which multiple processes are spawned to take advantage of multiple CPUs. In this case, each process would be locked to a different CPU. Performance is improved by reducing context switches, cache coherency problems and TLB misses.

The *pthread* library includes some new routines for implementing processor affinity in a threaded application. See the man page for *pthread_processor_bind_np(3T)* for more information.

8.7 Traps and Protection Violations

Another important category of CPU bottleneck is caused by traps. *Traps* are software interrupts that are caused by:

- Page faults
- Page protection violations
- Floating point emulation
- Integer and floating point overflow and underflow

Traps are costly in CPU utilization because whatever is executing is interrupted. A trap requires a switch to kernel mode, a save of state, and processing to determine the cause and take the appropriate action. A trap may also cause a context switch if the action causes an I/O such as a page-in, or if a higher priority process is ready to run.

Protection violations occur when a process attempts to access a page of memory for which the protection ID is *not* loaded into the control registers. *Control registers* are a special type of register that are set by the kernel for an executing process. *Protection IDs* are used to define ownership of a section of the VAS. Only processes whose protection IDs match the protection ID set on a page of memory are allowed to access that page. Figure 8-3 shows some examples of protection IDs. In the figure, Protection IDs 1 and 2 are both fixed for the life of the process and therefore would not cause violations. Protection IDs 3 and 4, however, are subject to change as a process accesses different memory segments.

NOTE: Shared libraries use the public protection ID if the file permission is 555 on the shared library. In this case, the shared library does not require a protection ID register.

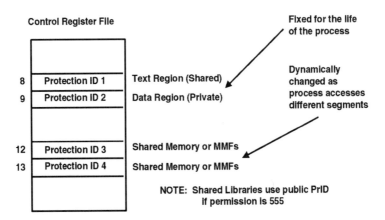

Figure 8-3 Protection Violations

PA 1.x systems have four control registers that are used for protection IDs, while PA 2.x systems have eight control registers for this purpose. Therefore, the chance of protection ID register thrashing is much lower on PA 2.x systems. Protection registers are needed for each non-locked shared memory segment, non-global shared library and memory-mapped file accessed by the process. Locking shared memory segments into memory uses only one protection ID for all locked shared memory segments.

8.8 Global CPU Metrics

A variety of global metrics are available for identifying potential bottlenecks in the CPU.

8.8.1 Global CPU Saturation Metrics

The following metrics are useful in determining whether the CPU is saturated, and in what areas saturation is taking place. They are expressed as percentages of total CPU, that is, they add up to 100%. Abnormally high values may indicate potential problems. Most metrics are easily visible with *glance*.

- *% User*—percentage of CPU consumed by processes in user mode
- *% Nice*—percentage of CPU consumed by niced processes in user mode
- *% Nasty*—percentage of CPU consumed by processes assigned a negative *nice* value
- *% Real-time*—percentage of CPU consumed by real-time processes running in user mode
- *% System*—percentage of CPU consumed by processes in kernel mode (system calls)
- *% Interrupt*—percentage of CPU consumed by kernel interrupt processing
- *% Context Switch*—percentage of CPU consumed by kernel scheduling
- *% V Fault*—percentage of CPU consumed by kernel memory management

- *% Traps*—percentage of CPU consumed by kernel trap handling
- *% BLOCK*—percentage of CPU consumed by spinlocks (SMP only, visible only with top)
- *% SWAIT*—percentage of CPU consumed by kernel semaphores (SMP only, visible only with top)
- *% Idle*—percentage of idle CPU

8.8.2 Global CPU Queue Metrics: Run Queue vs. Load Average

The global CPU queue metrics include the run queue and the load average. These metrics capture different aspects of the CPU load; together they provide a more complete picture. The *run queue* is the current instantaneous number of processes waiting to use the CPU (that is, they are in the SRUN or TSRUN state). The value is provided per CPU in an SMP system. Different tools may or may not count the current running process.

The *load average*, on the other hand, shows one-minute, five-minute, and 15-minute averages of CPU use. The load average is the count of processes in the run queue plus fast sleepers (that is, the processes in the SRUN or TSRUN state and some in the SSLEP or TSSLP state). These values are also per CPU in an SMP system.

Also significant is the global priority queue, which shows the number of processes blocked on PRIORITY. The global priority queue, available only from *glance*, *gpm* and *MeasureWare*, is analogous to the run queue but is calculated differently.

8.8.3 Other Global CPU Metrics

Other important global CPU metrics include the system call rate (global and per system call), the context switch rate, and the kernel profile. The global system call rate is an important metric because it reflects the rate of invocation of system services. It is related to system CPU utilization. The context switch rate is an indicator of application contention and kernel contention on SMP systems.

8.8.4 Per-Process CPU Metrics

Some metrics are also available to indicate CPU usage on a *per-process* basis. Saturation metrics include *% User*, *% System*, and user, system and elapsed times. Per-process CPU queue metrics include *% Blocked* on PRIORITY (runnable). Other per-process CPU metrics include per-process system call rate (total and per system call), context switch rate (forced and voluntary), CPU switch rate (for SMP systems), and the process profile.

8.9 Typical Metric Values

What, then, would be considered *normal* or *typical* values for these metrics? Of course, the best answer is given by **Rule #1**: "It Depends." Run-queue and load-average metrics have values that depend on the following, and it is not useful to provide a single rule of thumb for the values of these metrics.

• Whether the application is interactive or batch
• Whether the application is compute or I/O intensive
• Whether the application is a server or client application
• Speed of the CPU
• Time in queue (the *glance* metric *% Blocked on Pri* is a measure of this)

One heuristic can be provided for the global system call rate. A rate of 3,000 syscalls per second per CPU may be indicative of a CPU bottleneck, although this heuristic will increase as processors become faster. Context switch rates have a heuristic threshold of 1/3 of the system call rate. A system's exceeding these heuristic thresholds may be an indicator of possible poor performance, or the cause of poor performance. The types of system calls may also be signficant.

Figure 8-4 shows some ratios of values for system versus user CPU utilization.

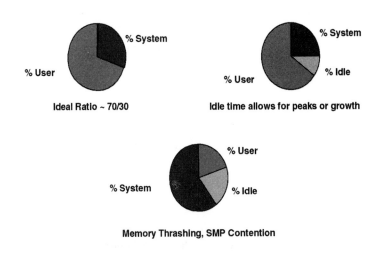

Figure 8-4   Ratios of System and User CPU Utilization in Unix

These ratios can be helpful in judging whether a given metric reflects a problem. An ideal ratio is 70% user to 30% system usage for a typical OLTP environment. Compute-bound environments may see ratios of 90% user to 10% system usage or more. Allowing a small percentage of idle CPU helps to provide for peaks or for expected growth in usage. The ratio at the bottom of the figure might indicate such problems as memory thrashing or SMP contention.

The ideal ratio shown above would not be the same for other operating systems. In Unix, system CPU utilization includes time spent in system calls on behalf of the user process. This is why the percentage of system usage (30%) is so high. Higher numbers do not necessarily indicate a performance problem. It may merely be that the application utilizes a lot of system calls.

8.10 Symptoms of a CPU Bottleneck

What are the symptoms of a CPU bottleneck? The four major areas are:

- Saturation of CPU
- Large queues
- Resource starvation
- User dissatisfaction with the system

8.10.1 Saturation

Saturation may be indicated by the following:

- Zero idle CPU
- A high percentage of user CPU usage
- A high percentage of system CPU usage

In the case of high system CPU usage, memory management, I/O management and SMP kernel contention involving spinlocks may cause false symptoms of saturation. Real causes of CPU saturation from heavy system CPU usage are:

- A heavy IPC system call rate
- Heavy *termio* load
- Evidence of process creation
- Heavy network traffic
- An SMP kernel contention, but only if caused by a user process

8.10.2 Expensive CPU Utilization

The factors that cause high levels of user CPU usage—normal, *nice*, or real-time, are:

- Computation
- Cache misses resulting from CPU switches or from the application
- Maintaining cache coherency after CPU switches or IPC activity

The factors that cause high levels of system CPU usage are:

- Time spent in system calls
- SMP contention involving spinlocks
- Cache misses

Context switching caused by process scheduling or SMP contention from kernel semaphores is expensive. Also expensive are processing hardware interrupts, processing page faults and TLB miss handling, processing traps (protection, emulation, computation), and spinning while waiting for DBMS latches to release.

8.10.3 Expensive System Calls

The most expensive types of system calls are *fork()* and *exec()* for process management, *select()* for I/O processing, and *semop()* (System V semaphores) and *msgop()* (System V message queues) for inter-process communication (IPC).

Figure 8-5 shows the expensive parts of a *fork()* call. Data structures must be copied at the time of the fork, and data pages must also be copied when accessed or written.

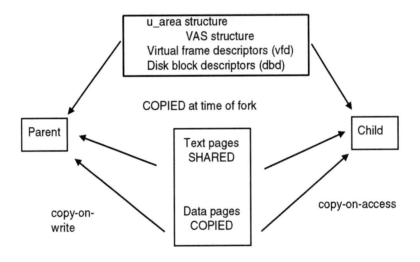

Figure 8-5   Expensive Parts of a *fork()* Call

NOTE: On a PA-RISC system, there are usually no instructions for a direct memory-to-memory copy operation. Copying items from one location to another in memory is done using a series of loads and stores, which can use many machine cycles. The V-Series systems have implemented data movers that make copy operations more efficient.

Figure 8-6 shows some of the costs of the *exec()* call. In this call, nothing is actually copied. Instead, pages for the new process must be created or loaded from disk.

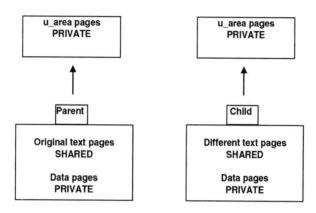

Figure 8-6   Elements Copied by the *exec()* Call

8.11 CPU Use and Performance Tools

Many tools provide useful data for dealing with CPU bottlenecks. Here is a summary.

Table 8-1   Tools that Provide Data on CPU Use

	glance/gpm	*MeasureWare*	*sar*	*top*	*vmstat*	*iostat*
user	X	X	X	X	X	X
nice	X	X		X		X
nasty	X					
real-time	X	X				
system	X	X	X	X	X	X
interrupt	X	X		X		
context switch	X	X		SSYS		
vfault	X					
trap	X				X	
block				X		
swait				X		

Table 8-1   Tools that Provide Data on CPU Use (Continued)

	glance/gpm	*MeasureWare*	*sar*	*top*	*vmstat*	*iostat*
wait I/O			X			
idle						
Run Queue	*	*	X	X	X	X
Load Average	X	X		X		

* Not shown by default; may be accessed through the Adviser.

8.12 Tuning CPU Bottlenecks

There are several ways to tune a CPU bottleneck:

- Hardware solutions
- Software solutions
- Application optimization
- Adjusting CPU-related operating system tunable parameters

8.12.1 Hardware Solutions

The simplest solution may be to move to a faster CPU. This solution will help most but not all applications with CPU bottlenecks. Another strategy is to move work to other systems—by creating a client/server environment, or by moving monolithic applications.

If the bottleneck is caused by increasing workload, the following strategies may help:

- Upgrade to a CPU with a larger cache
- Upgrade to a CPU with a different TLB
- Upgrade to an SMP system
- Add a CPU in an SMP system
- Remove CPUs to use *fewer* processors

WARNING: Not all applications benefit from an SMP system, and some applications may not scale well when another CPU is added.

8.12.2 Software Solutions

The following software solutions may be used to address CPU bottlenecks:

- Use PRM to control CPU allocation.
- Use workload balancing software in a distributed environment.
- Use *serialize( )* if large processes thrash memory (to be discussed in Chapter 9, "Memory Bottlenecks").
- Use the *nice* command to assign lower priority to less important processes.
- Consider using real-time priorities for processes, where appropriate.
- Restrict the RTPRIO and RTSCHED privilege groups.
- Change the time-slice value.
- Move work to other time periods; for example, use batch jobs.
- On SMP systems, use processor affinity with processes that communicate with each other.

8.12.3 Application Optimization

The following strategies are suggested for application development:

- Use compiler optimization.
- Minimize the use of expensive system calls. Specifically, switch from System V Semaphores to memory-mapped Semaphores (see *msem_init(2)*); switch from *fork( )* to *vfork( )*, if appropriate; switch from System V message queues to shared memory.
- If using *malloc(3)*, consider changing default behavior with *mallopt(3)*.
- Parallelize the application. Use threads or create a distributed architecture.
- Profile the application and rewrite routines that show a high CPU utilization.
- Minimize traps, including legal protection violations due to the number of shared segments.

From Bob's Consulting Log—I was called in to assess an X-windows application that drew maps with various data filled in, such as topology, structures, vegetation, etc. Performance was 50% of expectation for this application based on comparison with others. I found that the application was making 15,000 *ioctl()* calls per second. Further investigation showed that the application would check for keyboard input between drawing each vector on the map to see if the user wanted to abort the map. It was certainly not necessary to check for this user request 15,000 times per second! Changing the code to once per second doubled performance.

8.12.4 Tuning CPU-Related Parameters

The following CPU-related parameters may be tuned. In HP-UX 10.0 and later systems, they are in */etc/conf/master.d/*.*

- *acctresume*—pertains only to System V process accounting and has little overall effect on performance.
- *acctsuspend*—pertains only to System V process accounting and has little overall effect on performance.
- *netisr_priority*—refers to the priority of the network interrupt service routine. Its value should not normally be changed, because it is not applicable to all releases of HP-UX.
- *rtsched_numpri*—affects only the number of Posix real-time priorities.
- *streampipes*—refers to whether the original HP-UX implementation or the streams implementation is used for the pipe pseudo-driver. The HP-UX implementation is much more efficient but does not conform to the new desirable implementation paradigm.
- *timeslice*—It is not usually recommended to change the *timeslice* value. However, certain compute-bound workloads can benefit by disabling timeslicing. This is done by setting *timeslice* to -1.

NOTE: Disabling timeslicing is usually not a good idea with OLTP applications, due to added pressure on the scheduling resources.

Memory Bottlenecks

T his chapter describes major memory bottlenecks, starting with a review of some important concepts in the area of memory management. This is followed by a description of typical bottleneck symptoms and some techniques for diagnosing and tuning them. Chapter 9 covers the following topics:

- Virtual address space
- Types of magic
- fork() and vfork()
- Dynamic buffer cache
- Sticky bit
- Memory-mapped files and semaphores
- Shared libraries
- Paging, swapping, and deactivation
- Memory management policies
- Sizing memory and the swap area
- Memory metrics
- Types of memory management bottlenecks
- Expensive system calls
- Tuning memory bottlenecks
- Memory-related tunable parameters

9.1 Virtual Address Space

In order to understand the major bottlenecks that affect memory, it is necessary to know how virtual addressing works on a Precision Architecture machine, particularly at the individual process level.

While the amount of actual RAM available for HP-UX is determined by the number of memory chips installed on the computer, the system can make a much larger amount of space available to each process through the use of *virtual memory.* On 32-bit PA-RISC machines or on 64-bit PA-RISC 2.0 machines running in narrow mode, the virtual address space available to each process is 4 GB, spread over four 1-GB quadrants that are used for various kinds of memory objects. On 64-bit PA-RISC 2.0 systems (running HP-UX 11.0), the address space is 16 TB, spread over four 4-TB quadrants. Space registers (SRs) are used for short pointer addressing of these quadrants. Figure 9-1 shows the 32-bit implementation, and Figure 9-2 shows the 64-bit implementation.

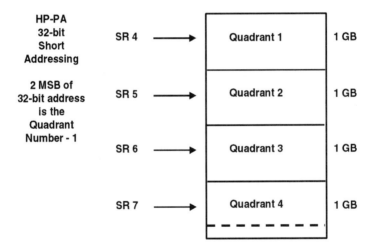

Figure 9-1 PA-RISC Per-Process Virtual Address Space (32 Bits)

Individual processes make use of areas of memory within all these quadrants. Specific areas are normally accessed by the use of short pointers consisting of a two-bit quadrant reference, and an offset into the quadrant where the required memory area starts.

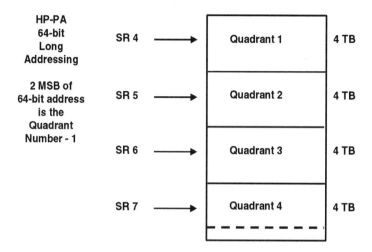

Figure 9-2   PA-RISC Per-Process Virtual Address Space (64 Bits)

Different levels of HP PA provide different amounts of virtual address space, as shown in Figure 9-3.

Level 0   **32-bit physical addressing only
            (Note: HP has never made a
            Level 0 system)**

Level 1   **48-bit virtual addressing
            2 ** 48 total VAS (272 TB)
            2 ** 16 (32768) spaces of 4 GB each**

Level 2   **64-bit virtual addressing
            2 ** 64 total VAS
            2 ** 32 spaces of 4 GB each**

Figure 9-3   PA-RISC VAS Levels

Pages of memory in HP PA can have two types of protection assigned to them: authorization, which is granted with a Protection ID, equal to the space number associated with the owner; and access rights (read/write/execute), which are the same as the actual file permissions for shared libraries and memory-mapped files. Space number 0 is always reserved for the kernel; non-zero space numbers are assigned to user processes. Note that in PA-RISC, text does not normally have write permission, which means that code cannot be modified in memory.

9.1.1   Variable Page Size

In HP-UX 11.0 and later on PA 2.0 systems, the size of a page of physical memory can be changed from the default of four KB. Because each page translation requires space in the TLB, one would want to define a larger page size when larger ranges of memory are accessed sequentially, or when application performance is poor due to a large number of TLB misses. PA 2.0 systems typically have smaller TLBs than earlier systems. They no longer have a block TLB, nor do they have a hardware TLB walker. These changes in the design were made to lower the cost and reduce the portion of the chip physically required for large TLBs.

The following page sizes are available by user request:

- 4 KB (the default)
- 16 KB
- 64 KB
- 256 KB
- 1 MB
- 4 MB
- 16 MB
- 64 MB

The page size associated with an executable can be specified by using the *chatr(1)* command. The kernel may also increase or decrease the page size according to access patterns that the application exhibits. If an application executes sequentially, the page size will be increased. If an application executes randomly, the page size will be decreased. When there is severe memory pressure, the memory management system may also reduce the page size rather than force large size page-outs with subsequent page-ins when the pages are needed again.

9.2 Types of Magic

Executable programs compiled for PA-RISC processors include a *magic number* in their *a.out* file. This number tells the operating system how to interpret references in the code to the four VAS quadrants described in the previous section. Different types of magic number have been used over time. They include SHARE_MAGIC, DEMAND_MAGIC, EXEC_MAGIC, and SHMEM_MAGIC.

9.2.1   SHARE_MAGIC

By default, a process is compiled with SHARE_MAGIC, which means that the address space is divided into four 1-GB or 4-TB quadrants in 32-bit and 64-bit versions of HP-UX, respectively. In the SHARE_MAGIC format, each quadrant has a specific purpose—such as text, data, or shared objects. *Shared text*, which is code that can be used by many processes, is in Quadrant 1. *Private data* is in Quadrant 2. This data includes

- Initialized data
- Uninitialized data (BSS)
- Dynamically allocated memory
- u_area
- Kernel stack
- User stack
- All data from shared libraries
- Private memory-mapped files

Originally, shared libraries occupied Quadrant 3 while Quadrant 4 was for shared memory. The last portion of Quadrant 4 is reserved for hard and soft physical address space, which is used for addressing hardware devices based on slot number.

In HP-UX 10.0 and in HP-UX 11.0 in 32-bit mode, the VAS with SHARE_MAGIC appears as in Figure 9-4.

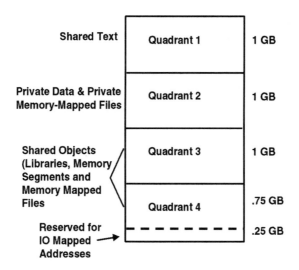

Figure 9-4   HP-UX VAS SHARE_MAGIC Format for 32-Bit HP-UX

In these versions, Quadrants 3 and 4 are globally allocated. Shared libraries, shared memory mapped files and shared memory can go anywhere within Quadrants 3 or 4, but no single segment can cross the boundary between them. This limits any one segment size to a 1 GB maximum on 32-bit HP-UX or 4 TB maximum on 64-bit HP-UX. Note that shared objects are mapped globally in HP-UX 10.x. Therefore, the total size of all shared objects must fit within Quadrants 3 and 4.

Note also the following limitations with the 32-bit SHARE_MAGIC format:

• Text is limited to 1 GB.
• Data is limited to 1 GB.
• Text is shared.
• Text is read-only.
• Text and data are demand paged in.
• Swap space is reserved only for the data.

In HP-UX 11.0 64-bit mode, the SHARE_MAGIC format is as shown in Figure 9-5.

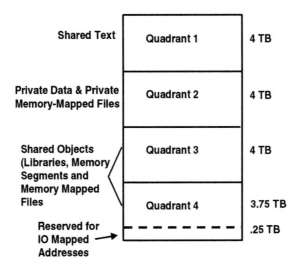

Figure 9-5   HP-UX VAS SHARE_MAGIC Format for 64-Bit HP-UX

While 64-bit architecture allows a far greater number of addresses, only a subset of the possible addresses within the 4 TB are normally used. The actual number of addresses used is constrained by the total swap space available.

9.2.2   DEMAND_MAGIC

DEMAND_MAGIC is functionally identical to SHARE_MAGIC, except for the fact that page alignment is guaranteed between memory and disk. A consequene of this alignment is that only exact page size I/Os are needed between memory and disk images. Very few users take advantage of this feature. Other characteristics and limitations of SHARE_MAGIC also apply to DEMAND_MAGIC.

9.2.3   EXEC_MAGIC

The EXEC_MAGIC format was introduced with HP-UX 10.0 on the Series 800 (HP-UX 9.01 on the Series 700). In this format, the data segment and private text segment could exceed 1 GB, as shown in Figure 9-6.

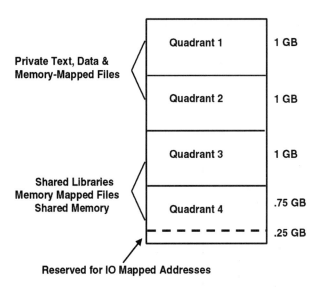

Figure 9-6   HP-UX VAS EXEC_MAGIC Format at HP-UX 10.0

In the 10.0 (and 11.0 32-bit) implementation, text and data together cannot exceed 2 GB. Also, text (code) is private, which means that there can be multiple copies in memory. Since text is writable, swap space must be reserved for it, although a lazy swap allocation scheme is used in which swap space is allocated only for text pages that are modified. Even this lazy swap is wasteful, since virtually no modern application uses modifiable code. Also, text is loaded entirely at *exec()* time rather than being paged in. This loading is inefficient, because you seldom need all the code in memory.

Because of the vastly larger quadrant size available on 64-bit processors, EXEC_MAGIC is neither needed nor allowed for 64-bit applications.

9.2.4   Shared Memory Windows for SHARE_MAGIC

Shared memory is normally a globally visible resource to applications. All shared objects must be placed in memory quadrants 3 and 4; therefore, the total size of all shared objects that 32-bit applications can access is 1.75 GB. This may be acceptable on smaller systems, but large systems, especially those where the total size of shared memory segments for different applications exceeds 1.75 GB, or those that are used for large databases, may need a much larger shared memory segment.

For HP-UX 11.0, an extension pack has been released that will allow 32-bit applications to access shared memory in windows that are visible only to the group of processes that are authorized through the use of a unique key. It is expected that this feature will be standard starting with HP-UX 11.10. Shared memory windows provide up to 2 GB of shared object space, which is visible only to the group of 32-bit processes configured to access it with the *setmemwindow(1m)* command. The total amount of shared memory in a shared memory window depends on the magic number of the executable. SHARE_MAGIC executables can use a shared window of up to 1 GB, whereas SHMEM_MAGIC executables can use a shared window of up to 2 GB.

The number of shared memory windows is configurable with the tuneable parameter *max_mem_window*. Each group of applications can access its own private memory window. The shared objects placed in Quadrant 4 remain globally visible. Therefore, HP-UX tries to load all shared libraries into Quadrant 4 when shared memory windows are used. Using memory windows has several side effects:

- Shared libraries that cannot be placed into Quadrant 4 are placed in Quadrant 3 and must be mapped into each shared memory window.
- The IPC_GLOBAL attribute must be used to force a shared memory segment into the shared memory window using shmat(2).
- The MAP_GLOBAL attribute must be used to force a memory-mapped file into the shared memory window using mmap(2).
- Processes must be in the same memory window to share data.
- Child processes inherit the shared memory window ID.
- The shared memory window ID may be shared among a group of processes by inheritance or by use of a unique key referred to by the processes.

The per-process Virtual Address Space (VAS) for processes that use SHARE_MAGIC shared memory windows is shown in Figure 9-7. Use of this feature constrains the globally accessible shared object VAS to .75 GB. This means that all shared libraries, memory-mapped files and shared memory segments that must be accessible to all processes on the system must fit into the .75 GB Quadrant 4. Therefore, this feature should be used with care.

Shared memory windows are not needed, at least today, for 64-bit applications, because the total shared object space may be as much as 3.75 TB.

9.2.5   SHMEM_MAGIC

SHMEM_MAGIC provides a means of extending the VAS available to global shared objects. SHMEM_MAGIC achieves this goal at the expense of the VAS available for process text and private data, which is limited to 1 GB together when using this option. Figure 9-8 shows this format.

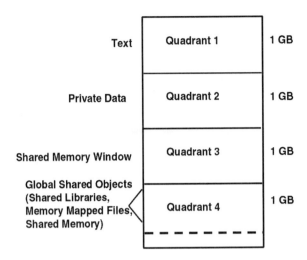

Figure 9-7   32-Bit SHARE_MAGIC Format with Shared Memory Windows

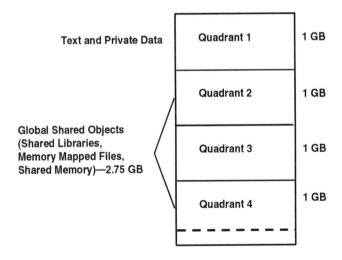

Figure 9-8   SHMEM_MAGIC Format

9.2.6   Shared Memory Windows for SHMEM_MAGIC

In a manner similar to that for SHARE_MAGIC, shared memory windows can be used to allocate VAS for shared memory segments that are visible only to a group of cooperating processes that are linked as SHMEM_MAGIC. Doing so makes 2 GB of VAS available for shared objects that are accessible only to the cooperating processes. Using this feature will constrain the VAS available for globally accessible shared objects to .75 GB, and it should therefore be used only when absolutely necessary. Figure 9-9 shows the SHMEM_MAGIC format with memory windows.

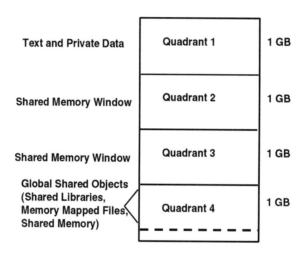

Figure 9-9   32-Bit SHMEM_MAGIC Format with Shared Memory Windows

9.3   fork() and vfork()

Virtual memory bottlenecks may also occur as the result of the *fork()* system call, which creates a new process derived from a currently running one. With *fork()*, the VAS data structures—virtual frame descriptors (VFDs) and disk block descriptors (DBDs)—are copied for use by the child process; this may even require page-outs to provide enough additional memory. Full swap space reservation is made for the child process. Furthermore, copy-on-write is implemented for the parent—that is, the child process receives a copy of the data page before the parent writes. Moreover, copy-on-access is implemented for the child, which means that a fresh copy of data is created whenever the child writes or reads data.

Vfork() allows VAS structures to be shared, which makes it much more efficient than *fork()*. No swap space reservation is necessary for the child. When using *vfork()*, the parent waits, suspending execution, and the child must be coded to call *exec()* immediately; these calling conventions must be used. *Vfork( )* saves the resources of CPU time and required memory for copying the VAS structures. The larger the process, the greater the amount of overhead that is saved.

From Bob's Consulting Log— I was called in to diagnose a workstation performance problem. The customer was running a large engineering design application. The application ran well until the engineer used a feature that allowed a shell escape, to type a system command. Performance suddenly degraded significantly: the disk drive could be heard performing I/Os for about 90 seconds, and then, finally, the shell prompt appeared.

What I found was that the system had only 128 MB of memory, and the engineer was calling up a model of a satellite that took over 150 MB of data space. This resulted in physical memory being totally filled, plus some of the data being written to the swap area.

When the engineer did a shell escape, the application called *fork()*, which copied all of the VAS structures associated with the application. These VAS structures were quite large, because of the 150 MB of data space. The copying not only took some time, but it also caused paging out to occur to make room for the new copy of the VAS structures. However, to do the shell escape, the application now called *exec()* to start up the shell. The *exec()* threw away the VAS structures that were just copied and created new ones for the shell process!

The solution was to convince the third party software supplier to change the *fork()* call to a *vfork()* call. When they made this change, the large VAS structures were no longer copied, and the shell prompt appeared in less than a second.

9.4 Dynamic Buffer Cache

The use of the file system buffer cache is another important area where memory bottlenecks can be observed. The storage of pages in buffers means quicker access to the data on the second and successive reads, because they do not have to be read in again. It is possible to set the size of the file system buffer cache, and the cache can be set up as either dynamic or static.

A dynamic buffer cache is enabled when the system parameters *bufpages* and *nbuf* are both set to zero; this is the default for HP-UX 10.0. The buffer cache grows as the result of page fault requests, which in turn result in pages being added. The cache shrinks as the page daemon *vhand* reclaims pages and *syncer* trickles out dirty buffers. (Trickling is a process by which the *syncer* process attempts to avoid large spikes of I/O by writing out pages in small groups.)

An advantage of the dynamic buffer cache is the fact that when buffers are not in use, the memory they occupy can be reclaimed for other purposes. The use of dynamic caches makes the most sense in scientific and engineering applications, which alternate between intensive I/O and intensive virtual memory demands.

Dynamic caches are not always the best strategy: most database environments and many other applications will run better with a fixed cache size. Growth and shrinkage of the cache may in fact cause performance degradation, as well as make application performance less predictable.

9.5 Sticky Bit

The *sticky bit* is a mode setting on executable files indicating that shared code is to be paged or swapped out to the swap area. Under these circumstances, startup of the executable may be faster from the swap area than from the *a.out* file itself, which is beneficial for frequencly executed programs like *vi*. However, text pages are almost always shared, non-modifiable, and merely deallocated when memory pressure occurs. In current implementations of the sticky bit (10.0 and later), the bit is honored when *a.out* is remote (for example, when it is mounted across an NFS mount), when a local swap area is present, and when the *page_text_to_local* parameter is enabled. This may be useful in distributed environments where programs are executed remotely.

9.6 Memory-Mapped Files and Semaphores

An alternative to the use of the file system buffer cache for file I/O is the use of memory-mapped files. The *mmap()* system call creates a mapping of the contents of a file to the process's virtual address space. Private memory-mapped files are mapped into the Private Data space; shared memory-mapped files are mapped into shared quadrants. With memory-mapping, I/O is not buffered through the buffer cache but is page-faulted in and paged out. The backing store is the original file, and *vhand* writes the pages to the original file, not the swap area.

The *madvise()* system call can be used to specify random or sequential access to a memory-mapped file; sequential access results in clustered reads. Starting in HP-UX 10.0, the kernel clusters the reads if sequential access is detected.

Advantages (+) of using memory-mapped files include the following:

+ After setup, data is accessd by pointer, so no system calls (such as *read()* and *write()*) are used to access the data; thus there may be fewer context switches.
+ Dirty data can be flushed by request. Reads cause page faults unless they are already in memory, and page-outs of dirty data directly to the file are initiated by *vhand*.
+ The data is not double buffered (meaning that it is stored only once in memory, in the process address space), and no swap space is allocated for the pages associated with the memory-mapped files. When memory-mapped files are not being used, data is stored in both the process VAS and in the buffer cache.

The use of memory-mapped files does not necessarily mean better performance. Here are some of their disadvantages (-):

- They require significant coding changes to the application. The most appropriate use is when you have a lot of data and do not want the swap area to be too large.

- Memory-mapped pages cannot be locked into memory, and are not trickled out to the disk by *syncer* as is the case with the buffer cache. Instead, they are written all at once.

- There may be protection ID fault thrashing.

Table 9-1 shows the maximum file size that can be mapped as well as the maximum combined size of all shared mapped files, all shared memory, and all shared libraries.

Table 9-1   Memory Mapped File Size Limits

	32-bit systems	**64-bit systems**
Maximum memory-mapped file size	1 GB	4 TB
Combined maximum size for shared mapped files, all shared memory, and all shared libraries without shared memory windows	1.75 GB	7.75 TB

Use of memory-mapped files requires considerable care. Concurrent access to the same file by traditional file system calls and by memory-mapping can produce inconsistent data at best and corrupted data at worst. The user cannot specify the mapped address range, and only one fixed contiguous mapping of a shared mapped file can exist; no address aliasing is possible. Even if more than one process is accessing the file, both processes must map the file in the same way. Separate calls to *mmap()* for the same file might result in non-contiguous virtual addresses, depending on what occurred on the system between calls; this may cause application problems. Finally, extending a memory-mapped file might result in an ENOMEM error to the application if global shared memory space is full.

9.6.1   Memory-Mapped Semaphores

Memory-mapped semaphores may be used with memory-mapped files or with an anonymous memory region created with *mmap()*. These semaphores require additional memory (at least one page), although multiple semaphores may be located on the same page. Memory-mapped semaphores are binary (set or clear) instead of counting. They are managed with the *msem_init()*, *msem_lock()*, *msem_unlock()*, and *msem_remove()* system calls. Although memory-mapped semaphores consume more memory than do traditional System V semaphores, they are much more efficient. Their use will usually improve both application and system performance.

Memory-mapped semaphores are mentioned here for consistency and completeness, since they are implemented as part of the memory-mapped file implementation. Their employment in a user process is really an application design or optimization choice that may improve CPU utilization. Application tuning is discussed in Part 4.

9.7 Shared Libraries

Shared libraries are used by default on HP-UX systems. With the use of shared libraries, the library on the disk is not made a part of the *a.out* file, and memory or disk space is saved as a result. However, shared libraries may consume more CPU and require more I/O activity.

With shared libraries, deferred binding is the default. Binding is done upon the first call to a procedure in the library. This means that unresolved symbols may not be detected until *exec( )* time. Shared libraries are compiled as position-independent code (PIC), which results in reduced performance compared with executables linked with archive libraries. This is because the code is bigger, and uses more CPU. Also, shared libraries cannot be locked in memory, and swap space is reserved for data required by every procedure in the library, even those that are not called.

Shared libraries are favored by software vendors because updates to the shared library do not require relinking of the *a.out* file. They are favored from a system perspective because they consume less memory and disk space; however, they consume more CPU. Performance tradeoffs with shared libraries are discussed further in the chapter on "Application Optimization."

9.8 Paging, Swapping, and Deactivation

Unix systems use a variety of strategies for handling high demand on memory resources. These include paging, swapping, and deactivation.

9.8.1   Paging

Paging is the process by which memory pages are brought into memory and removed from memory. Various algorithms for paging have been used in different HP-UX systems. *Page-ins* occur when a process starts up, when a process requests dynamic memory, and during page faults after a page-out, a swap-in or a reactivation. Page-ins are always done as needed. Code that is never executed never gets paged in unless the program is linked as an EXEC_MAGIC program.

Page-outs and *page-frees* occur when memory is scarce. The page daemon *vhand* (further described below) does page-outs only for dirty data pages; text (code) pages and unmodified data pages are simply freed.

9.8.2   Operation of vhand

Vhand, also known as the page daemon, is the system process that manages the paging out and freeing of data pages in a dynamic buffer cache. The name *vhand* was suggested by the two parts ("hands") of the daemon. The *age hand* cycles through memory structures, clearing the Recently Referenced bit in the PDIR (page directory) and flushing the TLB entry. The *steal hand* follows, freeing or paging out those pages that the age hand has cleared, and which the application has not accessed since the time the Recently Referenced bit was cleared. See Figure 9-10.

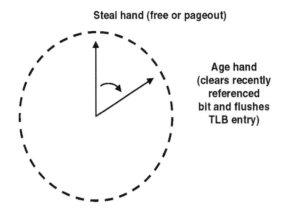

Steal hand (free or pageout)

Age hand
(clears recently
referenced
bit and flushes
TLB entry)

Figure 9-10   Two-Handed Clock Algorithm of vhand, the HP-UX Page Daemon

The TLB must be flushed to force a page fault, even though the page may still be in memory. Memory pressure has a negative impact on CPU utilization, because the CPU must deal with more TLB misses, page faults, and other memory management housekeeping.

9.8.3   Swapping

Swapping is an event that occured with user processes in HP-UX systems earlier than 10.0 when memory was very scarce or when the virtual memory system was thrashing. The algorithm for swapping depended on paging rates and on the amount of free memory in the system. In *swapping out*, the entire process, including private data, the u-area, and the *vfd/dbd* data structures, were written to the swap space in a series of large (up to 256 K) I/O operations. Shared text (code) was not swapped, but freed, and the process was not removed from the run queue. The opposite process, *swapping in*, required a large number of page faults to bring back code and data as the process started executing again.

Since a swapped process remains on the run queue, its priority will soon be improved to the point where it is the highest priority process again, and then it will then be swapped back in. This potentially starts the severe memory pressure again as the process that was swapped (and probably had a very large RSS) executes again, page faulting in its pages.

The swap area is used for both paging and swapping (pre-10.0). It is the backing store for private data, pageable process structures, shared memory, private text (executables with the EXEC_MAGIC format), and shared text (where the sticky bit is set and the executable is remotely accessed). *Swapper* is the process responsible for swapping processes out. Swapping is no longer implemented as all-or-nothing, but deactivated processes are the first to be paged out.

9.8.4   Deactivation

Swapping out has a tremendous negative impact on the system. Because of this, "swapping" has been implemented through *deactivation*, starting with HP-UX 10.0. Deactivation occurs when memory is very scarce, or when the virtual memory system is thrashing. The algorithm determines when deactivation is needed based on paging rates, the number of running processes, the amount of CPU idleness, and the amount of free memory.

In deactivation, a user process may be removed from the run queue for up to 20 minutes. Process structures (*u_area*) are written to the swap area after all the pages have been paged out. A candidate for deactivation is chosen based on the process size, priority, and time in memory, as well as on whether or not the process is interactive, whether or not it is serialized, and whether it is running or sleeping. *Glance* shows deactivation and reactivation statistics, but there is no utility that can give a list of processes that are currently deactivated. *Sar* and *vmstat* continue to refer to "swapping," although the term now means deactivation. The process *swapper* is now responsible for deactivating processes rather than for swapping them out.

The biggest advantages (+) of deactivation over swapping, from a system perspective, are:

+ Deactivation causes pages to be trickled out to the disk by *vhand* rather than all at once with multiple large I/Os.
+ With deactivation, the process stops executing for a while, so it does not soon cause its pages to be brought in again.

Of course, the user of the deactivated process may not like having to wait up to 20 minutes before forward progress continues.

9.8.5   Serialization

Serialize() is a system call and command that was introduced with HP-UX 10.0. It can improve performance when the overhead for paging in and out would be excessive. The use of the *serialize()* call provides a hint to the memory management system that the process is large, and that throughput will probably increase if the process is run serially with respect to other "serialized" processes. Serialization has no effect on processes that are not serialized.

Serialize() lets a process run for up to one hour before another serialized process is allowed to run; it is effective only when there is a shortfall of memory and when there are several serialized processes. There is no tool that shows you whether or not a process has been serialized.

The following is an example of using *serialize()*.

From Bob's Consulting Log—Five engineers were running a compute-bound application that used as its input a very large data set, each engineer supplying a different data set. I/O was only done at the end to write out the results. Normally, the five copies of the application would run concurrently and be timesliced, causing forced context switches. Accessing five very large data sets caused such severe memory pressure that the applications actually ran for a longer time than 5 X the average time for one copy because of this additional overhead.

Each user saw consistent slow performance and roughly the same execution time. After serializing these processes, the users saw inconsistent performance and total execution times. The first process would execute in one fifth the average time; the last process would execute in 5 X the average time. The important thing is that *overhead on the system had been significantly reduced.*

9.9 Memory Management Thresholds

The memory management system within HP-UX uses a variety of thresholds to enforce a consistent policy for memory management. Some of these thresholds—*lotsfree*, *desfree*, and *gpgslim*—are used in relation to *freemem*, the amount of memory currently free on the system.

A description of the basic HP-UX memory management parameters is in Table 9-2. Table 9-3 on page 197 shows how the default values of the variable parameters are calculated

Table 9-2   HP-UX Parameters for Memory Management

Parameter	Tunable	Description	Comment
lotsfree	Yes	Upper bound where paging starts and the threshold at which paging stops	The default is a variable number of pages based on physical memory size.
desfree	Yes	Lower bound where paging starts	The default is a variable number of pages based on physical memory size.
gpgslim	No— dynamic	The current threshold between *lotsfree* and *desfree* where paging actually occurs	Default = (*lotsfree* + 3*desfree). Recalculated every time *vhand* runs based on how often *freemem* = 0.
minfree	Yes	Threshold where deactivation occurs. Any process is chosen. VM system is thrashing and cannot keep up to provide enough free pages.	The default is a variable number of pages based on physical memory size.

9.9.1   Regions and Pregions

The HP-UX 10.0 and later memory management policy also has positive effects on the handling or regions and pregions. A *region* is a collection of pages belonging to all processes that are all of a certain type—for example, text, private data, stack, heap, shared library text, and shared memory segments. A *pregion* is a collection of pages belonging to a particular process that are all of a certain type. In HP-UX since version 10.0, the following policies are used:

- All regions are treated equally no matter the size.
- Shared regions are not more likely to be aged.
- All pages of a pregion are eventually scanned.

Pages belonging to lower priority ("niced") processes are more likely to be aged and stolen; pages belonging to higher priority processes are less likely to be aged and stolen. Processes blocked for memory are awakened in CPU priority order rather than in FIFO order, with interactive processes usually being favored. Page-ins are clustered unless too little memory is available. Page-ins cause process blocking as available memory approaches zero (amount depends on process priority). Finally, the buffer cache can shrink as well as expand.

9.9.2   Thresholds and Policies

Memory management thresholds vary based on the amount of physical memory and CPU speed, and are set at boot time. The value of *gpgslim* floats between *lotsfree* and *desfree*, depending upon demands on memory. When *freemem* < *gpgslim*, *vhand* runs eight times per second and scans a set number of pages (depending on need and swap device bandwidth) and uses no more than 1/16 of a particular pregion at a time and no more than 10% of the CPU cycles for that interval. Each time *vhand* scans a pregion, it starts scanning pages at the point where it left off the previous time. The *nice* value affects the probability that a page will be aged. When *freemem* < *minfree*, *swapper* runs to free up large blocks of memory by deactivating processes. (Although the name is still *swapper*, HP-UX no longer swaps.)

Starting with HP-UX 10.20, *lotsfree*, *desfree* and *minfree* are tuneable. However, unless you really understand the needs of the application and how it is affected by these parameters, it is highly recommended that you accept the default values. In 11.x and later versions, the default values for *lotsfree*, *desfree*, and *minfree* have been adjusted, especially for systems with large amounts of physical memory (> 2GB). This was done because it is much better to start paging sooner on such systems, so that the paging process can meet demands more effectively.

9.9.3 Values for Memory Management Parameters

In these sample calculations for the default values of the memory management parameters, N is the number of non-kernel free pages at boot time.

Table 9-3 Calculations for Default Values of Memory Management Parameters

Parameter	N <= 8K and physical memory size is 32 MB	8K < N <= 500K and physical memory size is 2 GB	N > 500K and physical memory size is 2 GB
lotsfree	MAX (N/8, 256)	MAX (N/16, 8192)	16384 [64 MB]
desfree	MAX (N/16, 60)	MAX (N/64, 1024)	3072 [12 MB]
minfree	MAX (*desfree*/2, 25)	MAX (*desfree*/4, 256)	1280 [5 MB]

9.10 Sizing Memory and the Swap Area

Choosing the right memory size and configuring the right swap area size can contribute to good memory performance. Only experience can determine the right values are for any particular installation, but some initial guidelines are provided in the next paragraphs.

9.10.1 Sizing the Swap Area

For the swap area, the old rule of thumb was to use two to three times the size of physical memory, with a minimum of 1 times physical memory. However, this is not always realistic. For large memory configurations, the use of *pseudo-swap* in addition to normal swap allows up to 75% of available memory to be used once the swap devices are full, without the need to reserve physical swap space.

When physical memory size is greater than 512 MB, a more realistic guideline is to use 25% of physical memory as a minimum, plus the following:

- The sum of all shared memory requirements (not including text, memory mapped files, and shared libraries) minus the amount of locked memory. (Note: if the shared memory segment is locked into memory, do *not* count it.)
- N times the private virtual memory requirements for each application (private VSS) where N = the number of users; use glance (Memory Regions) to calculate this for each process.
- The sum of shared text VSS requirements when accessing remotely with the sticky bit set
- 10% overhead for VAS structures and fudge factor

Beyond this, pseudo-swap should allow for peak periods.

9.10.2 Sizing Memory

The following determine physical memory size:

- The sum of all resident shared memory requirements (text, shared libraries, shared memory, memory-mapped files), including the amont of locked memory (shared RSS)
- N times the private resident memory requirements for each applcation (private RSS) where N= the number of users
- 10 to 20 MB for the kernel and static tables
- The size of the fixed buffer cache, if applicable
- Initial allocation for the dynamic buffer cache, if applicable (a minimum of 10% of physical memory is required; 20% is recommended)
- An estimate for networking needs (10% of physical memory)
- Additional memory for NFS

9.10.3 Controlling Memory Allocation with PRM

On HP-UX 10.20 and later systems, Process Resource Manager (PRM), working with the standard memory manager, lets you allocate memory amounts or percentages independent of CPU allocations. Process groups are guaranteed a minimum percentage of memory and optionally a maximum percentage. This guarantees a fair share to a process group, but not necessarily to a given process. Shares are enforced when paging is occurring; processes are suppressed by the requested method (today, only SIGSTOP is available). You can choose to suppress all the processes in a process group, or just the largest.

Some side effects of using PRM for memory allocation are:

- PRM reports available memory—the maximum amount of memory that is available for allocation to user processes.
- PRM does not suppress a process that locks memory; however, use of locked memory will affect other processes in the process group.
- Allocations may interact with CPU allocations in such a way that a process group may not use all of the CPU it is allocated if it cannot use any more memory.
- If the PRM memory daemon dies unexpectedly, processes will remain suppressed until prmrecover is used.
- Process groups will exceed their allocations, even with a cap, in the absence of memory pressure.

9.11 Memory Metrics

A variety of global and per-process metrics are available for identifying potential bottlenecks in memory.

9.11.1 Global Memory Saturation Metrics

Global memory saturation metrics (provided by *glance*, *gpm*, and *vmstat*) tell whether the memory system as a whole is saturated. These include:

- Free memory in KB or pages
- Active virtual memory (avm) in the last 20 seconds
- Available memory (physical memory, kernel memory, fixed buffer cache memory)

The most useful global saturation metric is free memory.

9.11.2 Global Memory Queue Metrics

The only queue relating to memory is the number of processes blocked on VM. *Measure-Ware* gives this as a count; *glance* and *gpm* show this as a percentage of time blocked on VM.

9.11.3 Other Global Memory Metrics

Other global metrics include:

- Page-in/page-out rate
- Page-in/page-out quantity
- Swap-in/page-out rate (before 10.0)
- Swap-in/page-out quantity (before 10.0)
- Deactivation/reactivation rate (10.0 and greater)
- Deactivation/reactivation quantity (10.0 and greater)
- Number of page faults and paging requests
- Number of VM reads and VM writes (clustered)

The following global metrics are the most useful in diagnosing memory bottlenecks:

- Page-out rate. Page-ins are normal, even when there is no memory pressure. Page-outs occur only when memory pressure exists.
- Deactivations. Deactivations only occur as a last resort when there is severe memory pressure, and when the paging system cannot keep up with demands.

9.11.4 Per-Process Memory Metrics

Per-process memory saturation metrics (provided by *top*, *glance*, and *gpm*) include Resident Set Size (RSS) and Virtual Set Size (VSS). Per-process memory queue metrics include the percentage blocked on VM. Other per-process memory metrics are:

- Number of VM reads and VM writes
- Number of page faults from memory

- Number of page faults from disk
- Number of swaps (before 10.0)
- Number of deactivations (10.0 and later)

Looking at the RSS will show you how much of a process tends to occupy memory. VSS shows you how large the process is, including:

- Text in memory as well as text not yet referenced from the *a.out* file (error routines may never be paged in if not needed)
- Data in memory and data not yet paged in from the a.out file
- Shared libraries in memory and not yet paged in from the .sl file
- Shared memory
- Memory-mapped files in memory and not yet paged in from the original file
- Private data that has been paged out to the swap area
- Shared memory that was not locked, and that was paged out to the swap area

9.11.5 Typical Metric Values

Page-ins occur normally, and thus do not indicate memory pressure. However, page-outs are an indicator of memory pressure. Page-outs of the following can cause pressure:

- Process data pages
- Process text pages for EXEC_MAGIC format executables
- Shared memory pages
- Writes to memory-mapped files (MMFs)
- Shrinkage of the dynamic buffer cache

Swapping or deactivation is an indicator of severe memory pressure.

9.12 Types of Memory Management Bottlenecks

What are the symptoms of a memory bottleneck? The four major ones are:

- Saturation of memory
- A large VM queue
- Resource starvation
- User dissatisfaction with response time

Saturation is indicated by low free memory, and by process deactivation (swapping in systems before 10.0). A large VM queue sustained over time is also indicated by a high percentage of processes blocked on VM, as well as by large disk queues on swap devices. Resource starvation occurs when a high percentage of CPU utilization is used for VM activity, or when the disk subsystem is consumed by VM activity. User dissatisfaction with the system results from poor transaction response time.

Lack of memory often results in other problems with the CPU and disk systems, and these problems tend to mask the true cause, which lies inside the memory-management subsystem.

From Bob's Consulting Log—One client had recently added 20% more users to an OLTP system, and performance degraded significantly compared to the state before adding the users. I was asked to recommend a CPU upgrade. On investigation, we found that the degradation of performance was much more severe than what you would expect for the number of users being added. I looked at how much memory each new user needed and found that the new users increased the memory beyond what was physically in the system. Memory was thrashing, and performance was degrading much more than expected. The actual solution to the problem—a memory upgrade—turned out to be a lot less expensive than the CPU upgrade the client thought he needed.

9.13 Expensive System Calls

The most expensive system calls from the standpoint of memory are *fork()* and *exec()*, *malloc()*, and *mmap()*. *Fork()* and *exec()* require extensive new memory allocation for VAS/pregion structures; *vfork()* offers a partial remedy (see the previous section on *vfork()*).

Malloc() and *mmap()* also are expensive calls simply because they are likely to increase memory utilization substantially.

9.14 Tuning Memory Bottlenecks

As with CPU bottlenecks, there are several ways of tuning a memory bottleneck:

- Hardware solutions
- Software solutions
- Application optimization
- Adjusting memory-related operating system tunable parameters

9.14.1 Hardware Solutions

The simplest hardware solution may be to increase the amount of physical memory. Another strategy is to use multiple interleaved swap devices if not enough physical memory can be used to prevent page-outs.

9.14.2 Software Solutions

Typical software solutions include the following:
- On small systems, reduce the size of the kernel (subsystems and tables).
- Carefully reduce the size of the fixed buffer cache.

- Use a dynamic buffer cache, and tune it carefully.
- Reduce and/or restrict the use of memory locking by defining the system parameter unlockable_mem.
- Use privileges (see *setprivgrp(1m)*) to regulate user access to memory.
    - Use the MLOCK privilege to lock processes into memory.
    - Use the SERIALIZE privilege on large processes and batch processes.
- Nice less important, large, or batch processes.
- Move work to other time periods, or run them as batch jobs.
- Reduce the number of workspaces in a VUE environment.
- Restrict maximum process size by setting the following parameters:
    - *maxdsiz*
    - *maxssiz*
    - *maxtsiz*
  Keep in mind that setting these values affects all processes on the system.
- Switch from hpterm to xterm or dtterm.
- Use the sticky bit for NFS-mounted executables (Doing this requires setting the PAGE_TEXT_TO_LOCAL parameter).
- Use *setrlimit(2)* starting in HP-UX 10.10.

It is recommended that database shared memory segments be locked into memory. These segments are caches, and it makes no sense to allow a portion of a cache to be paged out.

9.14.3 Application Optimization

Here are some suggestions for optimizing applications to best use memory:

- Minimize the use of expensive system calls:
    - Switch from *fork()* to *vfork()* if appropriate
    - Minimize the use of *mmap()*
- Use memory leak analysis software (for example, *Purify* from Rational Software).
- Use malloc() carefully, because it allocates memory in such a way that the virtual space cannot be returned to the system until the process exits. Using free() releases memory only at the process level; such memory is still considered to be in use by the system. Also, watch for malloc pool fragmentation.
- Minimize the use of resources that consume memory indirectly, such as user-space threads and semaphores.

9.15 Memory-Related Tunable Parameters

The following memory-related parameters may be tuned. These are found in the file */usr/conf/master.d/**. Items marked with an asterisk (*) are discussed in more detail in Chapter 10 on "Disk Bottlenecks."

- *bufpages* *
- *dbc_max_pct* *
- *dbc_min_pct* *
- *desfree*
- *lotsfree*
- *maxdsiz*
- *maxssiz*
- *maxswapchunks*
- *maxtsiz*
- *maxusers*
- *minfree*
- *msgmax, msgmnb*
- *nbuf* *
- *nclist*
- *netmemmax*
- *nfile* *
- *ninode* *
- *nproc*
- *page_text_to_local*
- *strmsgsz*
- *swapmem_on*. Should be enabled to reduce the amount of swap space required for large memory systems (greater than 512 MB).
- *unlockable_mem*. Can be used to limit the amount of memory that can be locked by processes.

While most of these parameters have only a small effect on memory utilization, system tables should not be sized arbitrarily large.

It is highly recommended that *desfree*, *lotsfree*, and *minfree* not be tuned unless HP support specifically tells you to do so.

For the buffer cache, use either *bufpages* to create a fixed size buffer or *dbc_max_pct* and *dbc_min_pct* to create a dynamic (variable size) buffer cache. These parameters will be discussed further in Chapter 10.

9.15.1 Logical View of Physical Memory Utilization

Figure 9-11 shows a logical summary of the components of physical memory that must be managed in performance tuning.

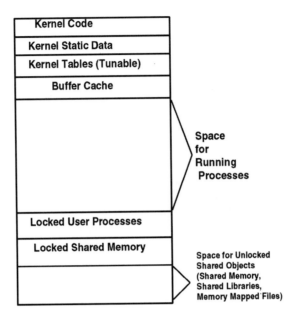

Figure 9-11   Logical View of Physical Memory Utilization in HP-UX

Disk Bottlenecks

Thisﾠchapter describes major bottlenecks related to the HP-UX disk I/O subsystem. A review of some of the basic concepts of disk I/O for HP-UX is followed by a description of typical symptoms, techniques for diagnosing them, and methods for tuning. Here are the topics:

- Review of disk I/O concepts
- Logical volume manager concepts
- Disk arrays
- SCSI access to disks
- File systems and the kernel
- File system types
- Disk metrics
- Types of disk bottlenecks
- Expensive system calls
- Tuning disk bottlenecks
- Database issues
- Disk related tunable parameters

Dealing with I/O often involves many choices. The wisdom of **Rule #2**, "Performance tuning always involves a trade-off," is good to remember in this arena.

10.1 Review of Disk I/O Concepts

The Unix operating system sees all input to and output from the CPU as a matter of reading from or writing to files. Disk files are one specific type of I/O governed by the same rules and using the same I/O stack as all the I/O operations. This stack as it applies to disk devices is shown in Figure 10-1.

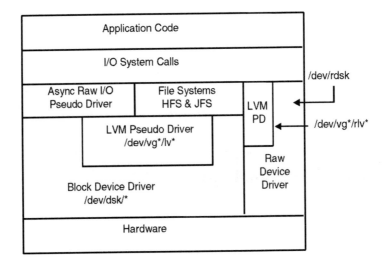

Figure 10-1   I/O Stack

The application code makes system calls to the I/O subsystem, specifying what is to be opened, closed, read, or written as a *filename*. The filename determines the type of object that is opened and accessed. Object types include whole disks, disk sections, or LVM volumes. I/O types used to access the data include raw (unbuffered) I/O, asynchronous raw I/O, buffered file I/O, and direct file I/O. Depending on the object type and I/O type, different *system calls* and different *device drivers* are used to access data. Each call or driver has characteristics that affect performance. The following sections describe the most important of these calls and drivers.

10.1.1 Disk Access Methods

Disk data may be accessed through a variety of methods. In HP-UX, these methods have evolved over time from the early use of disk sections, down to the current methods employed by specialized volume management software—for example, Logical Volume Manager (LVM). The following disk access methods are possible:

- Whole disk. This is accessed by a device file specifying section 0. Example:
    - */dev/[r]dsk/c#t#d0* (HP-UX 10.0 and later)
- Sections. Each brand of hard disk formerly had a set of fixed definitions contained in the file */etc/disktab* which described 16 potentially overlapping partitions of the disk. No sup-

port is provided for disks or arrays that have been introduced since HP-UX 9.04, though a pseudo-driver allows the continued use of the disk section access method.

• LVM. Logical Volume Manager replaces the use of disk sections in more recent systems. The additional overhead results in a 3 % performance degradation, but this is usually an acceptable price to pay for the added functionality provided by LVM.

Any of the access methods mentioned here may be used with each of the various I/O types described in the next sections.

10.1.2 Unbuffered (Raw) I/O

Unbuffered I/O does not use HP-UX file system buffers to pass data to and from applications. This means that raw I/O does not use a file system, but depends on the user's application to manage the organization of the data on the disk device. Raw I/O is performed by accessing the character (raw) device file associated with the disk on which the data resides. A typical example is */dev/rdsk/c0t0d0*. Two varieties of raw I/O are the basic and asynchronous types. A logical view of basic raw I/O is shown in Figure 10-2.

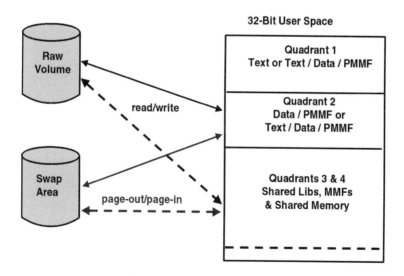

Figure 10-2 Logical Diagram of Basic Raw I/O Blocking

10.1.2.1 Basic Raw I/O

With basic raw I/O, data is transferred directly to or from the user's buffer. Only synchronous reads and writes are allowed. The process blocks until the I/O is complete, regardless of whether the application is performing a read or a write operation on the device. For this reason, raw I/O can actually be slower than buffered I/O in some circumstances.

10.1.2.2 Asynchronous Raw I/O

In asynchronous raw I/O (Figure 10-3), data is transferred to and from shared memory

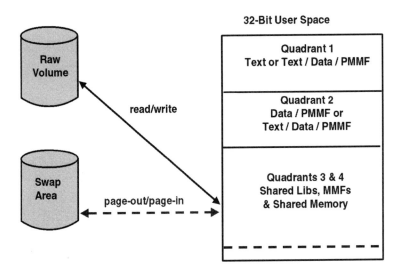

Figure 10-3   Asynchronous Raw I/O Blocking

segments. The process does not block, but you must check to make sure the I/O operation is complete before accessing the data in the shared memory area through the use of the *select()* system call. This type of raw access requires special *ioctl()* calls to configure the shared memory segment. Asynchronous raw I/O uses the block device driver, which has efficient sorting capabilities. Also, since the process is not blocked, it is possible to queue up I/Os, and this improves performance.

Asynchronous raw I/O has been implemented in the major relational database management software packages, which has resulted in substantial performance increases when using raw volumes. Databases almost always benefit by using raw volumes rather than using a file system (either HFS or JFS).

10.1.3 Buffered I/O

Buffered I/O (Figure 10-4) makes use of the Unix file system buffers. Synchronous reads are done from disk or from the buffer cache while the process blocks. Asynchronous read-ahead places additional pages of data from the file system into the buffer cache to speed up subsequent accesses. When the O_SYNC flag is used, synchronous writing blocks the process while data is copied to the cache from application data space and written to disk. When O_SYNC is not used, the default write on the Series 700 is an asynchronous copy to cache and write to disk without blocking the process if the last byte in the block has been written. (This is also known as write-behind.) Otherwise, the data is written in a delayed fashion by *syncer*. On the Series 800, when O_SYNC is not used, the default is an asynchronous copy to cache without blocking the process, followed by a delayed write to disk by *syncer*. Buffered I/O requires a copy of data between the kernel and the user spaces, and this impacts performance.

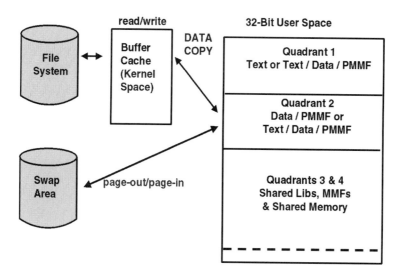

Figure 10-4   Buffered File I/O Blocking

10.1.4 Direct Files and Memory-Mapped Files

Direct file I/O (Figure 10-5) is possible only within JFS file systems. It is possible to have

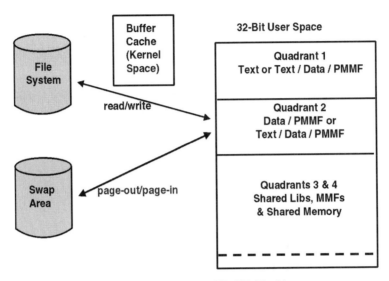

Figure 10-5   Direct File I/O Blocking

synchronous reads and writes, during which the process blocks. The performance advantage is that there is no copying of data between the kernel space and the user space, and data is unbuffered. This type of I/O is good only when the application does relatively large I/Os and does not reference the data again for a long time, meaning that the buffer cache performs no useful function. For instance, a scientific application that writes a very large output file when it completes, may benefit from direct I/O.

10.1.5 Memory-Mapped I/O

Memory-mapped I/O (Figure 10-6) provides unbuffered transfer of data in a file system to and from quadrants of user address space. Reading is done by page faults, and there are clustered page-ins (read-aheads) if the file is sequentially accessed. Writing is done via the *vhand* daemon or through the *msync()* and *close()* system calls.

10.2 Logical Volume Manager Concepts

Since HP-UX 9.0, Logical Volume Manager (LVM) has become the most common tool for creating and managing disk storage. LVM provides the capability to group multiple physical disks into a single volume group composed of one or more logical volumes. Logical volumes can contain file systems, or they can be accessed like raw files.

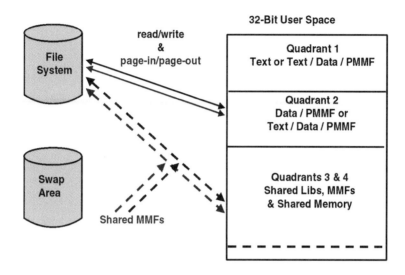

Figure 10-6   Memory Mapped File (/O

Although non-default naming is possible, LVM objects usually have device file names beginning with */dev/vg* (for example, */dev/vg00* for a volume group, and */dev/vg03/lvol9* for a logical volume). These objects are accessed via the LVM pseudo-driver, which in turn accesses either the block or character mode driver to perform actual I/O to the disk.

Volume groups offer a great deal more flexibility than the historical disk section access method. You can configure up to 256 volume groups (the default is 10), up to 255 physical volumes (disks or LUN's) per volume group, and up to 255 logical volumes per volume group. You can create logical volumes of any size up to 128 GB (HP-UX 10.10). Volumes can be striped or mirrored to enhance performance, and in HP-UX 11.0, volumes can be striped and mirrored at the same time.

10.2.1 LVM Striping

LVM striping is a software technique in which data is written to disks in a volume group in a manner that allows parallel reads and writes to speed up performance. The I/O is split into equal pieces, each of which is written to a different disk. The *stripe size* is the amount written to one disk. Logical volumes can be quickly created with stripe sizes of 4, 8, 16, 32, or 64 KB. Striping is done by the LVM pseudo-driver; no additional system calls are needed.

How does striping affect performance? It improves large sequential write performance by involving multiple disk drives in the I/O. Striping should improve small random read and write performance, because statistically the I/Os will be spread across multiple drives. Yet striping may reduce the performance gains expected from the I/O merging feature of HP-UX 10.0, where multiple I/Os that are physically contiguous are merged into a single I/O. The fewer I/Os made possible by merging may yield better performance than the larger number required for striping; fewer I/Os are almost always better than more I/Os.

10.2.1.1   LVM Striping Recommendations

Don't stripe everything everywhere. Instead, place a large file or file system on a separate striped group of disks. This allows you to detect "hot" files when necessary, and lets you control their placement. The use of smaller separate volume groups also can reduce the time needed to restore data in case of a mechanism failure. This is because you must restore the entire volume, not just the part that was on the failed disk. As a heuristic, keep striped volume groups less than or equal to four physical volumes. At four, you reach the point of diminishing returns.

Set the stripe size according to I/O size and access patterns. This is more difficult to do when you are using JFS, where the I/O size is variable. On HFS, the I/O size is equal to the block size, which is 8K by default. Typically, match the stripe size to the file system I/O size: the blocksize on an HFS file system, and the average extent size on a JFS file system.

10.2.1.2   LVM Extent-Based Striping

An older, "manual" way to stripe using LVM is *extent-based striping*. In this method, the administrator must issue a large sequence of *vgextend* commands, alternating among the physical volumes in the volume group. This method of striping is usually less effective than the built-in striping discussed earlier, because the minimum stripe size is the same as the minimum extent size, which is 1 MB.

10.2.2 LVM Mirroring

LVM mirroring in HP-UX is provided by the optional add-on product MirrorDisk/UX. LVM mirroring provides RAID 1 mirroring in software, and allows two-way or three-way mirroring (that is, one or two levels of redundancy), in addition to split/merge capabilities. (RAID levels are described in a later section.)

LVM mirroring gives better performance than application mirroring, which requires multiple system calls. Mirroring is done by the LVM pseudo-driver, so that no additional system calls are necessary. Reads are done from the mirror with the shortest queue, thus increasing potential read performance up to 40%. (You may only notice this when the disks are very busy.) Writes cause multiple I/O requests to the driver, thus decreasing potential write performance by as much as 10%.

Hardware mirroring may provide better performance, but this depends on the hardware implementation (remember Rule #1). Also, hardware mirroring does not provide three-way mirroring and split/merge, except for the EMC Symmetrix with the Symmetrix Multi-Mirror Facility (SMMF).

10.2.2.1   Mirror Scheduling Policy

You can select either a parallel or serial write policy with mirrored logical volumes. Parallel write (the default) is faster for raw access and for JFS file systems. A serial write policy may be faster for HFS in HP-UX 10.01 and later versions because of I/O merging.

10.2.2.2   Mirror Consistency

If you create a mirrored logical volume with the *-c y* option, LVM guarantees that mirror copies will be consistent with one another, even following a crash. In the event of a system crash, LVM must recover mirror copies to a consistent state. To speed up the recovery process, LVM provides a *mirror-write cache*, which keeps track of the changes in the logical track groups (LTGs) on each disk. You enable the mirror write cache by using the *-M y* option at the time you create a mirrored logical volume.

When the mirror-write cache is enabled, time-stamped mirror consistency records are written to the volume group data area (VGDA) of one of the disks where the logical volume resides whenever the status of that LTG changes.

Maintaining the mirror-write cache has definite performance implications. There is a trade-off between degraded online performance and fast recovery following a system crash. Online performance suffers because:

- In order to write MCRs, the disk heads can potentially move from the outer tracks (where the VGDA is written) to the inner tracks where user data resides.
- Additional writes occur to post the MCRs to each physical volume in the volume group.
- Delays are possible when the mirror write cache is full and there are I/Os in the queues pending for all entries in the logical track group.

The advantage of the MWC is that the synchronization of logical volume mirrors on reboot after a crash is very fast.

To check for MWC contention with *GlancePlus* or *gpm*:

- Choose I/O by Logical Volume ("v").
- Select a volume ("S"). Pick a logical volume, not the volume group or group file.
- Look at statistics for MWC hits/misses. Hits are good; misses are bad. Look at the metric "MWC Misses." For good performance, there should be few MWC misses.

You can help reduce contention by creating a larger number of smaller volume groups rather than a few large volume groups. In HP-UX 11.0, the MWC has been increased in size from 32 to 120 cache entries, so there should be less contention.

10.2.2.3   Mirrors and Volume Group Size

If you are using mirroring, the number of volume groups versus the number of logical volumes can be an important decision point. For most configurations, it is better to use more volume groups with fewer logical volumes in each.

The mirror-write cache has less impact on performance with a large number of smaller volume groups than with a smaller number of larger volume groups, because there is less contention for LTG entries in the mirror-write cache. (This is because each volume group has its own mirror-write cache.)

Smaller volume groups will normally result in shorter recovery times after a system crash This is because logical volume resynchronization is done serially within a volume group, but in parallel among volume groups.

Fewer volume groups are easier to administer in most instances.

10.2.2.4   Disabling the Mirror-Write Cache

You can disable the mirror-write cache for a mirrored logical volume by using the -M n option in creating the volume. This will not result in online performance degradation, but rather in a slow recovery following a system crash. In this scenario, one side of the mirror is chosen as current and is copied fully to the other side(s) of the mirror upon volume group activation after a crash; this can take in the tens of minutes. All the mirrored logical volumes within the volume group are resynchronized serially. On the positive side, volume groups are accessible during resynchronization. Once they are resynchronized, online performance is not affected.

NOTE: Although it is possible to disable mirror consistency by using the -c n option in creating mirrored logical volumes, this is never a safe alternative for anything other than a swap device, because it may result in inconsistent mirrors after a system crash.

10.2.3 Read-Only Volume Groups

LVM lets you configure read-only volume groups, which allow online read-only access to a split-off mirror of a mirrored logical volume by another SPU. This feature is designed to work only with mirrored logical volumes; a snapshot of the data is obtained when one mirror is split.

This feature is not meant to improve performance, and must be used only with a dormant logical volume such as a split-off mirror. If used on an active logical volume with a file system, a panic will occur on the read-only SPU as soon as a change is made to the file system by the read-write SPU. If used on a non-split raw logical volume, there will be data consistency issues.

10.3 Disk Arrays

Disk arrays offer larger capacity data storage, as well as a variety of options that facilitate high availability and multi-system access. Most of the features of disk arrays have performance implications.

10.3.1 RAID Modes

The acronym RAID stands for "redundant array of inexpensive disks." A RAID device consists of a group of disks that can be configured in many ways, either as a single unit or in various combinations of striped and mirrored configurations. The types of configuration available are called RAID levels:

- RAID 0: Disk striping
- RAID 1: Disk mirroring
- RAID 0/1: Sector Interleaved groups of mirrored disks. Also called RAID 1/0 or RAID 10
- RAID 2: Multiple check disks using Hamming code
- RAID 3: Byte striped, single check disk using parity
- RAID 4: Block striped, single check disk using parity
- RAID 5: Block striped, data and parity spread over all disks
- RAID S (EMC Symmetrix): Block striped with a stripe group of 4 and a stripe depth of 1 (a special case of RAID 5)

The various RAID levels can be implemented in either hardware or software. Hardware RAID and bit software mirroring is most often used as the data redundancy solution. One-way data redundancy is possible using RAID 1, 3, or 5.

10.3.1.1 RAID 1

RAID 1 performance implications include the following:

- Mirroring is done in the array, so that only one write occurs from the CPU, potentially improving performance.
- Reads occur using both sides of the mirror to increase performance with some disk arrays.
- The benefit that might be obtained by doing reads from a pair of LVM mirrors attached to separate SCSI buses is lost.

10.3.1.2 RAID 3

For RAID 3, performance degrades for small reads or writes (less than 64 KB). In this mode, performance is typically 20% of that of stand-alone mirrored disks.

10.3.1.3 RAID 5

For RAID 5, performance degrades for small writes (2KB, for example), but random small read performance (2 KB) approaches that of LVM striping. Although you cannot control the placement of data for tuning purposes, a large write cache on the array may reduce the penalty. Figure 10-7 shows how RAID 5 striping is done.

The use of RAID 5 for small I/Os causes the array controller to perform a read-modify-write operation. For a 2KB write, for example, the controller would read 4 KB of data, modify the 2 KB from the write, and then write out 5 KB—4 KB of data and 1 KB of parity.

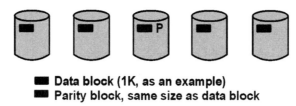

■ Data block (1K, as an example)
■ Parity block, same size as data block

Figure 10-7 RAID 5 Block Striping with Parity

10.3.1.4   RAID S

RAID S (a Symmetrix variant on RAID 5) provides a stripe group of 4, but blocks are sequentially laid out rather than striped. This provides good performance for both sequential and random reads (Note: you are likely to have multiple concurrent random reads). There may be degraded performance for small (less than 32 KB) writes, but the write cache should provide insulation against this for the application. Figure 10-8 shows the striping for RAID S.

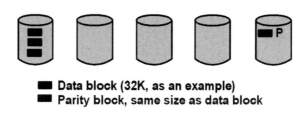

■ Data block (32K, as an example)
■ Parity block, same size as data block

Figure 10-8 RAID S Block Striping with Parity

The use of RAID S may cause the Symmetrix controller to perform a read-modify-write operation. For a write, for example, the controller would read 32 KB blocks of data and 32 KB parity blocks, modify the appropriate amount, compute XOR parity at the level of the individual mechanism controller, and then write out 32 KB blocks of data and parity.

10.3.1.5   Note on Symmetrix ICDA

LVM striping is not recommended with the use of EMC Symmetrix disk arrays. It can actually degrade performance, because of the segmentation of the array cache into 32K sections. All I/O's to and from the Symmetrix are via the cache, and all I/Os between the cache and the disks are 32K in size. It is often better to configure logical volumes contiguously on large Symmetrix logical devices, and let the Symmetrix optimize the access.

10.3.1.6 Note on Hardware Striping

Various disk array products provide the means to create striping in hardware as an alternative to using LVM. RAID modes can be used to achieve the performance benefits of striping as LUNs are configured on the array. One absolute rule to follow in this connection is: *Never mix hardware and software striping; use one or the other, but never both together.*

Hardware striping in arrays is not always superior to LVM striping. On HP Model 10 and 20 disk arrays in RAID 5, for example, the segment size is 128 KB. Each time data is modified, the array recomputes the checksum and writes out the corrected data. This is expensive, especially for database applications with many small writes. When comparing hardware and software striping, be sure to remember **Rule #1**: "It depends." With RAID 5, if the write I/O size is smaller than the stripe size multiplied by the number of disks in the stripe set, there is a condition in which a read/modify/write operation is done in the array, and this dramatically slows down performance.

10.3.2 PV Links

PV links are provided with LVM in HP-UX 10.0 and later, as a way to provide a redundant path to a disk hardware unit. Using PV links, you attach different buses to a multi-controller disk array so that access to the data is maintained even when the primary path fails. PV links are *not* used for concurrent access to the same logical device or LUN. However, if the disk device supports it, PV links can be used to increase potential performance by providing two separate I/O paths from the LUNs on the disk device to the computer. This behavior is supported with HP Models 10 and 20 disk arrays and with the AutoRAID array, as well as on the Symmetrix, as long as the I/Os are to different logical devices. You must carefully define the volumes, however, in order to achieve this potential performance improvement.

The operation of PV links is illustrated in Figure 10-9. When the volume group is created, two separate physical volume device files (representing paths to the disk array from two different SCSI controllers) are used for each LUN. This provides an alternate path to the data. In this example, link #1 is the primary link for LUN 0 and the secondary link for LUN 1, as determined by the device names specified in the *vgcreate* command (primary link) and *vgextend* command (secondary link). The order is reversed for LUN 2, therefore ensuring that both links are used for I/Os under normal circumstances.

10.4 Shared-Bus Access to Disks

The use of SCSI buses or FibreChannel allows for configuration of data storage with access by more than one system at a time. The type and number of buses used, particularly in mirrored configurations, can affect performance considerably.

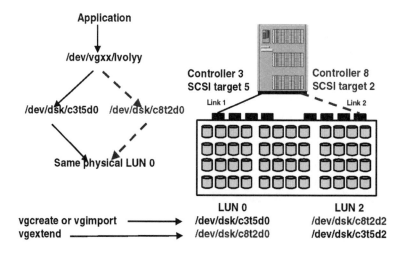

Figure 10-9 PV Links

10.4.1 Single-Initiator Configurations

A single initiator configuration is one in which a single SPU initiates access to a disk. An example is shown in Figure 10-10. This figure shows two configurations. At the top is a config-

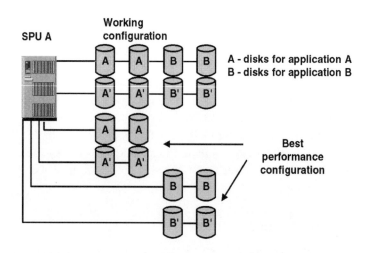

Figure 10-10 Single Initiator Disk Configurations

uration with disks for two applications attached to the same SCSI bus, and the mirrors on a separate bus for high availability. At the bottom is a better performing configuration, in which the disks for the different applications are separated from each other. The cost is, of course, more card slots and buses.

10.4.2 Multi-Initiator Configurations

In a multi-initiator configuration, more than one SPU accesses the disks from the same bus. A sample is shown in Figure 10-11. Again, two configurations are shown. The one at the

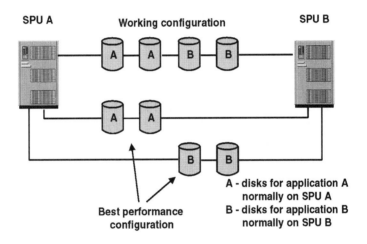

Figure 10-11 Multi-Initiator Disk Configurations

bottom performs better for two reasons: each application's disks are accessed on a different bus; and each SPU will normally access data for one application.

10.4.3 Performance Load on Multi-Initiator Buses

SCSI buses can easily become overloaded, especially in a multi-initiator environment. It is important to set SCSI priorities (determined by SCSI address) so that no device is starved for access to the bus. SCSI controllers (on the interface card attached to the SPU) should have the highest priority. Large disk queues or long service times on low priority devices indicate performance issues.

Table 10-1 gives a performance load factor (PLF) for typical devices attached to a Fast/ Wide SCSI bus. The values are based on peak transfer rates associated with devices and interfaces. For best results, the maximum PLF on a multi-initiator F/W SCSI bus is 11.5. The sum of the values for all active F/W SCSI interfaces on a single bus must not exceed this value, or severe performance degradation will result.

Table 10-1   Performance Load Factors for SCSI Devices

Device or Interface	PLF
F/W SCSI Host Adapter	1.5
Stand-alone Disk Drive (JBOD)	1.0
Disk Array with one Controller (Storage Processor) attached to the bus	2.0

10.4.4 Disk Drive Write Caches

Most modern disk drives and arrays contain RAM for a read and/or write cache that can be enabled or disabled. The read cache is usually enabled by default. Enabling the write cache is also called "turning immediate report on," and signals I/O completion when the data is written into the RAM cache. Enabling the write cache is especially good for sequential writes.

On some disk arrays (Models 10 & 20, for example), the cache can be split between read cache and write cache. This has some implications for performance:

• Cache sizes must be carefully chosen according to I/O patterns.
• The read cache is redundant if the application also caches.
• The write cache is less useful in read-mostly applications.

On the 700 Series, the kernel enables the write cache by default on all stand-alone disk drives. On the 800 Series, the kernel disables the write cache by default on all stand-alone disk drives. Default behavior can be modified with the following utilities:

• */usr/sbin/scsictl* for stand-alone disks
• */usr/hpC2400/bin/dcc* for Cascade disk arrays
• The Grid Manager for Model 10 and 20 Disk Arrays

WARNING: You must make a trade-off between loss of data integrity in case of power failure or device reset, and gain in performance from disabling the write cache. For mission-critical environments, it is recommended that immediate report be *disabled*.

10.5 File Systems and the Kernel

The Unix virtual file system (VFS) supplies a standard interface to various physical file systems. On HP-UX, supported file systems include *ufs* (known as HFS on HP-UX), JFS, *lofs* (loopback file system), *cdfs*, and NFS. NFS, while not a physical file system, is included because of its importance in networked environments. Hierarchical file systems are also available, as well other file systems offered by other Unix variants, including *dosfs* and *ramfs*. Tuning recommendations will be presented later in this chapter for HFS, JFS, and NFS file systems.

10.5.1 I/O Related Kernel Tables

Figure 10-12 shows the kernel tables that describe files and file systems. The user process

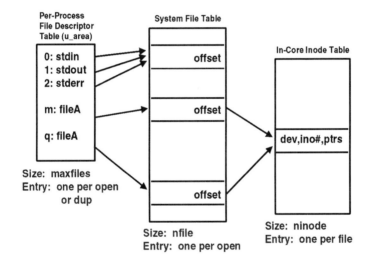

Figure 10-12 Kernel Tables for I/O

has a table of file descriptors that points to entries in the system file table. This in turn points to the in-core inode table, which contains one entry per open file. One entry in the per-process file descriptor table is used for each file *open(2)* or *dup(2)*. Its size is determined by the tuneable parameter *maxfiles,* which defaults to 60. Larger sizes can result in wasted space, fragmentation, and slower performance. Instead of increasing the size of this table for all processes, use *getrlimit(2)* and *setrlimit(2)* within the application, if possible, to increase the size of the file descriptor table for only that application rather than all applications.

An entry in the system file table is used for each *open(2)*. It contains the current file offset for the particular file descriptor used by a process. It may safely be sized arbitrarily large: each entry is small, and access to the table is very efficient.

The in-core inode table is used only for HFS file systems. Only one entry is used for a given file, no matter how many times it has been opened. This table often appears to be full. This is deceptive, however, since it is really a cache that contains both active and previously used entries. It should *not* be sized arbitrarily large, since the algorithm used for accessing the table is most efficient for table sizes of 4096 or smaller. Inode tables may need to be sized above 4096 entries according to real application needs. The inode table used by the JFS is initially sized at 50% of *ninode*, and will grow dynamically to 150% of *ninode*.

10.5.2 File System Limits

Files are limited in size by system architecture and other considerations. If you are not using LVM, the limit is 2 GB for the raw disk partition, which means that the file system (whether HFS or JFS) is also limited to 2 GB. It follows that the individual file cannot exceed two GB.

When using LVM, the following file and file system limits apply:

Table 10-2   LVM File and File System Size Limits

HP-UX Version	File Size Limit	File System Size Limit
10.01	4 GB	4 GB
10.10	128 GB*	128 GB

* When accessing files greater than 2 GB in size, 32-bit applications must be modified to use 64-bit pointers and to call *create64(2)*, *open64(2)*, *lseek64(2)*, etc.

10.5.3 Buffer Cache

The buffer cache is used to buffer file system I/O between the application and the disk. It supports the following patterns of reading and writing data from disk files:

• Synchronous reads: When data is not in the buffer cache, the process blocks until the data is read from the disk.

• Immediate reads from cache (does not involve I/O): When data is already in the buffer cache, it is copied to the process without blocking unless the inode or buffer are "busy."

• Synchronous writes: When the O_SYNC flag is specified, the process blocks until data is written to the disk.

• Asynchronous writes (write-behind): Queue the block to be written, but do not block the process.

• Delayed writes: The block is written by the *syncer* process some time in the future.

On typical large memory systems, the larger the size of physical memory, the larger the buffer cache that is desired. Buffer caches more than 500 MB in size may cause performance degradation, however, due to VAS allocation and overall management of the large number of buffers.

The cache can be no larger than 1 GB (one quadrant) for HP-UX version 10.0 and 10.10 systems; it can be as large as 3.75 GB in HP-UX 10.20 or later. You should reduce *dbc_max_pct* from the default of 50% on large memory systems if a dynamic buffer cache is used.

10.5.4 Fixed Buffer Cache

The cache was of fixed size only prior to 9.0 for Series 700 systems and prior to 10.0 on Series 800 systems. The default size = 10% of physical memory if *nbuf=bufpages=0*.

In 10.0 and later, you can fix the size of the buffer cache by setting *nbuf* and/or *bufpages* to non-zero values in the system file. A good default for *bufpages* is

sizeof(physmem) * 10% / 4096

if you don't know where to start. Note that there is usually no need to change the value of *nbuf* from its default value of zero.

10.5.4.1 Performance Implications

A fixed-size buffer cache often improves performance for commercial applications, or in cases where the environment is static. Buffer caches that are too large waste memory, and can cause memory bottlenecks. Buffer caches that are too small can cause disk bottlenecks. A fixed buffer cache does not adapt to changing conditions. The balance between VM and I/O can be controlled, however, by adjusting the fixed size of the buffer cache.

10.5.5 Dynamic Buffer Cache

A dynamic buffer cache became the default in HP-UX 9.0 for Series 700 systems and in HP-UX 10.0 for Series 800 systems. The starting size = 5% of physical memory, and the maximum is 50% by default. The dynamic buffer cache grows in size when VM demands are low and I/O demands are high by allocating new pages. The cache shrinks in size when VM demands are high and I/O demands are low. The use of the dynamic buffer cache is enabled when *nbuf* = *bufpages* = 0.

10.5.5.1 Performance Implications

Dynamic buffer caches often improve performance for technical (CAD/CAM) applications, or in cases where the environment is dynamic. With a dynamic cache, the size of the buffer cache changes according to demand, and additional overhead occurs for page allocation and freeing. Note that the system administrator cannot control the balance between VM and I/O.

A 50% maximum size is often too much for large memory systems (>= 1 GB). You should reduce the maximum size by setting *dbc_maxpct* to a value between 20% and 30% for most applications.

10.5.6 Maxusers, Maxfiles and Other Kernel Parameters

Maxusers is employed in formulas to size other parameters, including *nproc*, *nfile* and *ninode*. Removing the dependency on *maxusers* from the definitions of these other parameters is recommended. You can hardcode the values of *nproc*, *nfile*, and *ninode* as needed. *Maxusers* does not have anything to do with the user license level of the system. It is merely a convenience parameter for sizing several other parameters at once.

10.6 File System Types

This section describes several of the most common file system types together with some of the tunable parameters that relate to the creation and mounting of file systems.

10.6.1 HFS

The High Performance File System (HFS) is known by at least four names:

• HFS
• *ufs* (Unix File System)
• Berkeley File System
• McKusick File System

HFS is not the same as the System V File System, although some System V Release 4 variants may offer both. HFS was designed for environments with many small files; users of large files in HFS are deliberately penalized from a performance perspective, as will be seen in following sections.

10.6.1.1 HFS Layout

HFS file systems use the layout on disk shown in Figure 10-13. An HFS file system is composed of a primary and a secondary superblock containing structural metadata describing the layout, and one or more cylinder groups that contain both inodes (metadata for individual files) and data blocks. Note that kernel tables in memory also contain inode data for open files .

The design of the HFS file system allows the inode for a file and the data blocks of the file to be located in close proximity, to improve performance. The inode is written when the file is created and any time data blocks are added to the file.

Figure 10-14 shows how pointers to the data blocks operate when the default blocking of 8K bytes is used. There are always 12 direct pointers, each of which points to an 8KB data block. This results in very good performance for files of 96KB or less. As the file grows above 96KB, the indirect pointers are used. The single indirect pointer refers to an 8KB block of point-

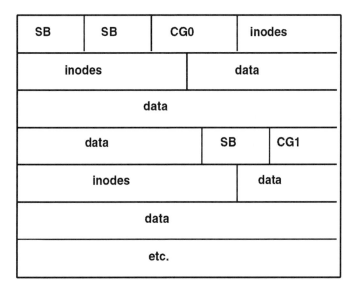

Figure 10-13   HFS File System Layout

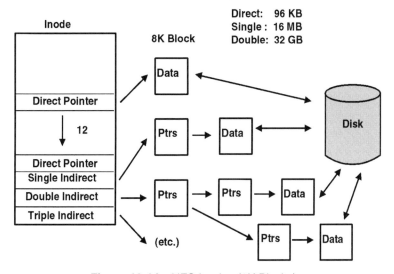

Figure 10-14   HFS Inodes (8K Blocks)

ers (2048 pointers) which in turn point to data blocks. Two I/Os are necessary to access the next 16MB of the file in the worst case scenario, in which the block of pointers does not remain cached. The use of double and triple indirect pointers further degrades performance for the largest files.

10.6.1.2   Disktab File

Prior to HP-UX 10.0, disk geometry for HFS was determined by the */etc/disktab* file, which defines numbers of cylinders, tracks, sectors, the rotational speed, size of the file system, block size, and fragment size. In HP-UX 10.0, section definitions other than section 0 (whole disk) were removed. Information in the disktab file was used to figure "optimal" block placement on the disk, not necessarily contiguous placement.

NOTE: By default, */etc/disktab* is no longer used by *newfs*. See the *newfs* man page for default geometries used. While the default geometries *may* cause performance degradation as compared to their use on pre-10.0 systems, disk geometries usually have little impact on the performance of modern disks.

10.6.1.3   HFS Block Allocation Policies

With HFS, the system attempts to allocate the first blocks of the file in the same cylinder group as the directory. When the file size exceeds that which is pointed to by direct pointers, the system places new blocks in a different cylinder group. Therefore, large files are deliberately scattered among multiple cylinder groups. By default, a single file is not allowed to occupy more than 25% of a cylinder group. As the file system becomes full, a block may be placed in any free location.

10.6.1.4   HFS Tunable Parameters

An HFS file system is created with either the *mkfs* command or the *newfs* command, although *newfs* is easier to use. The following can be chosen at creation time:

- Block size (minimum I/O size): default = 8K, choose from 4K, 8K, 16K, 32K, 64K. Larger block sizes improve sequential I/O performance at the cost of consuming buffer cache pages faster, and time to complete I/O. Smaller block sizes improve random I/O performance for small I/Os.
- Fragment size (minimum file size): default = 1K, choose from block size divided by 1, 2, 4, or 8. Larger fragments waste disk space for small files, but improve performance during large file creation. Smaller fragments use less disk space for small files, but degrade performance during file creation when the file size is < block size * 12.
- Cylinders per cylinder group: default = 16, minimum 1, maximum 32. There is little benefit in changing this, except where the file system contains only large files. In this case, increase to 32.
- Bytes per on-disk inode: default = 6144 (10.0), maximum 65536. This determines the maximum number of files per file system. Use of ACLs halves the maximum number of files per file system. Too many inodes wastes disk space. Change this value to 65536 for file systems which contain only a few large files, such as file systems used with databases.

- *Minfree* (minimum free space): default = 10%. New block allocation performance degrades as file system capacity exceeds 90%. Reserved space can be used only by the superuser. *Minfree* often wastes disk space for file systems containing databases because the space is preallocated, and the free space goes unused. For file systems containing only large, preallocated files, set *minfree* to zero.

You can also use the *tunefs* command to adjust the following:

- *Minfree* (see previous list)
- *Maxbpg* (maximum blocks per group): default = 25% of total blocks in CG, maximum 100%. Determines amount of scattering of large files. Increase to 100% for file systems with mostly large files by following these steps:

  - Step 1. Use *tunefs -v* to report the structural values of the file system.
  - Step 2. Look for the parameter *bpg*. This is the number of blocks in the cylinder group.
  - Step 3. Change *maxbpg* by using *tunefs -e <number>*, where *<number>* is the value found in Step 2.

- *Rotdelay* (rotational delay): default = 0 ms in 10.0, driver dependent in previous releases. Determines sequential block placement by using disk rotational speed and an estimate of the time delay for the OS to issue multiple sequential I/O requests. *Rotdelay* should be kept at zero so that files may be allocated contiguously on the disk. For today's disks, there is no longer a need to change the value.

10.6.1.5   HFS Inode Posting Behavior

The HP-UX HFS is more reliable than those provided with other Unix variants. Inodes are posted synchronously to the disk when an important field in the inode is modified (access times, file size, or pointers) causing the file to be inaccessible until the inode is written to disk. This can be seen in *glance/gpm* when processes block on "inode," virtually ensuring the structural integrity of the file system even if the system crashes.

Default posting behavior can be modified by using the file system mount option *fs_async* or by setting the kernel tunable parameter *fs_async* = 1. Although using this option *may* significantly improve performance, it is risky. If the system crashes, *fsck* may be unable to repair the file system, or at a minimum, some data will be lost. Since changing this parameter affects all file systems system-wide, it is recommended that the *mount* option be used instead, and only for those file systems where the risk is acceptable, such as a temporary file system.

10.6.1.6   HFS Mount Options

The following options may be used with the *mount* command to control the behavior of some aspects of HFS file systems:

- *-o behind*: Enables asynchronous write behavior for blocks in which the last byte has been written (default on Series 700). This is useful when buffers will not be modified again soon.

- *-o delayed*: Enables delayed write behavior for all dirty blocks unless the file is opened with O_SYNC (default on Series 800). This is useful when buffers are frequently modified

- *-o fs_async*: Enables delayed posting of modified inodes. There is a trade-off between potential data integrity problems if the system crashes and improved performance. This option is useful for temporary file systems, in cases where files grow, or when they are modified rapidly. This is a **high risk**. option.

- *-o no_fs_async*: Enables synchronous posting of modified inodes (default). There is a trade-off between increased writes and possible loss of structural integrity. This is the **lowest risk** option.

NOTE: Neither *fs_async* nor *no_fs_async* affects how data are written; these options only affect how file system metadata are written.

10.6.1.7   HFS syncer

Syncer is the daemon responsible for flushing dirty buffer cache pages to the disk. Its default scheduling of 30 seconds is divided into five intervals. Every six seconds, *syncer* flushes 20% of the dirty pages that are "older" than 30 seconds to disk, attempting to spread the I/Os and to age the buffers sufficiently to ensure that they are finished with.

The scheduling intervals can be adjusted by editing */sbin/init.d/syncer* to change the default. It is possible to reduce the scheduling interval when buffers will not be written to more than once, and increase the scheduling interval when buffers will be modified many times. The trade-off is between the risk of data loss and the possible occurrence of disk bottleneck problems.

NOTE: *syncer* calls *sync(2)*, which initiates a *sync* of all virtual file systems.

10.6.2   JFS

The Journaled File System (JFS) is a newer alternative to HFS. JFS has the following characteristics:

- *Fsck* is faster due to the use of an intent log.
- Intent log contains recently committed file system metadata and (optional) data.
- Size of intent log is configurable.
- Performance of JFS varies with the application and may differ from HFS performance.

• If used for the root file system, */stand* must be a mount point, must be *lvol1*, and must be HFS.

10.6.2.1 JFS Structures

JFS uses allocation units, extents, and blocks. An allocation unit is similar to an HFS cylinder group. Extents are groups of blocks occupying contiguous space on the disk; they default to *variable* length. (OnLine JFS offers a fixed length option.) Indirect extents default to 8 blocks, but may be up to 32 MB with a version 2 layout or larger with a version 3 layout. Blocks are similar to HFS fragments. They default to 1 K, and can be up to 64 K in size. Block size determines the smallest file size, but the extent size determines the size of the I/O, up to a maximum I/O size of 1 MB.

10.6.2.2 JFS File System Layout

The layout consists of primary and redundant superblocks, the intent log, allocation units, maps, extents, and inodes and data blocks. For more information, see the man pages on *fs_vxfs(4)*, *inode_vxfs(4),* and *mkfs_vxfs(1m)*. Figure 10-15 shows the layout graphically.

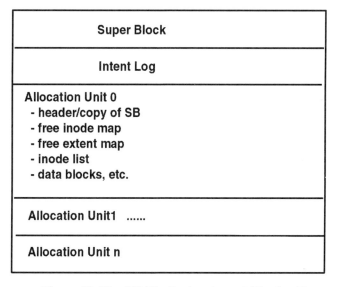

Figure 10-15 JFS File System Layout (Version 2)

Allocation units are similar to cylinder groups; extents are contiguous groups of data blocks.

NOTE: The Version 3 layout differs slightly from what is shown in Figure 10-15, but the differences are not important to this discussion.

JFS inodes are shown in Figure 10-16. The figure shows how pointers to the data blocks are used with the JFS file system. Ten direct pointers each point to one direct data extent whose size varies from one file to another depending on access patterns, I/O size and file system. Indirect pointers always point to 8KB extents containing 2K pointers which point to data blocks. Indirect data extents default to 64KB in size and may be increased. Thus, with a JFS, there is a potential for placing large files in large extents and for fewer I/Os needed to access data..

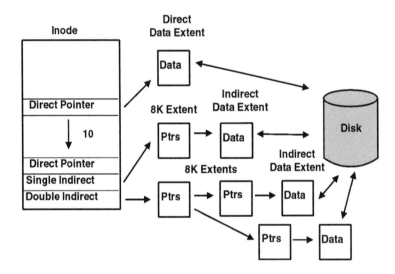

Figure 10-16   JFS Inodes

10.6.2.3   JFS Tunable Parameters

You can create a JFS file system with either *mkfs* or *newfs*. The use of *mkfs* is recommended, however, since it lets you specify a much greater number of the following options:

- *-o inosize=n* (on-disk inode size). Default = 256 bytes, maximum 512. No known reason to change from default.
- *-o bsize=n* (block size [minimum file size]). Default = 1K; choose from 1, 2, 4, or 8K. Larger blocks waste disk space for small files, but improve performance during large file creation.
- *-o ninode=n* (inodes per file system). Default = total # of blocks in FS/4. Increase if average file size < 4 blocks; decrease if average file size > 4 blocks
- *-o nau=n* (number of allocation units—AUs—per FS). Default <= 8; it is suggested not to exceed 10 for overhead reasons. More AUs should improve file locality; fewer AUs should improve performance for large files.

- *-o ausize=n* (size in blocks of AU). Alternative way to specify number of AUs.
- *-o aufirst* and *-o aupad.* Esoteric options for attempting to improve performance by aligning AUs and data blocks on cylinder boundaries.
- *-o logsize=n* (intent log size). Default = 512 blocks; range 32 to 1024. No reason to reduce size of intent log unless very short on space. Increase intent log size if modification rate is too high for posting routine to keep up.

10.6.2.4   JFS Mount Options

The following mount options are used with the *mount -F vxfs* command:

- *-o log.* Enables synchronous posting of modified inodes to the intent log (default). The trade-off is that logging means additional writes to disk (immediate write to the intent log, followed by the inode itself, later); not logging means longer recovery after a system crash. This is the **lowest risk** option.
- *-o delaylog.* Intent log writes are asynchronous. "Double" writes will still occur, but the process does not block while the intent log is being written to; there is a potential performance increase at small additional risk. This is a **low-risk** option.
- *-o tmplog.* Intent log writes are delayed; recent changes will be lost if the system crashes; *fsck* is still quick. This option is recommended for temporary file systems. There is **medium risk**. This option is similar to enabling *fs_async* for an HFS file system.
- *-o nolog.* Disables intent log; full *fsck* required after system crash. The trade-off is potential data integrity problems if the system crashes versus improved performance. This is a **high-risk** option.
- *-o blkclear.* Clears all data extents before allocation. The trade-off here is between increased security preventing access to deleted data versus the loss of performance due to an increased number of writes to clear the extents.
- *-o snapof.* Specifies snapped file system name. Here there is a trade-off between the ability of one process to access data as of a point in time while other processes are updating the data, versus the performance cost of the additional writes needed to copy the original data to the snapshot FS.
- *-o mincache= direct.* All reads and non-O_SYNC writes are unbuffered. This possibly *degrades* performance. The trade-off: reduced need for pages in buffer cache versus process not blocking. Useful for large I/Os direct from the application.
- *-o mincache =dsync.* Converts non-O_SYNC and non-VX_DIRECT writes to data synchronous. Data is posted synchronously but inodes are delayed if only the access times are being changed. This option *degrades* performance. The trade-off is increased data integrity when source code is not available versus performance.
- *-o mincache=tmpcache.* Disables delayed writes and extent clears when file is extended; explicit *fsync(2)* required to post changes. The trade-off is data integrity versus performance. This option is useful for temporary files.

- *-o mincache=closesync*. Enables automatic *fsync(2)* upon file close. The trade-off: risk of compromised file integrity and flurry of writes upon close versus the performance cost of waiting for the writes to be done by *syncer*.
- *-o convosync =direct*. Converts reads and O_SYNC writes to unbuffered. Possibly *improves* performance. The trade-off is a reduced need for pages in the buffer cache versus the process always blocking. This option is useful for large I/Os direct from the application; saves data copy
- *-o convosync=closesync*. Converts O_SYNC writes to delayed with *fsync* at close. The trade-off is between increased performance when source code is not available versus a possible loss of data integrity. This is a **high-risk** option if application robustness depends upon synchronous writes.
- *-o convosync = dsync*. Converts O_SYNC writes to data synchronous. Data is posted synchronously, but inodes are delayed if only access times are being changed. This option improves performance. It is an excellent **low-risk** choice for database and other file systems where files are preallocated; otherwise, it is **medum-risk** if access times are not critical.
- *-o convosync=delay*. Converts O_SYNC writes to delayed writes. *Improves* performance. The trade-off is increased performance when source code is not available versus a possible loss of data integrity; *high risk* if application robustness depends upon synchronous writes.
- *-o datainlog*. Posts O_SYNC writes to intent log as well as inode changes involving access times (default). The trade-off: disk heads stay over intent log longer versus potential increased performance by writing data only once with higher potential head movement (inodes to intent log, data directly to extents)
- *-o nodatainlog*. Posts O_SYNC writes of the data directly to the file. This is analogous to HFS behavior. *Improves* performance. The trade-off: fewer writes with possibly increased head movement versus double writes with less head moves.

10.6.2.5   JFS System Processes

The following system processes handle the flushing of buffers and other activities for JFS file systems in HP-UX 10.x:

- vx_sched_thread
- vx_iflush_thread
- vx_inactive_cache_thread
- vx_delxwri_thread
- vx_logflush_thread
- vx_attrsync_thread
- vx_inactive_thread

In HP-UX 11.x, there is a single process, *vxfsd*, that is composed of many threads to perform the various file system management operations.

10.6.3   OnlineJFS

OnlineJFS is an optional product starting with HP-UX 10.01. OnlineJFS requires a JFS file system. OnlineJFS gives the capability of online dynamic file system resizing without unmounting. It lets you create a snapshot file system for online backup by keeping a copy of the original data when modifications occur. There is also a file system defragmentation utility.

OnlineJFS also allows users to define additional *file advisories,* attributes of the file that instruct the file system to behave in particular ways. Advisories permit tuning at the level of the individual file.

10.6.3.1   OnlineJFS File Advisories

File advisories pertain to individual files, not to the file system as a whole. They must be set by the use of *ioctl* calls from an application, and they can be backed up only by JFS backup utilities. Here are the advisories:

- VX_SETCACHEVX_RANDOM. Donotperformread-ahead.Shouldimproveperformanceforran-domly-accessed files and conserve space in the buffer cache.
- VX_SETCACHE VX_SEQ. Perform maximum read-ahead. Should improve performance for sequentially accessed files.
- VX_SETCACHEVX_DIRECT.BypassthebuffercacheifitispagealignedandI/Osizeisamultiple of block size; otherwise default to VX_DSYNC. Should improve performance for large I/O sizes but process blocks.
- VX_SETCACHE VX_NOREUSE.Donotretainbufferpagesinanticipationoffuturereuse.Should free up buffers in the buffer cache more quickly.
- VX_SETCACHEVX_DSYNC.Writedatablockssynchronouslyanddo*not*writetheinodesynchro-nously if only access times have changed. Should improve performance because the inode is not posted to disk synchronously if only the access time has changed. Will *degrade* per-formance if file was not originally opened with O_SYNC.
- VX_SETEXT VX_CONTIGUOUS.Allocatecurrentfilesizecontiguouslyandfixtheextentsize. Should improve performance for large files, and for all files that are accessed sequentially.

In addition to the above, there are other file advisories that do not affect performance.

10.6.3.2   OnlineJFS *fsadm* Utility

The *fsadm* utility features online file system resizing (note that it will not shrink below currently allocated space); reporting on directory and extent fragmentation; and reorganization of directories and extents to reduce fragmentation.

Defragmentation reorganizes directories by placing all subdirectories first, by ordering regular files by decreasing time of last access, and by compacting to remove free space. Defrag-mentation reorganizes extents by:

- Moving aged files to the end of the AU

- Reorganizing non-aged files by minimizing number of extents
- Placing small files together in one contiguous extent
- Placing large files into large extents of at least 64 blocks
- Placing individual files into the same AU to improve locality of reference
- Migrating small files and directories to the front of the AU
- Migrating large files and inactive files to the back of the AU

It is recommended that defragmentation be performed once a day to once a month depending on the volatility of the file system. The trade-off is as follows: a severely fragmented file system will degrade performance, but defragmentation *may take a long time* and will definitely degrade online performance.

10.6.4 Comparison of HFS and JFS

The following table shows a summary of the two types of file systems, with some of their advantages and disadvantages.

Table 10-3   HFS and JFS Characteristics

HFS	JFS
syncer flushes data buffers	*syncer* flushes inodes and data buffers
Metadata is written to the inode synchronously	Metadata is written first to the intent log and later to the inode
Data is wirtten directly to blocks	By default, O_SYNC data is written to the intent log first and later to the extent
Enabling *fs_async* causes metadata to be posted by *syncer* (mount-time option or kernel parameter)	There are many mount-time options to control JFS behavior
High performance for small files	Equal performance for any size file
Low performance for large files (> 96 KB and > 16 MB)	Better performance with large files than HFS

10.6.5 NFS

The Networked File System (NFS) was authored by Sun Microsystems. It provides a mechanism for sharing files across a network. NFS tends to consume in-core inodes on the server. Performance is affected by:

- Number of *nfsd* daemons on the server. This can be adjusted by tuning NUM_NFSD in */etc/rc.config.d/nfsconf*. The default is 4; there is no performance hit for configuring too many, other than *nproc* limit
- Number of *biod* daemons on the clients. This can be adjusted by tuning NUM_NFSIOD in */etc/rc.config.d/nfsconf*. The default is 4. A heuristic for an appropriate setting is the number of concurrent files open for writing
- Export option
- Various mount options

10.6.6 NFS Options

You can configure export options on the NFS server and mount options on the NFS client. Some of these have performance implications.

10.6.6.1 NFS Export Options on the Server

The *async* option when set in the */etc/exports* file enables asynchronous writes. The *biod* process only waits until the data has been written to the buffer cache on the server by the *nfsd* process. The trade-off is potential data integrity problems if the server crashes after it has replied to the client, versus improvement of write performance. This is a **medium-risk** option, depending on application needs.

The default is synchronous writes. The *biod* process waits until the data has been written to the disk by the *nfsd* process and file system. Note that the process does not wait while the *biod* sends the write to the server.

10.6.6.2 NFS Mount Options on the Client

The following options to the *mount* command have performance implications:

- *-o acdirmax* or *-o acregmax*. Retain directory cache and inodes on the client for a maximum of 60 seconds (the default) if not modified. The trade-off is potential data integrity problems versus the frequency of inode reads from the server. Use the *getattr* metric in the NFS screen of *glance/gpm*.
- *-o acdirmin* or *-o acregmin*. Retain directory cache and inodes on the client for a minimum of 30 seconds for directories and 3 seconds for inodes if not modified.
- *-o noac* or *-o nocto*. Suppress inode and name lookup caching. Suppress inode rereads upon file open. The trade-off is the risk of stale information versus quick file reopens and I/Os.
- *-o rsize*. Set NFS read buffer size (default 8KB).
- *-o wsize*. Set NFS write buffer size (default 8KB) When buffers are smaller than blocksize, multiple I/Os are required. Make sure that wsize is >= the file system block size.
- *-o timeo*. Set NFS timeout (.7 sec default). Decreasing the timeout increases network traffic.

10.7 Disk Metrics

A variety of global and per-process disk metrics are available for identifying potential bottlenecks in disk I/O.

10.7.1 Global Disk Saturation Metrics

The only global memory saturation metric is the per-disk utilization metric provided by *glance* and *gpm*. Unfortunately, this is an unreliable metric for the following reasons:

- The metric refers only to the busiest disk.
- 100% utilization does *not* mean that more I/Os are not possible. 100% utilization means that each time the disk queue length is inspected, there are one or more I/Os in the queue. There could be one I/O or a hundred. It does *not* mean that the disk is fully saturated, merely that it is busy.
- The metric does not reflect the size of the queue. It merely means that there is always at least one I/O pending for the busiest disk.

10.7.2 Global Disk Queue Metrics

There are two global disk queue metrics, visible in *glance* and *gpm* only:

- Per-disk I/O queue length
- Number of processes blocked on Disk, I/O, Buffer Cache, Inodes

10.7.3 Other Global Disk Metrics

A variety of other global metrics reported by *GlancePlus* include:

- All disks (Disk Report-d), which includes:
    - Logical and physical read and write rates
    - User, VM, system, and raw I/O rates
    - Remote logical and physical read and write rates
    - Read and write cache hit rates
    - Directory name lookup cache hit rates
- I/O by File System Report (i), including:
    - Logical and physical I/O rates
    - For selected file systems

    a. Logical and physical read and write rates

    b. Logical and physical read and write bytes

    c. Mapping information
- I/O by Disk Report (u)
    - Utilization

    - Queue length

    - KB/sec

    - Logical and physical read and write rates

    - I/O rates

    - For selected disk drives

       a. Logical and physical read and write rates

       b. Logical and physical read and write bytes

       c. Queue length and utilization

       d. Mapping information

• I/O by Logical Volume Report (v)

    - LV read and write rates

    - For selected file systems

       a. Read and write rates

       b. Read and write bytes

       c. MWC hits and misses

       d. Mapping information

10.7.4 Per-Process Disk Metrics

The following per-process disk metrics are available. The amount of information is much more limited than the information available in the global metrics.

• Logical and physical read and write rates
• File system read and write rates
• VM read and write rates
• System read and write rates
• Raw read and write rates
• Byte transfer rate
• Remote logical and physical read/write rate

10.7.5 Typical Metric Values

Disk utilization metrics are misleading, because the graph shows only the busiest disk, and displaying it does not mean that it is incapable of more I/O. The Physical disk queue is the most meaningful metric: consistent queue lengths > 4 are indicators of bottlenecks.

Use logical and physical rates and buffer cache hit rates to check for the lack of repeated accesses, indicated by a read cache hit ratio < 90%, or a write cache hit ratio < 70%. Then use other metrics to drill down to the causes of physical I/O.

To determine whether the inode table or the buffer cache may be the problem, look at global and process wait states. Note that the cause of a problem may be usage (for example, O_SYNC) rather than too small a size.

Core dumps show up as physical I/O, user I/O and system CPU, but the file does not show up as open. Remember that memory-mapped file I/O shows up as *virtual memory* I/O.

10.8 Types of Disk Bottlenecks

As with other types of bottlenecks, the four types are:

- Saturation—indicated by 100% disk utilization on one or more disks
- Queue—indicated by *large* per-disk queues *sustained over time* or a high percentage of processes blocked on disk, cache, or inode
- Starvation—less than 100% CPU utilization, and memory bottlenecks
- User satisfaction—poor transaction response time

10.9 Expensive System Calls

Here are the expensive system calls for basic I/O:

- fsync()
- open
- stat
- sync

For NFS:
- open()
- Slow reads and writes

10.10 Tuning Disk Bottlenecks

The three ways of tuning disk bottlenecks include hardware solutions, configuration solutions, and application solutions

10.10.1 Hardware Solutions

There are a variety of hardware solutions, all of which can be thought of as "spending money" solutions. Here are a few common approaches:

- Add disks drives and rebalance the I/O load.
- Add disk adapters and rebalance the I/O load.
- Use faster disks.
- Use faster disk links (e.g., F/W SCSI versus SCSI).
- Use dual device controllers, if applicable.
- Switch from disk arrays to stand-alone disks.
- Use mirroring (stand-alone or arrays) to improve read performance.

10.10.2 Configuration Solutions

This set of solutions requires additional study of the existing configuration, as well as some trial and error to obtain the right results.

- Rebalance the I/O load across available disks and adapters.
- Use LVM disk striping if the I/O pattern warrants.
- Dedicate disks to a single application.
- Switch from file system to raw I/O.
- Use the *async* disk pseudo driver for raw I/O, if appropriate.
- Switch from JFS to HFS or vice versa.
- Tune the file system.
- Adjust the mount options.
- Change block size and other tunables.
- Change OnLineJFS file advisories.
- Minimize the use of symbolic link.
- Start with a clean, empty file system.
- Stop using *ksh* or Posix shell history files.

10.10.3 File System Solutions

Another set of approaches to tuning depends on the type of file system you are using. For HFS file systems, you can

- Defragment the file system by backing it up, recreating it, and then restoring it.
- Use *newfs* and *tunefs* to set block size, cg size, and *maxbpg*.
- Use *newfs* to reduce the number of inodes.

For JFS file systems:

- Use *fsadm* to defragment the file system.
- Try switching to direct I/O.
- Try switching O_SYNC to data synchronous if risk is acceptable.
- Try mounting temporary file systems with *-o tmplog*.

For NFS file systems:

- Increase the # of *nfsd* and *biod* daemons.
- Try switching to *async* writes on the server if risk is acceptable.

10.10.4 Application Solutions

Finally, there are application solutions:

- Review application I/O sizes and access patterns.
- Use relative path names.
- Preallocate files.
- Do not use `O_SYNC` if application integrity can be maintained.

10.11 Database Issues

The following tuning suggestions apply to databases and database applications, which have somewhat unique features and performance needs.

10.11.1 Use Raw Volumes

It is often recommended to use raw volumes with the async disk pseudo driver rather than file systems. File systems have the following disadvantages that are troublesome for databases:

- I/Os are double buffered (buffer cache).
- I/O size mismatches can cause read-modify-write.
- Large file fragmentation or scattering frequently occurs.
- Indirect pointers are used.
- There is additional OS overhead.
- File system recovery time is required after a system crash
- Files can be inadvertently removed.

There are disadvantages to raw volumes as well. These are relatively minor in comparison, but are often "emotional" issues rather than technical ones:

- Raw volumes require special backup tools.
- Moving objects to different disks requires deletion and recreation.
- Objects are not visible through simple Unix commands.

If you are using the file system, use a large buffer cache and possibly smaller shared memory segment. If using raw volumes, use a small buffer cache and large shared memory segment.

10.11.2 Data Placement Recommendations

The following are some recommendations for placing database elements on disk:

- Place tables and indices on different disks.
- Place logfiles on a separate group of disks.
- Place tables that are accessed concurrently on different disks.
- Place temporary disk areas (used for sorting) on separate disks.
- Stripe large tables across multiple disks.
- Don't stripe indiscriminately.

• Don't use LVM or hardware striping *and* database striping together.

10.11.3 Review and Tune Database Parameters

Here are a few more general suggestions for tuning the database:

• Tune the database parameters.
• Use the database performance monitors.
• Review locking methods (database, table, page, row).
• LVM mirroring is typically much more efficient than database mirroring (reduced system calls).
• Database striping features *may* be better than LVM striping, because the database "knows" where the data and holes are.
• The JFS intent log provides no benefit to databases, because database size and structure seldom change, and the database does its own logging anyway.
• If using JFS, direct I/O might improve performance.

10.11.4 Lock Database Shared Memory Segment

Use the following code to lock a shared memory segment. First, run the *ipcs* command to obtain the shared memory segment id, then pass the id to this program::

```
#include <sys/shm.h>
#include <errno.h>
main (argc,argv)
int argc;
char **argv;
{
    int shmid;
    int error;
            /* pass shm ID in run string */
    shmid = atoi (argv[1]);
    error = shmat(shmid,0,0);
    if (error == -1) {
        perror("shmattach:  ");
        exit(1);
        }
    error = shmctl(shmid,SHM_LOCK,0);
    if (error == -1) {
        perror ("shmctl:  ");
        exit(2);
        }
    error = shmdt(shmid);
    exit(0);
}
```

10.12 Disk Related Tunable Parameters

The following disk-related parameters may be tuned. In HP-UX 10.0 and later systems, they are found in */etc/conf/master.d/**.

- *bufpages*
- *create_fastlinks*
- *dbc_max_pct*
- *dbc_min_pct*
- *default_disk_ir* (10.X only)
- *maxfiles*
- *maxfiles_lim*
- *maxswapchunks*
- *maxvgs*
- *nbuf*
- *nfile*
- *ninode* (keep < 4096)
- *no_lvm_disks* (10.X only)

10.12.1 bufpages and nbuf

Bufpages and *nbuf* are used together to control whether a file system is of fixed size or is dynamically sized. When *bufpages* = *nbuf* = 0, the buffer cache is dynamically sized, subject to the limits specified in *dbc_max_pct* and *dbc_min_pct*. The performance of commercial applications is often improved by fixing the size of the buffer cache to an optimal value. It is easiest to set *bufpages* equal to the number of 4KB buffers in the buffer cache. If you don't know what size to pick, a good starting point would be 10%–20% of physical memory. Use the formula

bufpages = n*physmem/4096

where *physmem* is the size of physical memory in bytes and *n* is between .10 and .20.

If you choose a dynamic buffer cache, by leaving *bufpages* = *nbuf* = 0, the kernel starts with a size of *dbc_min_pct* (default 5%) of physical memory, and can grow to *dbc_max_pct* (default 50%) of physical memory. On large memory systems (512 MB or more), setting *dbc_max_pct* to 50% may cause excessive VM paging and, possibly, deactivations. It is better to set *dbc_max_pct* to 20% on large memory systems until there is a clear need for a larger value.

10.12.2 create_fastlinks

The *create_fastlinks* parameter is used to control whether symbolic link names less than 60 characters in length are stored in the inode, in place of the pointers, thus saving a disk I/O when the link is referenced.

10.12.3 nfile

The size of *nfile* should be increased, as necessary, to support the needs of the application to open many files. Use *sar*, *glance*, or *gpm* to determine when to increase this value.

10.12.4 ninode

The value of *ninode* should be increased only when absolutely necessary. It is used to size the in-core HFS inode table and indirectly the in-core JFS inode table, which starts at *ninode*/2 but grows dynamically as needed. The algorithm used to access the HFS in-core inode table degrades in performance when the table has more than 4096 entries. Remember that this table is a cache of the inodes of currently and previously opened HFS files. Even when it appears full, it may not be necessary to increase its size, because the inodes of closed files are flushed to make room for newly opened files. Increase the size if:

- You see application errors
- Applications often repeatedly open and close a large number of files
- There is a console error message "inode table overflow"
- You see overflows for the inode table in the output of s*ar -v*

10.12.5 maxvgs

You will need to increase *maxvgs* if you want to create more than ten LVM volume groups.

10.12.6 maxfiles

The *maxfiles* parameter controls the maximum size of the per-process file descriptor table, and defaults to 60. Some applications require more than 60 file descriptors. Since the algorithm for accessing the table is inefficient when the table gets large, it is better, if possible, to increase the size of the table only for those applications that need it. You do this by modifying the application code to call *getrlimit(2)* and *setrlimit(2)*.

10.12.7 default_disk_ir, maxfiles_lim, and no_lvm_disks

It should not be necessary and it is not recommended to change the values of these parameters.

10.12.8 HFS Specific Tunable Parameters

There is only one HFS-specific tunable parameter, *fs_async*. This is a frequently misunderstood parameter. People often think it controls whether data from an HFS file system in the buffer cache is written synchronously or asynchronously. In fact, it refers to how HFS meta-data (superblocks and inodes) are written.

By default, when *fs_async* is set to 0, HFS meta-data is written synchronously; that is, any time meta-data changes, it is written synchronously to the disk, thus blocking any other I/Os to that file (inode) or file system (superblock) until the physical I/O completes. This default behavior is intended to ensure structural integrity of the HFS file system in case of a system crash. However, it does so at the expense of diminished system and application performance.

Setting *fs_async* to 1 is generally very risky, although it can substantially improve performance. It is recommended that you leave this parameter at 0. If you are willing to accept the increase in risk that file system structural integrity cannot be repaired by *fsck(1m)* after a system crash, you should change this value on a per-file system basis, using the *-o fsasync* option with the *mount* command.

10.12.9 JFS Specific Tunable Parameters

In HP-UX 10.0, there are no JFS-specific tunable parameters. However, recent 11.0 extension media have added some new tunable parameters:

- *vx_ncsize*—This is used to size the kernel file system directory name lookup cache (DNLC), which improves performance for frequently accessed directories. Default is 1024. This parameter was added because the structure was originally sized based on *ninode*, which is the size of the HFS in-core inode table. The DNLC is now sized based on both HFS and JFS needs. Usually, this parameter does not need to be changed.
- *vxfs_ra_per_disk*—Controls the maximum number of read-aheads on a given disk with JFS file systems. Default is 1024. Usually, this parameter does not need to be changed.
- *vxfs_max_ra_kbytes*—Controls the maximum bytes for a read-ahead operation during sequential access of a file. Default is 1024. For applications or systems where there are many large sequential I/Os, it may be useful to increase this value to 65536 (64KB).

Application Tuning

Part 4 introduces the complex topic of application tuning. Tuning the operating system is not always enough; it is equally important to understand application design when evaluating the performance of existing applications, and to design for performance when creating new applications. The chapters are:

- Compiler Optimization
- Designing Applications for Performance
- Application Profiling

Compiler Optimization

One technique for improving performance in executable code is optimization at the compiler and linker levels. Compiler optimization creates machine code that is more efficient for each unit of compilation. Linker level optimization can create more efficient programs at higher levels than that of the compilation unit. Here are the topics covered in this chapter:

- Compilers and optimization
- Optimization levels
- Compiling for a target architecture
- Other compiler and linker options
- Why does optimization "break" applications?
- Debugging optimization problems
- Options for Fortran and COBOL
- Profile-based optimization
- Porting applications
- Code to demonstrate optimization effects

Note that compiler optimization only fixes performance problems relating to CPU and memory. As with any kind of performance tuning, there are tradeoffs, and these will be described in detail.

11.1 Compilers and Optimization

Compiler optimization uses compiler command options or directives to perform specific types of code modification as the compiler is building object code. For most compilers, the first step is the creation of System Low Level Intermediate Code (SLLIC), which the optimizer then modifies in specific ways. Depending on the optimization level you choose, the optimizer may create object code directly, or it may output *ucode*, another intermediate level of code that can be further optimized at link time when the scope of the optimization is broader.

Figure 11-1 shows the relationship of various programming languages, compilers and the linker.

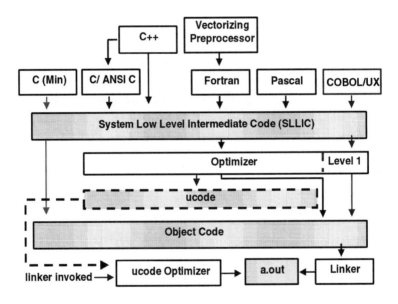

Figure 11-1   Languages, Compilers, and Optimization

Optimization is invoked with command line options, or through the use of compiler directives embedded in the source code.

11.1.1 Advantages and Disadvantages of Optimization

The use of compiler optimization has many advantages (+):

+ Ensures the optimal use of registers.
+ Takes advantage of processor parallelism, tailoring the code to run with a specific pipeline, coprocessor architecture, or multiple computational units, if available. The goal is to achieve as much parallelism as possible.

+ Reduces memory accesses. Remember that loading from cache may require one or two cycles, whereas loading from memory may require as many as 60 cycles or more. This is a vital area of performance improvement. Keeping something in a register that will soon be accessed again can significantly improve performance.

+ Improves application performance as much as 200% to 300% for typical commercial and technical applications, and by as much as 1000% for some scientific and engineering applications.

There are also disadvantages (-) to optimization:

- Optimization is not the default compiler behavior, and people easily forget to use it.

- Optimizing may cause applications to break, especially at Level 2 or greater.

- Optimized code consumes significant resources during compilation. Optimization uses more CPU time, virtual memory, and disk bandwidth at compile time.

- Optimized code is more difficult to debug, because code is rearranged and/or removed.

- The standard C compiler does not optimize; only the optional ANSI C compiler can optimize.

- Compiling for specific CPU models may cause degradation when the executable is run on different models.

- Optimization Levels 3 and 4 are not compatible with symbolic debugging; you can debug code optimized at Level 3 or 4 only at the assembly language level.

11.2 Optimization Levels

Table 11-1 shows the basic optimization levels that are included in many compilers, and indicates how they are invoked:

Table 11-1 Compiler Optimization Levels

Level	Description	Command Line Option	C Directive	Fortran Directive
0	No optimization. This is the default	none	#pragma optimize off	$Optimize off
1	Local optimization within block boundaries only	+O1	#pragma opt_level 1	$Optimize level 1 on
2	Global optimization within procedures only	-O or +O2	#pragma opt_level 2	$Optimize level 2 on

Table 11-1   Compiler Optimization Levels (Continued)

Level	Description	Command Line Option	C Directive	Fortran Directive
3	Full optimization across all procedures within a single file	+O3	#pragma opt_level 3	$Optimize level 3 on
4	Full optimization across the entire application program. This also involves linker optimization	+O4	#pragma opt_level 4	$Optimize level 4 on

11.2.1   Level 0 Optimization

Level 0 optimization, the default, only optimizes a little. The compiler only carries out constant folding and simple register allocation. Here is an example of constant folding that takes place when the compiler converts from source code to object code:

```
x = 3 * 5
```

is replaced by

```
x = 15
```

Since the value of the product of two constants does not vary as the program executes, the answer is a constant.

11.2.2   Level 1 Optimization (+O1)

Level 1 optimization is sometimes called *local* or *peephole optimization* because it can only be carried out on a small visible window of the application, namely, a basic block of code. In a typical piece of code having *if*, *then*, and *else* statements, each of these statements represents one block of code, resulting in a very narrow window. The following code shows examples of basic blocks inside boxes:

```
if ( i < 3 || i > 5 ) {

        j = i * 5;
        k = j + 6;
}
else {

        j = 3;
        k = 9;

}
```

Local optimization requires very little additional compile time, and does result in better register allocation and branch optimization. It performs simple instruction scheduling, and eliminates dead (impossible to execute) code. There is a low risk of breaking the application with Level 1 optimization.

11.2.3   Level 2 Optimization (-O or +O2)

Level 2 optimization is also known as global optimization. It requires longer compile times—twice as long or more. The optimization occurs across block boundaries, but is limited to the procedure level only. Level 2 initializes uninitialized variables to zero, and analyzes loops, expressions, data flow and memory usage. It attempts to find ways to minimize memory references, and to control how long a variable stays in a register. It may move loop invariant code from an inner loop to an outer loop or to a place outside the loop. It also performs advanced constant folding.

Two especially important techniques of optimization at Level 2 are loop unrolling and software pipelining.

11.2.3.1   Loop Unrolling

Loop unrolling changes the stride or increment in a loop and duplicates some code in an effort to reduce pipeline flushes due to top-of-loop branching. (Remember that pipeline flushes are inefficient; refer to Chapter 7, "Hardware Performance Issues.") This is most helpful for tight loops with few instructions and many iterations. The default loop unroll factor is 4; this can be changed on the command line with the option *+Oloop_unroll=<n>*. This technique, also used in the Fortran optimizing preprocessor, trades off increased memory consumption for reduced CPU utilization. The following example shows how a loop may be unrolled:

```
for (i=0;i<6000;i++) {
    x[i]=y[i]*z[i];
    }
```

becomes

```
for (i=0;i<6000;i=i+4;){
    x[i]   = y[i]   * z[i];
    x[i+1] = y[i+1] * z[i+1];
    x[i+2] = y[i+2] * z[i+2];
    x[i+3] = y[i+3] * z[i+3];
    }
```

11.2.3.2   Software Pipelining

Software pipelining optimizes loops by rearranging the order in which instructions are executed. It attempts to overlap operations from different loop iterations. Pipelining is effective only for instructions that reference floats and doubles, because these instructions may take multiple cycles to complete. The goal is to avoid CPU stalls due to memory or pipeline latencies.

Pipelining moves a portion of the loop code to a position before the loop, and moves a portion of the last iteration to a position after the loop. The loop is unrolled twice, and operations from different iterations are interleaved. The following is an example:

```
float x[10000], y[10000];
int i;
for (i = 0 ; i  <= 10000 ; i++); {
    x[i] = x[i] / y[i] + 4.0
    }
```

This is transformed into something like the following:

```
r1 = 0                          initialize array index
r2 = 4.0                        load constant
r3 = y[0]                       load first y value
r4 = x[0]                       load first x value
r5 = r4 / r3                    divide (multiple cycles to complete)
loop:  do {

                                Unroll level 1:

r6 = r1                         save current array index
r1++                            increment array index
r7 = x[r1]                      current x
r8 = y[r1]                      current y
r9 = r5 + r2                    add prior row (after divide is complete)
r10 = r7 / r8                   divide current row
x[r6] = r9                      save result of prior addition
r6 = r1                         save current array index
r1++                            increment array index

                                Unroll level 2:

r3 = y[r1]                      load next y value
r4 = x[r1]                      load next x value
r11 = r10 + r2                  add current row
r5 = r4 / r3                    divide next row
x[r6] = r11                     save result of current row
}  while (r1 <= 10000)          end of loop

r9 = r5 + r2                    add last row
x[r6] = r9                      save result of last row
```

11.2.3.3   Level 2 Min and Max with the Fortran Compiler

In Fortran, you can specify minimum and maximum optimization at level 2. Minimum optimization turns off dangerous assumptions about the source code. Maximum optimization turns these assumptions on. There is a greater risk of breaking the application with Level 2 Maximum. Assumptions are further described later. See "Why Does Optimization "Break" Applications?" on page 257.

11.2.4 Level 3 Optimization (+O3)

Level 3 optimization is also known as inter-procedural optimization because it does full optimization across all procedures within a single source file. Techniques used at level 3 include transforming loops for improved cache access, and procedure in-lining (described in the next section). These transformations may result in code expansion, although the code will run faster.

11.2.4.1   Procedure Inlining

Inlining replaces a procedure call with the actual code, which results in code expansion. However, there is no procedure calling convention overhead, which may be significant, especially when the procedure is short. The process uses more memory, but it decreases the use of CPU. It may also reduce the number of cache faults, page faults, and longjump operations.

11.2.5   Level 4 Optimization (+O4)

Level 4 optimization includes full inter-procedural optimization, as well as support for linker level optimization. (See the section on Linker Optimization below.)

Level 4 provides full optimization across an entire application program, including procedure in-lining and global and static variable optimization (described in the next section). Level 4 transformations can result in an executable that consumes a large amount of virtual memory (about 1.25 MB per 1000 lines of non-commented source code). However, it usually results in significantly faster execution.

11.2.5.1   Global and Static Variable Optimization

The goal of this technique is to reduce the number of instructions required for accessing global and static variables. Normally, two instructions are generated to reference a global variable. Depending on the locality of the global variables, it may be possible to use a single "load offset" instruction. The linker rearranges the storage location of global and static variables to increase the number of variables that can be accessed with a single instruction. When using this level of optimization, you should *avoid* some common though undesirable programming practices:

• Making assumptions about relative storage location of variables

• Relying on pointer or address comparisons between variables

• Making assumptions about the alignment of variables

11.2.6   Linker Optimization

Linker optimization is invoked with the +*O4*, +*Oprocelim* and +*Ofastaccess* options of the *ld* command. In order to use linker optimization, you need to use interprocedural optimization options with the compiler (-*Wl*, -*O*, or +*O3* and higher) at compile time. These options result in the generation of *ucode* rather than object code, and the final optimization is deferred until link time. Optimization is done across the entire program. Global and static variables are optimized by rearranging the variable address so as to be referenceable by an offset, saving one instruction for each reference.

11.2.7 Finer Control over Optimization

The following options allow you to obtain additional control over the optimizer. The default values are shown in the list; use the *no* modifier to turn off a particular option. See the compiler man page and/or the compiler reference manual for details.

- *+Oinitcheck*—variable initialization
- *+Oparmsoverlap*—assumption
- *+Onovolatile*—keep variables in registers
- *+Oinline*—procedure inlining
- *+Onolibcalls*—inlining of particular library call and use of math millicode routines
- *+Omoveflops*—conditional floating point in loops
- *+Opipeline*—software pipelining
- *+Onoentrysched*—instruction scheduling at entry/exit
- *+Onoregionsched*—aggressive instruction scheduling
- *+Onosignedpointers*—signed pointer usage
- *+Onosideeffects*—assumption
- *+Oregreassoc*—register reassociation
- *+Onofastaccess*—linker optimization for global data; default is *fastaccess* with +O4
- *+Ofltacc*—floating point precision tradeoff
- *+Onoinfo*—information about optimizations that are being made

11.2.8 Tradeoffs Between Memory Expansion and CPU Utilization

Additional compiler options allow you to specify your preference in the tradeoff between memory and CPU:

- *+Olimit*—suppresses optimizations that significantly increase compile time or consume a lot of memory. This is the default.
- *+Onolimit*—allows optimizations that significantly increase compile time or consume a lot of memory.
- *+Osize*—suppresses optimizations that significantly increase code size.
- *+Onosize*—allows optimizations that significantly increase code size. This is the default.

11.3 Compiling for a Target Architecture

In designing applications, you may or may not know what kind of system will run them. On HP-UX systems, you can use specific compiler options to indicate either a specific architecture or a range of architectures. You can specify either the model number as returned from the *uname* command or the PA revision number. Refer to the file */opt/langtools/lib.sched.models* for a list of HP 9000 systems.

Two particular options are of use in specifying the architecture: *+DA* and *+DS*.

11.3.1 +DA

The *+DA* option lets you specify the instruction set that should be used. It is important to set this option correctly, since code compiled for higher level architecture will not execute on lower levels. Different levels generate a different magic number in the *a.out* file. As a rule, you should choose the lowest level where code must execute. However, code will execute slower on newer systems if a lower level instruction set is chosen. Choices are *+DA1.0*, *+DA1.1*, and *+DA2.0*. You can also use *+DAportable*, which runs on both PA 1.1 only and PA 2.0.

For instance, if your application must run on PA 1.0, PA 1.1, and PA 2.0 systems, use *+DA1.0*. However, if the application will be used only with PA 2.0 systems, use *+DA2.0*, so that it makes use of all the instructions available on PA 2.0 systems. Choosing the wrong value will have one of two results:

- The code will not execute at all on certain systems; or
- The code will run less efficiently than it might otherwise.

The default value is the architecture of the system where the compilation is occurring.

11.3.2 +DS

The *+DS* option lets you specify the instruction scheduling level. No matter what level is chosen, code will execute on all systems, although not optimally. Choose the level where the code will most commonly execute, specifying the model number of the system, or PA 1.0, 1.1a, 1.1b, 1.1c, 1.1d, 1.1e, or 2.0.

Choosing the wrong value will result only in less efficient code. The code will still run on all systems. Moreover, systems using newer architecture (PA 2.0 and later) provide out-of-order execution for instruction bundles. This minimizes the need for choosing a particular scheduling level.

11.4 Other Compiler and Linker Options

This section lists a few additional options. The first group permits notification of floating point traps. By default, the application is not notified of floating point traps; therefore, it may be producing incorrect results or performing poorly due to trap handling. The *+FP* compiler option can be used to provide floating point traps. The following options may be used at link or compile time, and may be changed at run time by using *fpgetround(3M)*:

- *+FPV*—enable signal on invalid FO operations (IEEE FP)
- *+FPZ*—enable signal on divide by zero
- *+FPO*—enable signal on floating point overflow
- *+FPU*—enable signal on floating point underflow
- *+FPI*—enable signal on inexact results (e.g., 1./3.).

- *+FPD*—enable sudden underflow of denormalized values
  - Flushes denormalized values to zero in hardware
  - Eliminates software traps for denormalized calculations
  - Undefined on PA 1.0
  - May significantly improve computation performance
  - May produce inaccurate results when performing arithmetic operations on several very small numbers

Note that integer overflow does not generate an error in C; integer divide by zero generates a floating point exception (SIGFPE) in C. Integer overflow and divide by zero do not generate an error in Fortran unless enabled with the ON statement. Example:

```
ON integer div 0 abort
ON integer overflow abort
```

These examples also require the use of the `$Check_overflow` directive.

11.5 Why Does Optimization "Break" Applications?

As indicated earlier in this chapter, optimization can sometimes break an application that executes correctly without optimization. Why does this happen? The most frequent reason is that the code violates the assumptions that the optimizer makes about the language. Sometimes the code does not conform to language standards. In other cases, code is poorly structured, or expects architecture-dependent behavior that is not applicable. This problem is typical of old code that has not been modified to run on a newer machine. Other assumptions involve local variables appearing as static, and the automatic zero initialization of variables.

Optimizer assumptions are language dependent as well as optimization level dependent. A few generalizations are provided in the next sections. For details about which assumptions a compiler is making, refer to the appropriate language reference manual.

11.5.1 C and ANSI C Assumptions

These compilers assume knowledge of all variable references; however, this may be violated with shared memory or signal handlers. There is also an assumption that the application does not dereference a pointer with the & operator, or dereference a pointer outside object boundaries.

The compilers also assume that all functions *might* modify global variables; this assumption can be changed by using the statement

```
#pragma no_side_effects
```

To keep your code consistent with the compiler's assumptions, you should *avoid* the following programming practices:

- Referencing outside the bounds of an array
- Referencing outside the bounds of an object (structure)
- Passing the incorrect number of arguments to a function (exception: VARARGS)
- Accessing an array in an array subscript. See the compiler manual or man page for clarification.
- Using variables that are accessed by external processes or are modified asynchronously unless declared with the volatile attribute (for example, in shared memory, or through signal handlers)
- Using local variables before they are initialized
- Relying on a memory layout scheme when manipulating pointers

11.5.2 Fortran Assumptions

The optimizer makes a number of assumptions about Fortran code. It assumes there are no parameter overlaps [as in CALL SUBA (L, L, N), where L is used twice]. It assumes no side effects; in other words, that procedures modify only local variables. Further assumptions are that there are no parameter type mismatches, no external parameters, no shared parameters, no floating invariants, and no hidden pointer aliasing

11.6 Debugging Optimization Problems

The following steps are suggested for debugging problems that appear after optimization:

1. Determine the level at which optimization is breaking the application. Most likely, it will be Level 2.
2. Coding with *#pragma* statements, use the binary search method to find the portion of code that is responsible:
   - Compile half at the lower optimization level.
   - Compile half at the higher optimization level.
   - Keep splitting the problem source code in half, repeating the process until the problem is found.
3. Once you have found the problematic source procedures, decide whether to fix the source or compile only the problematic procedure at the lower optimization level.

Application profiling can help determine whether a given problem is worth fixing. If an application spends very little time in a procedure that breaks at optimization level 2, then it is better to compile it at level 1 than it is to spend time to fix the problem. On the other hand, optimization problems may actually point out underlying programming errors. Therefore, all optimization problems should at least be reviewed to determine whether the application is providing incorrect results even at the lower optimization level where the problem is not detected.

See Chapter 13 for information about application profiling.

11.7 Options for Fortran and COBOL

11.7.1 Fortran Optimizing Preprocessor

A special Fortran preprocessor performs source code optimization and vectorization. You use the +*OP* and -*WP* options to invoke **ftnopp** to pre-process the source code. The preprocessor is currently supported only for Fortran, and must be invoked at initial compile time. It makes actual changes to the source code, including many special optimizer directives to control optimization. Changes also include the vectorization of DO loops by invoking vector libraries, and the substitution of procedure in-lining and loop unrolling.

Performance of Fortran applications can be significantly improved by using the optimizing preprocessor.

11.7.2 Special COBOL Considerations

There are limitations on the degree to which you can optimize COBOL. The highest optimization level is Level 1 for compiled COBOL; interpreted COBOL cannot be optimized at all.

Various executable formats of COBOL have different performance characteristics:

- <*programname*>.*int*—interpreted. This is the slowest form of COBOL, and cannot be optimized. It needs the COBOL runtime environment. Symbolic debugging may be done with Animator.
- <*programname*>.*gnt*—demand loadable generated native. This form also needs the COBOL runtime environment.
- <*programname*>.*snt*—shareable *gnt*. This also needs the COBOL runtime environment. HP technology was incorporated into the *gnt* format by MicroFocus.
- *a.out*—HP-UX executable, including COBOL runtime linked *int*. This is the fastest format, but has the longest compile time.

Use the following commands and options to obtain the different types of COBOL executables:

To obtain *prog.int*, use *cob prog.cbl*

To obtain *prog.gnt*, use *cob -u prog.cbl*

To obtain *prog.snt*, use *cob +u prog.cbl*

To obtain *a.out* with shared libraries, use *cob -xo prog.cbl*

To obtain *a.out* with archive libraries, use *cob -xo prog.cbl -Q -aarchive*

To provide optimization for any of the above except *prog.int*, use *cob +O1*

11.8 Profile-Based Optimization

Profile based optimization (PBO) is a technique for building an application so that information about its runtime behavior is incorporated into the code during the compile process. You first build a special executable containing instrumentation, and you run it to create a profile database. Then you build again using the profile database.

With PBO, the goal is to reduce instruction page faults and instruction TLB misses. PBO may be invoked at any optimization level.

PBO rearranges the position of procedures in memory based on actual execution profiles. It attempts to place the code of called procedures on the same page of memory as the calling routine. PBO should be used only in *final stages* of application development. PBO should be particularly effective when using large page sizes available with HP-UX 11.0 and later.

Here are the steps for using profile-based optimization:

1. Instrumentation. Compile the program with the *+I* compiler option.
2. Data Collection. Execute the program one or more times with various characteristic input data. This step writes profile information to a database in *flow.data*.
3. Optimization. Relink or recompile the program with the *+P* option, which uses the profile information in *flow.data*.

Figure 11-2 shows the steps involved in using PBO.

11.9 Porting Applications

When moving an application from one type of system to another, use the following procedure to phase in the types of optimization that are most effective:

1. Develop, port, and debug the application without optimization.
2. Test the code with test data sets to obtain a known set of outputs.
3. Use *lint* (C) or *lintfor* (Fortran) to help discover problems.
4. In C, you might need to use the *-z* option, since it is usually incorrect to dereference a null pointer.
5. First use *-O*, which defaults to Level 2; then increase the level of optimization if the application continues to execute correctly.
6. If there are problems, back off to a lower optimization level, or turn off some or all of the optimizer assumptions.
7. Look for warnings on uninitialized variables.
8. Use the binary search technique to discover the areas where optimization does not work.

Level 2 is usually sufficient for commercial applications. Higher optimization levels are most useful for engineering and scientific applications.

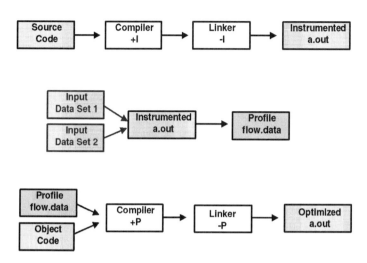

Figure 11-2 Steps in Using Profile-Based Optimization

11.10 Code to Demonstrate Optimization Effects

The following code can be used to observe the effects of optimization at the different levels and for different architectures:.

```
main()
{
        int i,j,k,l,m,n;
        for (i=0; i<2; i++)
        {
        j=i*5;/* constant multiplication */
        k=j*1000;/* constant multiplication */
        l=i+1;
        m=l*j;/* variable multiplication */
        printf("loop=%d, j=%d, k=%d, m=%d\n",i,j,k,m);
        }
}
```

This code, when compiled with different options, results in quite a variety of performance characteristics. Some of this is revealed in the assembly language view of the compiled code.

Using the command *cc +DA1.0 -go intnoopt int.c,* the code is compiled with no optimization. (The same output is obtained using *+DA1.1.*) The result is shown in the following listing:

Assembled Code for Source Program without Optimization

```
1 :              00004130   main       STW       %r2,-20(%r30)
                 00004134   main+0004  LDO       R'80(%r30),%r30
4 :              00004138   main+0008  STW       %r0,-120(%r30)
                 0000413C   main+000c  LDW       -120(%r30),%r1
                 00004140   main+0010  COMIBT,<=,N   2,%r1,main+009c
6 :    i*5       00004144   main+0014  LDW       -120(%r30),%r31
                 00004148   main+0018  SH2ADD    %r31,%r31,%r19
                 0000414C   main+001c  STW       %r19,-116(%r30)
7 : j*1000       00004150   main+0020  LDW       -116(%r30),%r20
                 00004154   main+0024  SH2ADD    %r20,%r20,%r21
                 00004158   main+0028  SH2ADD    %r21,%r21,%r22
                 0000415C   main+002c  SH2ADD    %r22,%r22,%r1
                 00004160   main+0030  SH3ADD    %r1,%r0,%r31
                 00004164   main+0034  STW       %r31,-112(%r30)
8 :              00004168   main+0038  LDW       -120(%r30),%r19
                 0000416C   main+003c  LDO       R'1(%r19),%r20
        I*j      00004170   main+0040  STW       %r20,-108(%r30)
9 :              00004174   main+0044  LDW       -108(%r30),%r26
                 00004178   main+0048  LDW       -116(%r30),%r25
                 0000417C   main+004c  LDIL      L'2000,%r31
                 00004180   main+0050  BLE$$mulI  R'430(%sr4,%r31)
  ────►          00004184   main+0054  NOP
                 00004188   main+0058  STW       %r29,-104(%r30)
10 :             0000418C   main+005c  ADDIL     L'fffff800,%r27
                 00004190   main+0060  LDO       R'730(%r1),%r26
                 00004194   main+0064  LDW       -120(%r30),%r25
                 00004198   main+0068  LDW       -116(%r30),%r24
                 0000419C   main+006c  LDW       -112(%r30),%r23
                 000041A0   main+0070  LDW       -104(%r30),%r21
                 000041A4   main+0074  STW       %r21,-52(%r30)
                 000041A8   main+0078  LDIL      L'4000,%r31
                 000041AC   main+007c  BLE printf  R'118(%sr4,%r31)
                 000041B0   main+0080  LDO       R'0(%r31),%r2
4 :              000041B4   main+0084  LDW       -120(%r30),%r22
                 000041B8   main+0088  LDO       R'1(%r22),%r1
                 000041BC   main+008c  STW       %r1,-120(%r30)
                 000041C0   main+0090  LDW       -120(%r30),%r31
                 000041C4   main+0094  COMIBF,<=  2,%r31,main+0014
  ────►          000041C8   main+0098  NOP
12 :             000041CC   main+009c  LDW       -148(%r30),%r2
                 000041D0   main+00a0  BV        %r0(%r2)
```

Note the NOP instructions filling the branch delay slots at main+0054 and main+0098. This represents wasted cycles. Also note the branch instruction BLE at main+0050 in the code for multiplying l*j. The multiplication is done by branching to software routine $$mulI, which is expensive in processor time.

Using the *+DA1.0 -O* options results in several improvements, which are shown below:
Assembled Code for Source Program with *-O* Optimization

```
 1 :                 00004130   main       STW      %r2,-20(%r30)
                      00004134   main+0004  STWM     %r3,R'80(%r30)
                      00004138   main+0008  STW      %r4,-124(%r30)
 4 :                 0000413C   main+000c  ADDIL    L'fffff800,%r27
       C:  4         00004140   main+0010  LDI      0,%r19
                     00004144   main+0014  LDO      R'0(%r1),%r3
 6 : C:  6           00004148   main+0018  SH2ADDL  %r19,%r19,%r24
 7 :                 0000414C   main+001c  SH1ADDL  %r24,%r24,%r23
                     00004150   main+0020  SH3ADDL  %r23,%r24,%r31
       C:  8         00004154   main+0024  LDO      R'1(%r19),%r4
                     00004158   main+0028  SH2ADDL  %r31,%r31,%r20
                     0000415C   main+002c  LDO      R'0(%r24),%r26
                     00004160   main+0030  BL       $$mulI,%r31
                     00004164   main+0034  LDO      R'0(%r4),%r25
                     00004168   main+0038  STW      %r29,-52(%r30)
       C:  7         0000416C   main+003c  SH3ADDL  %r20,%r0,%r23
 8*:                 00004170   main+0040  LDO      R'730(%r3),%r26
       C: 10         00004174   main+0044  BL       printf (hpux_imp
       C: 10         00004178   main+0048  LDO      R'0(%r19),%r25
 4 :                 0000417C   main+004c  COMIBF,<= 2,%r4,main+0018
       C:  4         00004180   main+0050  LDO      R'0(%r4),%r19
12 :                 00004184   main+0054  LDW      -148(%r30),%r2
                     00004188   main+0058  LDW      -124(%r30),%r4
                     0000418C   main+005c  BV       %r0(%r2)
       C: 12         00004190   main+0060  LDWM     -128(%r30),%r3
```

In this case, there is no NOP in the branch delay slot, and the BLE instruction has been converted to a BL. Both of these modifications result in major performance improvement.

Finally, using the *+DA1.1* **and** *-O* options results in still more improvement due to the use of the multiply instruction (XMPYU), which is available on 1.1 systems.

Assembled Code for Source Program with *+DA1.1* and *-O* Optimization

```
1 :                    00003000   main        STW       %r2,-20(%r30)
                       00003004   main+0004   STWM      %r3,R'c0(%r30)
                       00003008   main+0008   STW       %r4,-188(%r30)
4 :                    0000300C   main+000c   ADDIL     L'fffff800,%r2
    C: 4              00003010   main+0010   LDI       0,%r25
                       00003014   main+0014   LDO       R'0(%r1),%r3
6 : C: 6              00003018   main+0018   SH2ADDL   %r25,%r25,%r24
7 :                    0000301C   main+001c   LDO       -168(%r30),%r3
                       00003020   main+0020   STWS      %r24,-16(%r31)
    C: 8              00003024   main+0024   LDO       R'1(%r25),%r4
                       00003028   main+0028   STWS      %r4,-12(%r31)
                       0000302C   main+002c   SH1ADDL   %r24,%r24,%r19
                       00003030   main+0030   FLDWS     -16(%r31),%fr4
                       00003034   main+0034   FLDWS     -12(%r31),%fr5
                       00003038   main+0038   SH3ADDL   %r19,%r24,%r20
                       0000303C   main+003c   LDO       -52(%r30),%r29
                       00003040   main+0040   XMPYU,SGL %fr4L,%fr5L,%f
                       00003044   main+0044   SH2ADDL   %r20,%r20,%r21
                       00003048   main+0048   FSTWS     %fr6R,0(%r29)
    C: 7              0000304C   main+004c   SH3ADDL   %r21,%r0,%r23
8*: C: 10             00003050   main+0050   BL        printf (hpux_i
    C: 10             00003054   main+0054   LDO       R'730(%r3),%r2
4 :                    00003058   main+0058   COMIBF,<= 2,%r4,main+001
    C: 4              0000305C   main+005c   LDO       R'0(%r4),%r25
12 :                   00003060   main+0060   LDW       -212(%r30),%r2
                       00003064   main+0064   LDW       -188(%r30),%r4
                       00003068   main+0068   BV        %r0(%r2)
    C: 12             0000306C   main+006c   LDWM      -192(%r30),%r3
```

i*5

l*j

j*1000

Designing Applications for Performance

Preceding chapters have dealt with *system* performance tuning, which is comparatively easy to accomplish. Designing the application with performance in mind is much more difficult, though doing so may have the largest impact on overall performance. You cannot always control every aspect of the design, especially if the application is already written or if the source code is unavailable. Unfortunately, too many application development organizations leave performance considerations until the end of the process. Features often have precedence over performance when development resources are assigned. However, designing an application for performance from the beginning of the development process will most often ensure that the application performs satisfactorily.

To design an application for performance, one must have a good understanding of the target operating system on which the application will run, including knowledge of the choices for various OS services such as inter-process communication (IPC). This requirement is a large reason why applications previously written to work with one OS that are quickly ported to another OS do not perform well.

This chapter gives some advice on designing the application to enhance performance. The recommendations all assume that you have access to the application source code. Topics are:

- Tips for application design
- Shared versus archive libraries
- Choosing an inter-process communication model
- Shared memory
- Instrumenting an application for performance monitoring

12.1 Tips for Application Design

Here are some tips for good application design:

- Design the best possible algorithm first. Spending time up front to tune this algorithm so that it performs well often has the most impact on application performance. It is also more difficult to go back to analyze and tune the algorithm after it is written.
- Choose an IPC mechanism based on performance rather than ease of coding. This subject will be discussed more fully in the section on choosing IPC mechanisms.
- When large amounts of data must be shared among parts of the application, one should carefully evaluate relative performance differences among the following:

    - Using kernel threads
    - Employing user-space threads
    - Using child processes
    - Creating independent processes

Prototyping may be the best way to try these quite different designs.
- Data sharing can be accomplished via

    - Structures in the private data segment
    - Structures in the shared data segment (shared memory)
    - Using IPC mechanisms that transfer rather than share data
    - Passing data via files

Each of these choices has an entirely different performance profile. Carry out evaluations to choose the best design based on frequency and volume of data, efficiency of the mechanism, and prototyping.
- When coding the application, do not always choose defaults for parameters to system calls and library routines. For instance, the behavior of the dynamic memory allocation routine *malloc(1)* can be changed by calling *mallopt()*.
- Specific tips for using *malloc()* are:
    - Remember that *free()* returns previously allocated memory only to the *malloc* pool not back to the OS.
    - The *malloc* pool can easily become fragmented, and you can end up requesting much more memory from the OS than you expected. This may result in processes that are larger than they really need to be. Such processes hoard precious VM resources that are unavailable to other processes on the system.
    - An application that makes extensive use of *malloc()* may benefit from the larger virtual memory page sizes available in HP-UX 11.0 and later.

- Use compiler optimization to improve application performance. Doing so can save a considerable amount of time.
- Analyze the application for memory leaks that consume precious system resources and degrade performance. Commercially available software can help greatly with this task.
- If the application is to be used on a symmetric multi-processing (SMP) system, extreme care must be taken to ensure that performance is not negatively impacted. As discussed in the chapter on "Hardware Performance Issues," cache coherency problems can be caused by the process's being switched among the CPUs by OS load balancing, or when various parts of an application communicate extensively by IPC mechanisms. Remember also that poor application design is often a source of kernel contention and/or application deadlocks when running on an SMP system.

The following tips benefit engineering and scientific applications the most:

- Understand how the programming language works, and code accordingly. For example, C stores multiply-dimensioned arrays in row-major order, while Fortran stores them in column-major order. Accessing the arrays in the wrong way will have a large detrimental impact on performance by causing unnecessary page faults, in addition to cache and TLB misses.
- Consider using the vector library for vector math operations.
- Use the Fortran optimizing preprocessor, *ftnopp*, if coding in Fortran.
- Use the higher compiler optimization levels 1 and 2.

12.2 Shared versus Archive Libraries

Choosing between using shared libraries and archive libraries involves a classic memory versus CPU utilization tradeoff (Rule #2). Shared libraries, which are the default, are easier to use and consume less virtual memory. However, archive libraries consume less CPU while consuming more memory. When deciding whether to use shared or archive libraries, consider their advantages and disadvantages, as described in the next sections.

12.2.1 Shared Libraries

Shared libraries have the following advantages (+) and disadvantages (-):

+ They are linked by default.
+ They use less memory and disk space, because they are not included in *a.out* and are shared among all processes in memory that invoke the same routines.
+ They make it easier to maintain the application without relinking it entirely.
+ They make it easier to add support for new graphics devices if specified at run time.
+ There is a revision-control feature.

+ They can potentially extend the VAS of a process because they are loaded into a different quadrant.

- There is slow access on first call of a procedure because of binding.
- They cannot be locked into memory.
- Data for shared libraries are private, requiring swap space reservation.
- They are incompatible with *prof* and *gprof* profilers.
- They are slower because of the use of position-independent code (PIC) and cross-quadrant branching.

12.3 Archive Libraries

The use of archive libraries is optional, requiring one of the following options at compile or link time:

- *cc/f77 -Wl,-a,archive*
- *LDOPTS="-a archive"*
- *ld -a archive*

Archive libraries have the following advantages (+) and disadvantages (-):

+ Faster process execution is typical.
+ All procedures are fully bound at link time.

- A copy of the called routine is linked to each process, consuming more memory and disk space.
- Modification of a library routine requires relinking the entire process.

12.4 Choosing an Inter-Process Communication (IPC) Mechanism

The use of different types of inter-process communication can have a significant impact on performance. When considering which IPC mechanism is right for your application, recall that copying data on a RISC-architecture system consumes a lot of CPU, and may cause page faults and cache and TLB misses. Also remember that system calls cause execution to transfer to the OS, which interferes with the multi-tasking of user processes.

The following sections describe several types of IPC, each with its advantages (+) and disadvantages (-).

12.4.1 Pipes

+ They are universally available.

+ They are easy to code, because they are accessed by a file descriptor, in the same way a file is accessed.

- They are uni-directional.
- There is a limited of 8K bytes in the pipe at any one time (previously 5K).
- They are slow, since data is copied from user space to kernel space and back to user space.
- Named pipes cause inode accesses at *open* time and *read* or *write* time.

12.4.2 Message Queues

+ They are easy to code, although special system calls are required—*msgsend()* and *msgrecv()*.
+ They are bi-directional.
+ There can be multiple recipients of a message.
+ Queues can be blocking or non-blocking.
+ Synchronization and prioritization are done by the kernel.
+ Queues are persistent, even if a process terminates.

- They are optional in the kernel.
- One process can consume all available message queue space.
- They are limited to a total of *msgmax* bytes, and *msgmnb* for each queue; there is a hard upper limit of 64 KB for any one message queue.
- They are slow, since data is copied from user space to kernel space and back to user space. Thus additional system calls cause more overhead.

Messages should be kept small and infrequent.

12.4.3 System V Semaphores

+ They are easy to code, although special system calls are required (*semget*, *semctl*, *semop*).
+ They are bi-directional.
+ They can be blocking or non-blocking.
+ Synchronization and prioritization are done by the kernel.
+ They are persistent, even if a process terminates.

- They are optional in the kernel.
- One process can consume all available semaphores.
- System call utilization can be quite high.

It is recommended that you try memory-mapped semaphores if the application makes extensive use of semaphores.

12.4.4 Memory-Mapped Semaphores

Memory-mapped semaphores are implemented on one or more pages of mapped memory in shared quadrants rather than in the OS. The kernel code path is much shorter for these semaphores than the code path for System V semaphores. Memory-mapped semaphores therefore have less overhead. Here are the advantages (+) and disadvantages (-):

+ They are standard in the kernel.

+ They can be blocking or non-blocking.

+ Synchronization and prioritization are done by the kernel.

+ The number of semaphores is limited only by memory-mapped file limit.

- They are more difficult to code, mostly because of unfamiliarity—*mseminit()*, etc.

12.4.5 Shared Memory

Although shared memory segments require system call invocation for allocation and attachment, they are the most efficient IPC mechanism, having the least overhead. Access to the shared memory segment by either the writer or the reader is as easy as accessing a private variable or structure. However, extensive use of shared memory in an SMP environment may create cache coherency problems, depending on access patterns and CPU switching. (See Chapter 7, "Hardware Performance Issues.") In spite of this potential problem, shared memory segments remain the best-choice IPC mechanism.

Make sure that you type shared memory structures in C and C++ as *volatile,* so the optimizer will correctly treat the references. Doing so will keep shared memory from being a reason that compiler optimization breaks the application.

Advantages (+) and disadvantages (-) of the use of shared memory segments for IPC are:

+ Setup and control are done via system calls—*shmget()*, *shmat()*, *shmctl()*, *shmdt()*.

+ Access is by normal variable/pointer access—no system calls.

+ They are the most efficient IPC mechanism.

+ They are bi-directional.

+ They can be blocking or non-blocking.

+ They are persistent even if a process terminates.

- They are optional in the kernel.

- One process can consume all available shared memory space.

- They are more difficult to code due to synchronization requirements.

- They can cause protection register thrashing if too many shared memory segments are accessed by a single process. (See Chapter 7, "Hardware Performance Issues.")

It is recommended to use semaphores to synchronize no more than two shared memory segments per process.

12.4.6 Berkeley Sockets

Here are some of the advantages (+) and disadvantages (-) of using Berkeley sockets:

+ They are standard in the kernel.
+ Setup, transfer and control is done via system calls—*socket( )*, *setsockopt( )*, *accept( )*, *connect( )*, *send( )*, *receive( )*.
+ They are bi-directional.
+ They can be blocking or non-blocking.
+ Caching may be identical for both local and remote IPC.
+ Unix domain sockets are used when client and server are on the same system.
+ Internet Domain sockets are used when client and server are on different systems.

- They are more difficult to code.
- The use of internet domain sockets when client and server are on the same system causes unneeded overhead.

Recommendations: Code for both local and remote cases, and use *setsockopt( )* to appropriately size the send and receive socket buffers, to control the acknowledgement window size and to improve network utilization and performance.

12.5 Instrumenting an Application for Performance Monitoring

Hewlett-Packard has joined with other vendors and end user customers to form the Application Response Measurement (ARM) Working Group. This working group has agreed on an application programming interface (API) specification that application developers can use to instrument their applications for performance monitoring. The ARM Software Developer's Kit (SDK) is available at no charge on the following URLs:

http://www.openview.hp.com/solutions/application/
http://www.tivoli.com/ (see "Downloads")

Additional information about the ARM Working Group is available from:

http://www.cmg.org/regions/cmgarmw

12.5.1 Metrics Available by Using the ARM API

Instrumenting the application with the ARM API can provide metrics that can be used to monitor:

• Application availability
• Application performance
    - Business transaction response time
    - Workload throughput
    - Service levels as seen by the user
• Application usage, including data for chargeback accounting

The transactions measurements may be correlated among multiple systems to measure end-to-end response time in a distributed and/or client/server environment.

12.5.2 Run-Time libraries

API run-time libraries are available with *MeasureWare* on the following platforms:

• HP-UX 10.x and 11.x
• IBM AIX
• NCR MP RAS
• Sun Solaris

The ARM API is intended to work with various vendors' management applications, such as HP *MeasureWare*. The ARM agent (supplied by the management application vendor) receives metrics from the instrumented application when it calls the procedures in the run-time library, and sends the metrics to the management application.

12.5.3 Calls Available with the ARM API

The ARM API includes calls to:

• Identify a transaction with a label
• Indicate when a transaction starts
• Indicate when a transaction has completed
• Indicate the parent/child relations among pieces of transactions that may run on multiple
  systems in a distributed or client/server environment

Using the API is not difficult, but it does require access to the application source code and the ability to modify that source code. The benefits from instrumenting an application in this manner should provide the impetus necessary to convince the organization that the work should be done.

12.5.4 Using the ARM API to Measure Application Performance

The following steps are necessary to measure application performance using the ARM API:

1. Establish which business transactions are important from a measurement perspective. This may be done in conjunction with Service Level Agreement (SLA) creation.
2. Modify the application source code to include calls to the ARM API in appropriate places, to provide the data necessary to measure the business transactions defined in Step 1.
3. Link the application with the actual ARM library available from the management application vendor.
4. Run the instrumented application using various workloads over a suitable period of time.
5. Analyze the results with the management application, such as MeasureWare or PerfView.
6. Use the anlayzed results to modify the application to improve its performance or to meet the established Service Level Objective (SLO).

Instrumenting an application with the ARM API is the most accurate way to actually determine how the application is performing. Only then, can developers take knowledgeable actions to modify the application to improve its performance.

Application Profiling

Application profiling is a technique that uses a group of special tools to create executables that are designed to be analyzed for performance. This chapter describes the use of the following profiling tools:

- *CXperf*
- *gprof*
- *puma*

Profiling provides information on where the application spends its CPU time. *CXperf* and *puma* also provide information on virtual memory utilization. You can use the results of an application profile to:

- Tune the algorithms used by the application
- Improve the overall performance of the application
- Decide whether or not it is worth spending time on tuning the application
- Decide which routines or procedures are worth tuning

After profiling an application, apply the following simple rule of thumb: it is worth tuning a single procedure if the profile shows that it consumes more than 5–10% of the CPU utlization *and/or* has significant virtual memory problems.

13.1 CXperf

CXperf is an interactive runtime performance analyzer for programs writen in Hewlett-Packard Fortran 77, Fortran 90, ANSI C, ANSI C++, and Assembler. *CXperf* also profiles multiprocess (threaded) applications, message passing parallel programming models (including the Message Passing Interface, an API from HP), object files and archive libraries, and shared memory applications, including those that employ *pthreads* and user-specified parallel directives. *CXperf* can only be used on D-, K-, N- and V-Series HP 9000 systems because it requires special hardware instrumentation that is available only on these models. Additionally, *CXperf* runs only on HP-UX 11.0 (9806) or later.

    CXperf provides a powerful tool for application optimization by giving measurements of the following metrics on a procedure basis:

- Procedure execution count
- CPU time
- Wallclock time
- Instruction counts
- Instruction and data TLB misses
- Instruction and data cache hits and misses
- Context switches
- Thread CPU switches

CXperf also provides a complete call graph that shows the parent/child relationships of each of the procedures.

    The main *CXperf* executable is **cxperf**, which has the following syntax:

cxperf [executable] [pdf-filename] [-options...]

where *executable* is the program to profile (the default is *a.out*) and *pdf-filename* is a performance data file (PDF) created by *CXperf* for analysis. The default is *<executable-program-name>.pdf*.

    Both GUI and command line execution are available, and there is a batch mode. Man pages for *cxperf*, *cxoi*, and *cxmerge* contain detailed examples.

13.1.1 Steps in Using CXperf

There are five main steps for using *CXperf* to obtain data on an application's performance:

1. Insert data collection "infrastructure" into the application using the +*pa* flag at compile time or by placing it directly into object files or archived libraries using the *cxoi* utility. You would use the *cxoi* utility if you don't want to recompile the program, or if you do not have access to the source code. However, without the source code, it may be very difficult to analyze the results or to decide how to improve the application design.
2. Link the resulting .o and .a files with *CXperf's* monitor routines (*cxperfmon.o*). The result of this second step is an *instrumentable* application. (This link step is usually automatic;

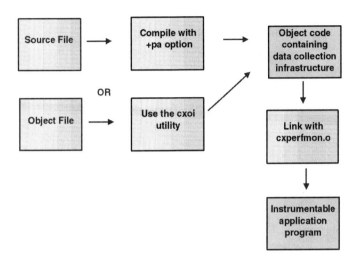

Figure 13-1   Preparing for Instrumentation with CXperf

after compilation, the *+pa* flag is also passed to the linker which knows to link *cxperf-mon.o*.) Steps 1 and 2 are both shown in Figure 13-1.

3. Instrument the application by specifying which functions and/or loops within functions to instrument for data collection. Also, choose which metrics you wish to obtain, bearing in mind that some metrics, such as call graph data, have a high overhead. This step can be done with the *CXperf* GUI, as shown in Figure 13-2.

4. Run the application, using whatever data inputs are normally used. You may want to run several profiles, because different data may cause different behavior in the application. On exit, a special data file is dumped that contains all the run-time performance data.

5. Analyze the resulting data file using any of several different report formats and queries. See the *CXperf* manual for more information on report formats and interactive commands.

A recommended method of using *CXperf* is as follows:

• First, get the CPU time for all routines in the application.

• Second, with a separate data collection run, get call graph information for all procedures.

• Third, focus futher data collection on only those routines that consume most of the CPU time. For example, you might focus on only the top 10% out routines in CPU consumption, or just those routines using more than 5–10% of the total CPU.

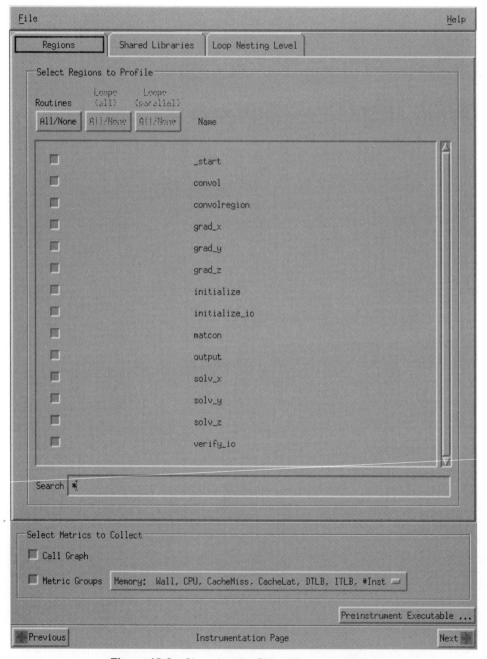

Figure 13-2 Choosing the CXperf Instrumentation

A summary screen showing call graph data from the *CXperf* GUI is shown in Figure 13-3. The

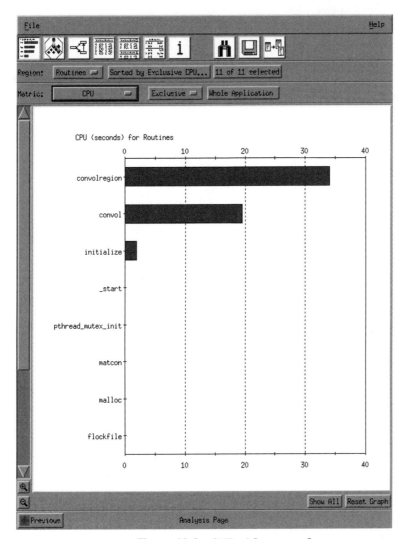

Figure 13-3   CXPerf Summary Screen

GUI allows you to jump from the summary page to a page of detailed data (Figure 13-4) for a given metric. From the detail screen, you can jump to the source code (Figure 13-5) for which the data is displayed.

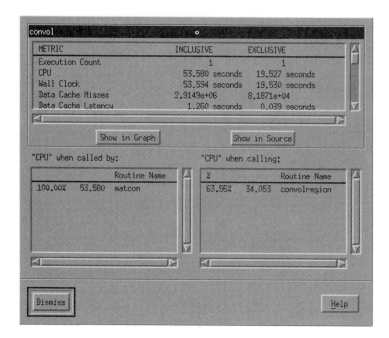

Figure 13-4   CXPerf Detail Metrics Screen

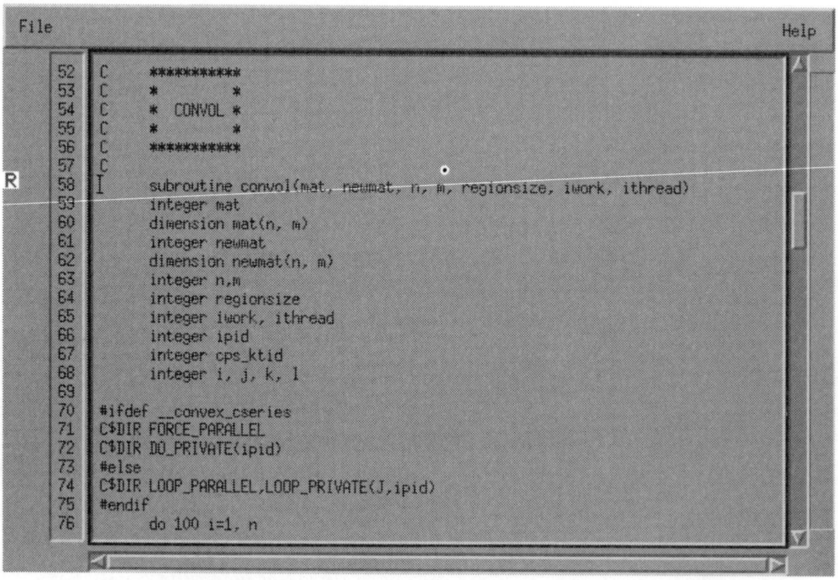

Figure 13-5   CXPerf Source Code Screen

13.1.2 Metrics in CXperf

The following metrics are provided by *CXperf*:

- Wall clock time
- CPU time
- Ratio of CPU/wall time
- Execution count
- Instruction count
- MIPS
- TLB misses
- Context switches and thread migrations
- Cache misses

13.1.3 Advantages and Disadvantages of CXperf

A major advantage of *CXperf* is its ability to collect information on cache and TLB misses. No other profiling or system performance tool provides this information. Disadvantages include the large instrumentation overhead needed for some metrics; this can create biased values for some metrics such as CPU time and wallclock time; however, metrics such as TLB misses and execution counts will be accurate.

13.2 gprof

Gprof is the Berkeley application profiling tool. *Gprof* provides a superset of the functionality available with *prof*, the System V version. Therefore, it is recommended that *gprof* be used rather than *prof*. Profiling an application with *gprof* involves the following steps:

1. Special compilation and linking
2. Program execution
3. Profile generation

13.2.1 Step 1: Special Compilation and Linking

Application profiling is available for programs written in the C, C++, Fortran, and Pascal languages. The program must be specially compiled with the *-G* switch to prepare the application for profiling. This special compiler option causes calls to the procedure *_mcount( )* to be inserted at the beginning of every procedure. In addition to recording the parent and child relationships of the procedure being monitored, *_mcount( )* collects call count information and total procedure execution time. The program is also linked with the profiled version of several of the system libraries which are located in */lib/libp*. Only the system libraries *libc.a*, *libm.a*, and *libM.a* are supplied in profiled form. The compiling and link steps are shown in Figure 13-6.

The program should be linked with *archive libraries* using the one of the following sets of options:

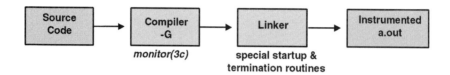

Figure 13-6   Compiling and Linking Steps with Gprof

- At compilation: *Wl,-a,archive*
- At link time: *-a archive*
- Using an environment variable: *LDOPTS="-a archive"*

This is done in order to get an accurate profile, because the profiling routines expect a contiguous instruction address space. Shared libraries should not be used, because they are loaded at an address that is not contiguous with the rest of the application code.

Finally, the application must be linked with the special startup routine */lib/gcrt0.o* which causes *monitor(3c)* to be called before application startup and after the application calls *exit(2)*. *Monitor(3c)* is an interface to the system call *profil(2)* that tells the kernel to record the application's program counter (*PC*) in a buffer at every clock tick.

By default, a maximum of 600 procedures can be profiled. This limit may be increased by making an explicit call to *monitor(3c)*. Explicit calls to *monitor(3c)* may also be made to change the range of memory addresses that are profiled. Otherwise, it is recommended that *monitor(3c)* not be called directly. See the *man* page for *monitor(3c)* to learn the proper format of the calls.

13.2.2 Step 2: Program Execution

After special compilation and linking, the application is executed one or more times to generate profile data, as shown in Figure 13-7. Each execution must terminate normally by call-

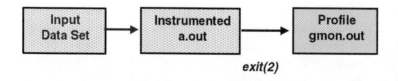

Figure 13-7   Executing the Application to Create Profile Data

ing *exit(2)* explicitly, or by returning from the *main* routine. Thus, programs in an infinite loop or those that are aborted will not produce a profile. A program which does not normally terminate could have a signal routine added to call *exit(2)*. Program termination calls *monitor(3c)* which turns off profiling and causes the *gmon.out* file to be written to the disk.

13.2.3 Step 3: Profile Generation

After one or more profiling runs have been completed, the profile data is analyzed and printed with the utility *gprof*. *Gprof* reads one or more *gmon.out* files, and may read the summation file *gmon.sum*. Then it produces a printed profile that can be used to determine where the program is spending the most time. Figure 13-8 shows this graphically.

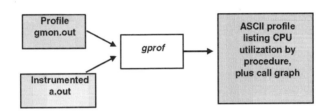

Figure 13-8   Creating the Profile

Procedures that are not profiled have the times of their profiled children propagated upward to them, but are shown as spontaneously invoked (the parent is shown as *<spontaneous>*), and the execution times are not propagated further upward. This results in the $START routine showing something less than 100% of the execution time.

Advantages (+) and disadvantages (-) of *gprof* are as follows:

+ It provides a call graph with parent and child relationships. *Gprof* tracks the number of times that a routine is called by specific callers, and also the number of times that it calls other routines; this is the parent/self/child relationship. *Prof* does not perform this function. This type of information helps determine where to spend time in optimizing the application.
+ It follows program execution into the system call code. The kernel keeps track of when a process is executing system call code, and allocates this time appropriately in the profile. This helps to show how a program spends its time.

- It requires special compilation and linking. The source code of the application must be available in order to profile it, and special compilation options must be used.
- The application process must terminate normally. Long-running programs are difficult to profile; programs that never have a normal termination cannot be profiled.
- Accuracy is affected by multi-tasking. Results of the profile can vary by plus or minus 20 percent due to varying CPU cache hit ratios, because the cache is shared by other processes.

- *Gprof* does not work with shared libraries. The program must be linked with archive libraries in order to provide an accurate profile, because the profile tools require a contiguous instruction address space.

- Not all system libraries are available in profiled form. Because of disk space limitations, only a few system libraries are supplied in profiled format. Therefore, it is difficult to get full propagation when non-profiled libraries are invoked.

13.3 Puma

Puma has been available in the HP Performance Analysis Kit (HP PAK) since the release of HP-UX 10.0. Written by HP, *puma* replaced *dpat* and *hpc* at HP-UX 10.20. It monitors the program counter, the call/return stack, and other performance statistics to show where a program is spending most of its time. Data is stored in a file that can subsequently be viewed in a number of ways. In the following example, *puma* is run from the command line with the *-invoke* option against the sample program *vanderbilt*.

```
hpgsyha9/B.11.00:/opt/langtools/bin/puma -monitor -invoke vanderbilt
Initializing image '/opt/langtools/hppak/examples/vanderbilt'...done.
Monitoring lasted 13 seconds.
Target ran 12 seconds and used 11 CPU seconds.
Monitoring stopped after 112 samples.
```

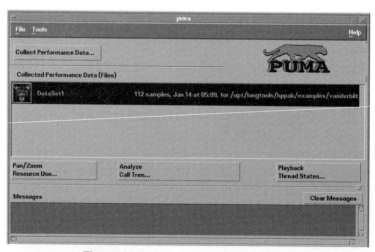

Figure 13-9   Graphic Display of Puma

The effect of this run is to generate a file (named *DataSet1* by default) containing performance data. DataSet1 is displayed on the screen (shown in Figure 13-9), and may be selected for further analysis.

Puma supports different types of analyses. As an example of one type, *puma* generates a bar graph showing the calls in the program and the percentage of time the program spends in each routine. The call tree analysis is shown in Figure 13-10.

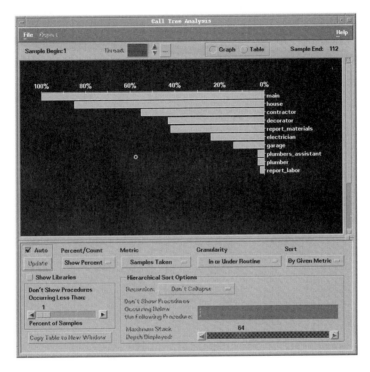

Figure 13-10 Puma Call Tree Analysis

The advantages (+) and disadvantages (-) of *puma* are as follows:

+ It reports data on multi-threaded applications.

+ It produces a dynamic histogram of CPU time for each procedure as the process executes and a call graph.

+ It shows parent and child relationships with no special compilation (only if the *a.out* file has not been stripped).

+ Optionally, it shows a histogram of CPU time at the source-code line level (requires compilation with the *-g* option).

- Because of its sampling method, it is less accurate on a multi-user system.

- It seems to work best on compute-bound programs.

Index

Hewlett-Packard Computer Education and Training

Hewlett-Packard's world-class education and training offers hands on education solutions including:

- Linux
- HP-UX System and Network Administration
- Y2K HP-UX Transition
- Advanced HP-UX System Administration
- IT Service Management using advanced Internet technologies
- Microsoft Windows NT
- Internet/Intranet
- MPE/iX
- Database Administration
- Software Development

HP's new IT Professional Certification program provides rigorous technical qualification for specific IT job roles including HP-UX System Administration, Network Management, Unix/NT Servers and Applications Management, and IT Service Management.

In addition, HP's IT Resource Center is the perfect knowledge source for IT professionals. Through a vibrant and rich Web environment, IT professionals working in the areas of UNIX, Microsoft, networking, or MPE/iX gain access to continually updated knowledge pools.

http://education.hp.com

In the U.S. phone 1-800-HPCLASS (472-5277)

Prentice Hall: Professional Technical Reference

Home | Reload | Images | Open | Print | Find | Stop

://www.phptr.com/

ew? | What's Cool? | Destinations | Net Search | People | Software

PRENTICE HALL

Professional Technical Reference
Tomorrow's Solutions for Today's Professionals.

Keep Up-to-Date with
PH PTR Online!

We strive to stay on the cutting-edge of what's happening in professional computer science and engineering. Here's a bit of what you'll find when you stop by **www.phptr.com**:

@ Special interest areas offering our latest books, book series, software, features of the month, related links and other useful information to help you get the job done.

Deals, deals, deals! Come to our promotions section for the latest bargains offered to you exclusively from our retailers.

$ Need to find a bookstore? Chances are, there's a bookseller near you that carries a broad selection of PTR titles. Locate a Magnet bookstore near you at www.phptr.com.

! What's New at PH PTR? We don't just publish books for the professional community, we're a part of it. Check out our convention schedule, join an author chat, get the latest reviews and press releases on topics of interest to you.

Subscribe Today! **Join PH PTR's monthly email newsletter!**

Want to be kept up-to-date on your area of interest? Choose a targeted category on our website, and we'll keep you informed of the latest PH PTR products, author events, reviews and conferences in your interest area.

Visit our mailroom to subscribe today! **http://www.phptr.com/mail_lists**